# THE MAKING OF WHITAKER WRIGHT

By

Douglas Hamilton

Copyright © Douglas Hamilton 2018
This book is sold subject to the condition that it shall not, by way of trade or otherwise, be lent, resold, hired out, or otherwise circulated without the publisher's prior consent in any form of binding or cover other than that in which it is published and without a similar condition including this condition being imposed on the subsequent publisher.
The moral right of Douglas Hamilton has been asserted.
ISBN: 9781983139536

# DEDICATION

*For Trudy Hamilton.*

Information in this book is true and complete to the best of author's knowledge. This book is presented solely for educational purposes. The author disclaims any liability in connection with the use of this information or with respect to any loss or incidental or consequential damages caused, or alleged to have been caused, directly or indirectly, by the information contained herein.

# CONTENTS

FOREWORD ..................................................................................................1
CHAPTER 1 *Making the Man*..........................................................................3
CHAPTER 2 *Making the Way*........................................................................18
CHAPTER 3 *Making the American Fortune*..................................................34
CHAPTER 4 *Making the English Fortune*....................................................49
CHAPTER 5 *Making the Name*.....................................................................62
CHAPTER 6 *Making the Home*....................................................................73
CHAPTER 7 *Making the Losses*....................................................................92
CHAPTER 8 *Making the Fall*......................................................................115
CHAPTER 9 *Making the Witness*................................................................131
CHAPTER 10 *Making the Flight*.................................................................145
CHAPTER 11 *Making the Moment*.............................................................162
CHAPTER 12 *Making the Defence*..............................................................175
CHAPTER 13 *Making the End*....................................................................189

# ACKNOWLEDGMENTS

Record offices, museums and history organisations provided immediate, useful and cogent information. Their willingness to help was evident and their enthusiasm was infectious. Thanks are due to many, too numerous to name. However, I should particularly acknowledge two people who were both helpful and encouraging. Ann Laver at Godalming Museum gave access to her own collection of well-researched and expertly assessed material and to the photographs of Lea Park House. Dan Plazak, author and engineer, was amazing. His chapter on Whitaker Wright in his *A Hole in the Ground with a Liar at the Top* gave a good read and his supply of contemporary newspaper cuttings of the man was generous to a fault.

# SYNOPSIS OF CHAPTERS

**1. Making the Man** sets out the modest background of his parents in Macclesfield. His father becomes a New Connexion Methodist Minister and the family lives in various midlands and northern towns in England. The social and economic conditions of the times at these places are highlighted and the rise and role of Methodism are described. Whitaker Wright is born in 1846 and is brought up in the religion.

**2. Making the Way** charts Whitaker's departure from Methodism and a failed business venture with his brother. On the death of his father in 1870, Whitaker and his brother emigrate. He becomes an assayer and starts to deal in mines in the American west. He gravitates to Philadelphia where he becomes a successful stock broker.

**3. Making the American Fortune** deals with the considerable wealth he makes floating companies to exploit the silver mines of Leadville in Colorado and Lake Valley in New Mexico in the early 1880s. The life in the mining camps and the role of the Apaches are featured. He makes a fortune although many of the mines ultimately fail. His family and wealthy social life are portrayed.

**4. Making the English Fortune** features his return to England in 1890 and details his floatation of large companies during the next decade principally to deal in the Australian gold mines. His business methods are described particularly his employment of aristocratic figures with little business acumen on the company boards to give credibility to his companies.

**5. Making the Name** deals with his further rise to become one of the wealthiest men in the country. His business methods are examined. His commercial empire expands worldwide and vast fortunes are made by him and others. He is described as a Midas when the Victorian empire and its commercial enterprise are at their height.

**6. Making the Home** describes how he uses his wealth to acquire Lea Park in Surrey and to build a large country house. The works to the house and grounds take years. His other assets include a Park Lane house, a flat in Whitehall Court and racing yachts. He rises socially and even entertains the Prince of Wales. He spends lavishly and is immensely popular locally.

**7. Making the Losses** deals with the period in 1899 and 1900 when he gambles on the stock exchange to acquire a particular company he believes will secure his financial future but is defeated by the 'bear market' of the time. He manipulates the balance sheets of his major companies to show a false financial position. At the end of 1900, the empire collapses leaving stock exchange members, shareholders and creditors bankrupt. Vast sums have been lost.

**8. Making the Fall** concern the events of 1901 when he tries to rescue his companies and his financial empire. His strategies and negotiations to deal with the aftermath are chronicled. His character and colossal status are tested.

**9. Making the Witness** goes through his appearance at various judicial inquiries and court cases in 1902 to examine the financial collapse of his companies which completely expose his dubious business methods. The discoveries of the Official Receiver challenge his credibility.

**10. Making the Flight** highlights the increasing public pressure to have him prosecuted and includes a Parliamentary debate on his case. A private prosecution for fraud is initiated and he flees to New York where he is arrested, imprisoned and extradition proceedings commenced. He returns to England to face trial.

**11. Making the Moment** sets out his famous trial and the prosecution led by Rufus Isaacs in January 1904 including the evidence given by an array of witnesses on his business activities. It is the sensational trial of the moment.

**12. Making the Defence** is the evidence given by him and the devastating cross-examination by the prosecution.

**13. Making the End** charts the trial verdict and his immediate suicide. An inquest is held and he is buried in the local churchyard. The newspapers highlight his life and business methods and take differing views on his activities and ethics. The arguments about his motives and behaviour are considered. The aftermath for his family and his estate conclude the story.

# FOREWORD

Whitaker Wright was one of the leading characters of the late Victorian era and his fraudulent label has been roundly used by various authors of short stories and by newspaper writers in their articles about him. He was both a product and a maker of the times and reflected many of the contemporary social and economic issues in England and America. So much has been concentrated on his last years to seal his reputation that his earlier life is overlooked. This is the true and full story about this great Victorian entrepreneur based on extensive research of historical records and contemporary newspaper accounts. Verdicts have readily been given about him both in the Victorian era and latterly. The reader can make their own assessment and be his judge.

This story makes few judgments but simply sets out his life and what it was actually like. His words and those of his contemporaries about him as they appeared in the archived material have been used to interpret his decisions and actions, what led to the events in his life and the reasons for them. The story is based upon and incorporates the available material but certain events have been surmised and some inventive narrative to some situations has been provided to give the flavour of his life and not simply a series of facts. The narrative is written without any anticipation of future events.

The original financial figures have been used and, except where important, have been rounded up as they deal with tens and hundreds of thousands and, in some instances, millions of either dollars or pounds. There were then about five dollars to the pound.

The figures look colossal even by modern equivalents. Their value is even more startling when the ordinary workers of the time received weekly wages of dollars or pounds in single figures.

Everything about him has been researched for this story – what he apparently said, what has been said about him, the places he lived and visited, the contemporary times. The details have been checked against verifiable records. Contemporary records, particularly public documents and countless newspaper reports have been used but also general historical information provided to give the background and environment in which the events occurred.

# CHAPTER 1

## Making the Man

He knelt down in the chapel and prayed. Alone and in the darkness, he humbled himself before the glory of God. He gave solemn thanks and gently cried with joy. His head was full of gratitude and his heart full of peace. His service had been recognised and God had planned his life. The years of faith to the Word and of devotion to the Rule had been for the greater purpose. The silence confirmed his profound belief.

James Wright owed a great debt to his mother for his early religious path. From his birth on 12$^{th}$ September 1815, she had planted in his mind the precepts of life and had nurtured them by her example and piety. He had lived all his life with his family at Prestbury on the outskirts of Macclesfield. It was a tiny settlement in Cheshire of some four hundred people. His father was a brick-maker at the local works. The family circumstances meant that James started work early in his life at one of the local silk factories.

But the demand for silk products varied annually, certainly seasonally and often weekly. There were periods of plentiful work and times of depression. It meant huge variations in the income of the silk workers. They could be working for months and then have a similar period of unemployment. And it could vary between the factories depending upon the orders they had for their particular product. There was competition from other towns and from abroad.

There were inevitably times of unrest and political agitation depending mainly on the economic situation. It was a growing industrial town at the forefront of the industrial revolution then taking shape. By the time James was ten years old in 1825, the population of the town had grown to 30,000 people more than three times its size in 1800. It meant volatility among the workers and a variety of outlets for their thinking.

Work was the ethos of survival and it started early in James' life. He began work at the factory at five years old along with many other children. His first job was mending the broken strands of silk, called 'piecing'. It was ideal work for his small and nimble fingers. He progressed to become a quill winder which meant laboriously winding the silk onto the small bobbins for a shuttle. At eight or nine years old, he recalled moving on to plain weaving and then his apprenticeship. His hours had been long. Starting at six in the morning, it meant he had to rise early and walk the mile or so to ensure attendance on time. Time was only measured by the factory clock and there were severe fines for any lateness. He worked until eight in the evening with breaks for meals. A twenty-minute break was allowed at eight o' clock, an hour was given between two and three for a mid-day meal and at five, and a further twenty minutes was given for tea. But he felt that conditions were better than the cotton mills. There was less humidity and dust, cleanliness was paramount not least for the quality of the product and discipline was generally reasonable. He never gave any trouble. From Monday to Saturday, he toiled with everyone else.

But there was deliberately no work on Sundays. It was the day for attendance at a religious service and, more importantly for youngsters, attendance at Sunday school. It was their major opportunity to gain some kind of basic education. It was endorsed by the employers both as a practical means for giving their workforce the simple and useful skills required in various industries and trades and as a moral framework for giving their workforce a sober and obedient framework in society. The teaching concentrated on reading and writing and arithmetic and was hugely successful in providing literacy and numeric skills to most children. A large Sunday school had been built in 1814 in Roe Street in the town. It was non-denominational and provided places for some 2,000 children.

At twelve years old, James was formally admitted to his Church and Sunday gave him time to become useful, and as he grew up, he made his way through the ranks of the congregation. At four o' clock in the morning, every Sunday, he would attend one of the classes for scripture reading and other religious exercises. At seven o' clock, there was the regular prayer meeting in the chapel vestry. The regular Sunday services for the wider congregation would follow. He became a Sunday school teacher, passing on, usually by rote, the lessons he had been given as a child. A little older, he distributed religious tracts and was a district visitor. Later still, he became a class leader and a local preacher. Such was his fervour that he was recognised as a local evangelist, visiting areas and homes in and around Macclesfield. He was particularly responsible for forming a congregation at the nearby village of Bollington. He was modestly proud of the part he had in the small but growing movement, itself a part of the national rise of Methodism.

James had witnessed much of the movement's growth and influence. Methodism had begun in the eighteenth century and had been one of a number of nonconformist religions founded to challenge the Church of England in its complacent approach to the religion of the country. The Established Church was generally under the control and patronage of the local gentry and there was little apparent concern for the ordinary working man whose life was being dramatically changed by the advancing industrial revolution. Many of the existing churches in the rural areas were without resident clergy and many of the newly industrialised towns had neither churches nor clergy. John Wesley had started Methodism to promote the fundamental belief that each man deserved to have his soul saved and be given spiritual guidance in a practical way for his everyday conduct. A significant part of the teaching related to self-rule and self-improvement. Wesley meant to supplement the Established Church with bible study and prayer meetings, often in adherents' houses. The movement endeavoured to reach out to the ordinary person to lead a better life. Wesley had a dream of Christian perfection to which he considered everyone could aspire and reach with the right attitude and belief.

James learned how John Wesley had encouraged small domestic gatherings held by travelling preachers. Wesley undertook the regulation of local affairs and established a National Annual Conference held in May or June of each year to discuss major affairs.

Initially, Methodist preachers were not ordained. Wesley introduced practices started by others and built them into a recognised body. He organised travelling preachers to make better use of them. It principally prevented their work from overlapping. The movement gradually developed into a structure. At the base were groups of twelve with a class leader mainly for bible studies and collecting the penny contributions. These formed into societies usually centred on a local chapel. In turn, Circuits were formed of groups of two or more societies under a Superintendent Minister who with other ministers served the several chapels. In large towns, there might be several circuits. The hierarchy meant that there was scope for individuals either to rise through the ranks according to their ability or to remain at a level to make their contribution whilst in full-time employment. A nationwide 'connexion' was developed with regular meeting of the Circuits to take stock of progress, highlight areas of concern and discuss improvements to the organisation. The Annual Meeting dealt with policy and the appointment of ministers on a three-year tenure to each Circuit.

James was also acutely aware of the fractures in the movement that had developed into the current sects of Wesleyan, Primitive, New Connexion and others. The divisions had been anticipated by Wesley but only realised on his death. The differences were not about their beliefs but principally about the role of their supporters. The Wesleyan minister, Alexander Kilham, had created one of the splits in Methodism as he had long advocated the greater involvement of the laity in its administration. He was expelled by the Methodist Conference in 1797 and with a number of other ministers, founded the Methodist New Connexion in 1799. They wanted the times of Sunday services to be determined by those who wished to attend, they wanted holy communion to be administered by Methodist itinerant ministers in their own meeting houses and they wanted lay members to share in the government of the church at district, circuit and annual conference levels. Otherwise, their beliefs and methods remained almost identical to mainstream Methodism. It was during James' formative years that the Methodist New Connexion Society grew significantly in numbers. James became one of those ordinary men who typified and contributed towards that growth.

The simple chapel gave James the quietness and time to reflect on the movement and the circumstances that had fostered its growth.

The change in agricultural methods and the development of the factory system in many industries led to a period of rapid social changes. Not only was there a mass migration from countryside to the town but the population itself grew. Whole areas suddenly became unrecognisable with the advent of expanding industries and commerce. For many families, their whole way of life changed. Their village life of a few hundred was replaced by the town life of thousands. These changes were recognised and addressed by the Methodist organisation. Itinerant preachers went to the people. Wesley's creation of Circuits was pivotal in the development of the movement. This network of voluntary societies extended into new areas from remote hamlets, isolated mining and fishing communities to the growing industrial villages and towns of the midlands and north. Methodism harnessed the ordinary people and made full use of lay abilities.

Accordingly, Methodism tended to establish itself in the very places where the Church of England either had never been or had apparently abandoned or was failing to deliver the Christian message. By the time James became actively involved in the organisation, it was already a separate church. Its heart was the industrial midlands and the north of England together with other major cities like London and Bristol. Whilst it had a socially diverse appeal, its principal target came to be the industrial poor of those communities. The Macclesfield area was a typical location. Although still rural in many respects, it had become significantly industrialised particularly through the growth of the silk industry and its resultant impact on local trades.

James Wright felt a belonging to Methodism. The movement promoted 'social holiness', meaning a commitment to meeting regularly for prayer and bible study, helping others and seeing social justice done. It aimed to involve the ordinary man like James in many appropriate roles within its organisation including as its ministers. It was determined to reach the whole of the community by providing a religious framework for the whole family. James felt the social unrest and political agitation around him. Occasionally, his own religion would become involved with his minister, supporting changes like the legislative reform of the factory hours and conditions. But Methodism was never particularly reformist in its approach to society and did not advocate major changes in society. Ordinary working people felt comfortable within its ranks. It required no revolutionary or political thought that would highlight an individual to an employer, as membership of a trade union inevitably did. Indeed, adherence to the movement brought a degree of respectability. Methodist teaching wanted individuals to lead improved lives largely through self-help and self-reliance, through their own efforts and the support of their families. By adopting an approach to life that depended on their own hard work and their individual determination, every person could rise above their surrounding usually impoverished circumstances. All could lead useful lives through quiet ambition and self-discipline.

This chapel in Park Street, Macclesfield, in which James knelt down, had been started in 1836 by the Methodist New Connexion. James recalled its first service on 12$^{th}$ March 1837 and the glory that had been felt by its congregation. Although only in his early twenties, he had played his part in its establishment and over the ensuing years his ability to serve the movement had been increasingly recognised. He thanked God for his gifts. He looked up during his solitary prayers and viewed the solid simplicity of the chapel in the early morning light. It reflected his being and the purpose chosen for him. The strong central pulpit, the absence of decoration, the smooth stonework and the polished woodwork shone in the growing morning light falling through the long windows. It was simple, strong and structured, reflecting the movement that had embraced him, and continued to meet his quiet aspirations. It gave the sense of belonging he craved.

The call of God had come to end his factory work. His piety, zeal and usefulness had been recommended by the Macclesfield Circuit in 1840 for the regular work of the Ministry. Accepted by the Conference, he had been appointed to Stourbridge in Worcestershire at the start of the regulated three years of probation. In his third year, his preaching and his work made a particular mark at Portwood in Stockport where at the request of the local Circuit, he was re-appointed. He was one of the 140 ministers in a Church of 20,000 members attending some 330 chapels with nearly 40,000 Sunday school scholars.

In his prayers, James thought of Matilda. To complete his life, on 21$^{st}$ May 1845, he married the woman he had known since his childhood. Both had been born in Macclesfield in 1815. Her father was a tailor. He recalled how before their wedding, he and Matilda had prayed together at the nearby small Methodist chapel at Bollin Green, then walked up beside the River Bollin, over the old bridge, to the local Church of St Peters in Prestbury. The marriage had been arranged by licence as his chapel minister had no power to marry them. The simple service was conducted by the local vicar, Henry Pearson. James' father, John, and Lydia Hall, were the witnesses. Matilda Whittaker shared in her husband's beliefs and purpose and looked forward to her role as a minister's wife. They both knew it would be an arduous and somewhat itinerant life. Appointments to any particular Circuit lasted a maximum of three years and they could be sent anywhere. But it was a commitment and a life both felt had been their destination. And it was a life beyond what they might have anticipated earlier in their lives. From humble beginnings, the couple had progressed through their devotion and work within their faith. They were no longer destined for the drudgery of the factory. They had belief and they would have purpose.

James' first full appointment was to the Stafford Circuit in Staffordshire and the newly married couple started their life together in a small house in Foregate Street in Stafford. Their first child was born prematurely at their home on 9$^{th}$ February 1846. Their son was named James after his father and Whittaker after his mother's maiden name which was a popular means of preserving the name of the female side of the family.

His congregation were largely the working people of this bustling midlands town with its pottery and shoe-making works recently linked by railway to the rest of the country. But there were other smaller outlying settlements in the surrounding countryside that required ministry. He preached at the small chapel in County Road but as the Methodist New Connexion thrived, James was instrumental in helping to raise the funds and support to build the new Snow Hill Chapel in Goal Street. However, the family had moved on before it was opened in 1848.

Great Yarmouth, Norfolk, was their new home. It was another growing town. The fishing industry dominated with its vast herring fleet and increased trading links particularly after the railway had arrived in 1844. Life was hard on this east coast and religion an important part of many lives. Sunday religious observance was high and James Wright could expect to have many hundreds of adherents attend one or more of the day's devotions. The congregation were mainly working people who earned their living either from the land or from the sea. The Wright family itself grew with the birth of another son, John Joseph, on 11$^{th}$ December 1847. There was then a brief stop in Mansfield, Nottinghamshire, where Matilda, their only daughter was born in the summer of 1850.

By July 1850, when the young James was just four years old, the family moved to Alnwick in Northumberland where he began to experience something of the England of the time. It was a small and quiet town with a large agricultural hinterland. They lived in South Street, with tradesmen and at least one other minister for neighbours. The property, on the edge of the town, was large and comfortable enough to support the growing family. Another son, Robert Henry, was born there in 1852. Lydia Hall had become their house servant and helped Matilda with the heavy work and the family.

It was a short walk along Percy Street past the Catholic church and down to the Bethel Chapel in St. Michaels Lane off Market Street which was the centre of the town. The Rev. James Wright was paid £23. 18s per quarter. It was roughly £2 per week which was something like four or five times an agricultural labourer or a domestic servant in a large house. Additionally, his house rent of £11 per year and his local poor and health rates were paid by the Circuit. A steady and relatively comfortable life ensued for the minister and his family. The young James would attend the services with the other family members and listen to his father's preaching.

In 1853, Derby became their home. They had a house in Parliament Street in the recently built residential area to the south-east of the town. Methodist New Connexion was one of the longest serving nonconformist bodies in Derby. The original chapel had been built in Devonshire Street in 1824 but by 1836, the Connexion had purchased the New Jerusalem Church in London Street from the Swedenborgians. As at Stafford, James Wright faced much competition from other denominations. Indeed, in the County of Derbyshire, there were hundreds of nonconformist churches and chapels. In Derby itself, there were four or five nonconformist chapels within a short distance with Wesleyan, Primitive Methodist,

Congregational and Baptist vying for membership. However, the Methodist New Connexion movement thrived.

The town typified the industrial revolution that had transformed the English midlands. Derby was at the centre of the sought-after natural resources including coal, limestone, iron and lead which fuelled many aspects of the insatiable appetite of industry. The railways had arrived relatively early in 1839. The North Midland Railway had established its main works there in 1840 and the Midland Railway its headquarters there in 1844. The mining, quarrying, milling and manufacturing expanded and the need for workers increased. Cotton and silk mills employed a good number in their factories. The population of the town had risen from 15,000 in 1801 to nearly 50,000 in 1851. Many had come from the agricultural villages in the hinterland. The town exemplified the major economic and massive social changes of the country.

There was grinding poverty exhibited in the form of poor diet and inadequate housing. Ordinary lives consisted of long hours of repetitive, often hazardous work begun at an early age. Education was limited to the Sunday school for most working children. People had little prospect of any change to their daily fare of work. This was the fertile ground for the role of Methodism. It identified with the search by many for some stability within the vast economic and social changes. Methodist services were full of bible-centred preaching and its relevance in dealing with the ordinary person and their daily issues. There was an enthusiasm in the services with spirited hymns, plain-speaking prayers, and rousing and direct sermons. James' role was to guide and support, admonish and cajole, sympathise and encourage the congregation to lead morally better lives. Much work of his work occurred within the Circuit not only using the chapels as focal points but supported by visits to individual houses and the outlying villages and hamlets.

There was a vast spectrum of life in Derby for the eight-year-old James. Its industrial scale was greater than anywhere he had previously experienced. With its vast growth in population, it was an area where men and women worked hard to survive. They were employed on the land, in the factories and industries, in the engineering works and in the mines. Most workers were unskilled labourers, some were semi-skilled being able to operate machinery or engage in a specialist process, and a few were highly trained. There were long hours and precious little time for anything else. Some turned to drink and a few to religion. He would see people advance and others barely able to sustain themselves. He witnessed huge differences between those with and those without money. He saw the few who largely through their own efforts ventured into betterment and the majority who stayed in their impoverished condition.

The Wright family grew again with Frederick Theophilus being born in the town on 1$^{st}$ September 1854. The two older boys, James and John, then aged eight and six, had become inseparable. The young James Wright's childhood had been one of constant change of location and at the time of a changing society, the stable family environment and his father's work provided great structure to his early life. His home life was modest but not poor. The family were almost inevitably very close given their regular changes of location and environment. Few friends could be maintained and James inevitably developed a close relationship with his brother. His contacts were with his father's congregation and similarly minded adherents to the faith.

Naturally, he was heavily influenced by his parents' beliefs and his father's ministry. His father was a man of high moral worth and sterling integrity. He had the pious look of a minister and the slight appearance of a biblical prophet with his closely cropped beard encompassing his angular jaw. His talents were solid rather than brilliant but were duly appreciated. He had usually remained the full three years in each of his appointments. He thought much of his congregation and had a strong sense of duty. He made the Methodist Rule his study and was careful to both practise and to enforce discipline. He would visit adherents in their homes and share their spiritual victories and failures. He objected to Sabbath-breaking, gaming, wrestling, and tippling. As with many of the nonconformist movements, the challenge of alcohol had become particularly relevant to the preaching. His own home was the model of his faith and had to provide an example to others. It was a caring but strict upbringing for the young James. His mother had a matronly appearance and demeanour. As the eldest child, the young James had to set the example. His life was engineered in basic Methodist principles. Progress was made by personal hard work and strength of character. It meant a sober and industrious disposition. It meant getting on with people of all classes and backgrounds. It meant adapting to changes and to different places. Most of all, it was about self-belief.

James received his education wherever his father was located and his father was keen to ensure that his family received better basic learning than he had obtained. By this time, National Schools had been established both by the Church of England and by the nonconformist movement. In some places, Sunday schools had expanded into day schools. Generally, a basic education of literacy and numeric skills was provided. Reading was paramount. Copperplate script was important. Basic arithmetic was learned by chanting times tables. Other skills centred on the technical rather than the academic. The purpose was often to fit the youngsters to the range of basic tasks that would make them employable in the local industries and trades. His family background ensured that he was a diligent pupil. James learned and developed his skills. He applied himself to the tasks. His bold, clear and upright writing demonstrated his assurance. He was particularly numerate. He read and studied. He enjoyed his lessons and the process of learning. His parents gave him the encouragement and atmosphere to learn.

By 1860, the Wright family had moved to Ripon in Yorkshire. It was another significant change of environment. Ripon was a market town of an overwhelmingly agricultural area of northern Yorkshire with a population of only a few thousand. The industrial revolution had barely touched the town. There was an iron works and a varnish works but none of the heavy manufacturing works or factories. It served a large local area with its shops, its weekly market of animals and its produce stalls in the central square. There was a mix of residences from simple terraced houses to the more palatial villas of prosperous tradesmen and professionals.

The Wrights lived at Bondgate Green by the side of the River Skell. It was a typical residential street of brick-built terraced properties in sight of the magnificent Ripon Cathedral situated high above and dominating the town. The house was just large enough to accommodate James, Matilda and their five children who settled to the peaceful pace of the town. The Methodist New Connection Church was at Blossomgate. It was a large and imposing building constructed in solid redbrick with large windows. The congregation was sedately manageable by the Reverend Wright but there was plenty of choice from the usual religions. There was the High Anglican Cathedral, the Anglican Holy Trinity, the Catholic St. Wifrid's and the rival Wesleyan Methodists at Coltsgate.

For the fourteen-year-old James, Ripon was an entirely different feel compared to previous places his family had resided. He walked daily to his work from Bondgate Green, through Skellgarths, up Kirkgate, into the town square and then to High Skellgate. He saw the range of market town businesses. The shops and services dealt with everything from Rayner's drapers to Parkin's chemists, from Hebden's ironmongers to Moss's cabinet makers, besides grocers, bakers, butchers and a host of public houses. It was a town of professionals and their office staff, tradesmen and their assistants, artisans and their apprentices, farmers and their labourers, with domestic servants, carters and provincial town workers. The town gently thrived and life moved slowly.

The young James worked as a printer in the town. Thirlways had been owned and managed by Henry Steel Thirlway since his father had handed over the business to him in 1850. It was a printing, bookbinding, bookselling and stationery business situated in High Skellgate on the corner of the main square. Henry Thirlway was a leading member of the Anglican Church and the local community. Under him, James learned something of the business. He worked with print machinery and the various chemicals and materials that were used. He saw the shop and business in operation with its products, orders and management. He was now bringing home a weekly wage whilst his siblings were still at school.

But Sunday remained set aside. He sat beside his mother, brothers and sister in the Blossomgate church. He knelt and prayed. He rose and sang. He listened attentively to his father's words. He was now set on the course similar to that which his father had undertaken. His footsteps were those of the Methodist New Connection movement. The bible classes and the Sunday school had taught him the words and his family had fostered his faith. He had become actively involved in the teaching. He had seen the duties and work of his father. He reflected on the way forward with times for study and for thought. Although he was learning the printing trade, he was steeped in the Methodist movement. It was a sober and modest life but where family and church dominated.

In 1863, James' father was appointed to the Sheffield North Circuit. It was a considerable Circuit with many societies and chapels which had a team of ministers to manage. Under Alexander Kilham, Sheffield was the founding locality of the New Methodist Connexion and of great importance to the movement. It was another major change for the young James. Like Derby, Sheffield had erupted with the advent of industrial development and the expansion of the railways. However, it was five times the size of Derby and contained over 250,000 people. The original town had been swamped by its industrial expansion although the beautiful Pennine Hills lay largely undisturbed close by. Derby had been a wonder to the ten-year-old James. Sheffield was equally amazing to the seventeen-year-old man. Industries flourished and soaked up the poor displaced from the countryside. Vast factories, metal works, engineering establishments produced an array of goods. The railways led the transportation of raw materials into and finished products out of the town. Vast areas of new housing had grown up to accommodate the increasing population. Commerce and finance ensured that the wheels of industry turned to profit. The metropolis only confirmed his reflections of Derby with a colossal gulf between rich and poor. Indeed, the town was a focal point of conflict generated by the growing organisation of the labour movement. Working conditions were the subject of much discontent and in this period there were violent incidents directed principally at employers but also involving fellow workers who would not join unions.

New Methodist Connexion was not immune from the unrest and was naturally in competition with other movements for the hearts and minds of the people. There were many religious movements, there were new groups of workers, political organisations, charitable institutions, social and economic bodies working to secure their place and their support within the population. The economic changes had fostered social and cultural reactions that were manifest in a huge variety of philosophies concerning the way life should be undertaken. Young men sought to find their place and their comfort in the vast array of bewildering movements. There was every attraction, from the public houses that met the basic pleasures to libraries and colleges that provided educational needs; from the trade unions that harnessed the aspirations of the workers to the political parties that largely represented the middle and upper classes; from the clubs and sporting societies that gave physical outlets to the charities that met social deprivation.

James was now a young man of seventeen and he had witnessed the reasons that had fostered the various movements. He had grown up with the massive changes in the country. Not least was the huge increase in the population evidenced by the growth of the towns. Industrial progress had been made by a combination of business initiative and technical invention. There were vast contrasts with glaring examples of social harmony and disharmony, prosperity and destitution, enterprise and drudgery in both urban and rural areas. One person was well-housed, well-fed, educated and had a good job while another had inadequate housing, poor diet, illiteracy and a subsistence wage. He could see that there was much spiritual destitution. People lived with the constant fear of unemployment and the consequences of the poor law institution of the workhouse. He resolved that it would not be for him. James believed in the gospel of work, seriousness of character, respectability and self-help. He knew that the individual was free to get on by self-help, character, thrift, punctuality and duty.

Whilst there were alternative routes, his beliefs ensured continued service to the New Methodist Connexion. As he matured, he naturally and enthusiastically followed the same path his father had some thirty years before. He became a class teacher, tract distribution and leader. The movement came to dominate his thoughts and any aspirations were encouraged by his parents. The New Connexion Methodist movement itself had grown over those same thirty years. By the mid-1860s, it had 650 chapels, 250 preachers, nearly 1,300 local preachers, over 30,000 members, over 3,000 probationers, some 550 Sunday schools, 12,000 teachers and 75,000 scholars. There were also overseas missions in Canada and China. Methodist New Connexion had come a long way in its seventy-odd year history. It had virtually doubled in size in the twenty years of the life of the young James. There were opportunities within the movement to take a role.

It meant that there was a critical decision to be made. He had to contemplate the direction of his life. There was some heart-searching, some discussion between father and son and between mother and son. There was a great deal of prayer and considerable thought. Whilst he was content with his training in the printing field, the religious path beckoned. But there would be consequences. It would mean a life away from his family. It would mean strict adherence to the Rule and an itinerant life. His name was put forward. The Circuit recommended him to the Conference. James followed his father. At age twenty, James Whitaker Wright entered the ministry.

He had to serve his probationary period. In 1866, he started at Shields in the Tyne and Wear Circuit in north-east England and then moved the next year to what had been his father's probationary Circuit at Stockport. It was his moment to leave the family home and venture out on his own. His family were modestly delighted with the start that their son was making. All of their Christian pride went with the young James. Father and son had seen this huge growth in the movement. Indeed, they were playing their individual parts in its progression. Both were part of a substantive movement with a strong sense of purpose. James Whitaker Wright considered that the destiny of his life was settled. He embarked on his probation with a view to becoming a minister with the New Methodist Connexion.

# CHAPTER 2

# Making the Way

He realised that his decision would disappoint his father and mother. He had tried his utmost to pursue the role his upbringing apparently determined for his life. He had endeavoured for two years. He had prayed. He had reflected. It meant a rejection of all that his family architecture had built for him. But what the movement had destined for him was not what he wanted. He reconsidered his father's life and decided that it was not for him. He craved something different. He was single and spent much time alone with his thoughts. He was away from his family for the first time in his life. And the anxiety had gradually increased as the major decision approached. It made him sick with worry. He could not continue in the task. There was the heart-searching and discussion with his father. And there was respect and understanding for his wishes. It was a close family who had supported each other on their many travels. The young James gave up his probationary ministry in 1868, relinquishing on the grounds of ill health.

The Wright family had moved in 1866 to Halifax in Yorkshire for a new ministry by James senior. His father had been delighted to be appointed Superintendent to the Halifax South Circuit along with a number of other ministers. The Circuit covered seven chapels. The town had a strong association with John Wesley who had initially preached there in August 1748 on the edge of Ogden Moor. The address had led to the formation of a house meeting and eventually to the building in 1773 of a chapel known as Mount Sion at Bradshaw. Wesley came to visit in April 1774 and again in May 1790 when he was a frail old man of eighty-seven years. The Kilhamites took over the chapel for Methodist New Connexion after Wesley's death.

Like nearly every northern industrial town, Halifax had grown significantly in the previous fifty years and thereby altered its character. It retained its town centre and market but industry had arrived to dominate the landscape. Its original wool base had encouraged a host of textile factories but with cotton latterly dominating. There were nearby coal mines and quarries, chemical and iron works and over one hundred trades operating within the town. It had an extensive commercial heart with the usual shops and services. However, within a mile or so of its centre lay the open countryside of the Pennine moors peppered with tiny villages. Vast open countryside lay around the dense residential and industrial town.

Both in their early twenties, the two brothers, James and John, started a business in Halifax in May 1868. They began as partners of a business as stationers and printers under the trading name of 'Wright Brothers'. They opened for business at 77 Northgate appropriately opposite the Temperance Hall. There was an eagerness to succeed. They used their basic education and their later training. James had trained as a printer and John as a millwright. They built on their inherent philosophies of the work ethic and personal improvement. Methodist teachings had instilled self-reliance and self-belief. They relied on their own characters and their regard for each other. It was a powerful combination. They had every hope that the business would thrive. They advertised on the front page of the *Halifax Courier* for their opening two months. They strived for over a year but their enterprise did not succeed. In early July 1869, the brothers sold off their stationery and book stock with a view to concentrating on the printing but by the end of the month and owing much more than the business could support, they made a composition with their creditors. The settlement was only accepted when their father assisted. The brothers agreed to pay their creditors eight shillings in the pound, only some 40% of their debts, by equal instalments on 25th September and 25th December 1869 and a final instalment on 25th March 1870. Their father, the Reverend James Wright, guaranteed payment of the last instalment. The arrangement was registered in the Bankruptcy Court on 31$^{st}$ July 1869. It was another disappointment and had a profound effect on the young James. It was the second time in only about year or so that he had given up. His path to a religious career had ended in resignation and his venture into business had ended in bankruptcy. Both were personal humiliations for him and challenged his confidence and self-belief.

At this time, the Reverend James Wright had completed his time at Halifax and was appointed to the Oldbury Circuit at West Bromwich near Birmingham. It was with mixed feelings and some relief that he and the family were to move. However, shortly before he left for his new appointment, he contracted a severe cold and during that winter, it became clear that he was not recovering. The family moved to Oldbury but the Rev. James Wright was not able to take up his ministerial duties. He wrote to a friend that he was very much distressed on account of the Circuit and that his personal sufferings were like dust in the balance compared with the anxiety he experienced on this account. But he considered it all in the order of divine providence and, dark and painful as this dispensation was, he thought it was God's will that was being done. He knew that he was dying. He lingered painfully for many months until 21$^{st}$ April 1870, when he died peacefully in the expectation of his salvation. He had served thirty years in the Ministry. He was fifty-five years old. His life was eulogised in the Methodist 1870 Annual Conference minutes with all the respect that the movement could muster. He had been a faithful servant to the cause and was praised for his steadiness of purpose.

The death meant dramatic changes had to be undertaken. It was a time for the family members to consider their future individually and collectively. All of the children were adults capable of work and self-determination. Their financial circumstances had to be addressed. The Reverend James Wright had left only a spiritual legacy. Matilda Wright, aged fifty-five, took a grocer's shop in Bordsley, a suburb of Birmingham. She set up business and home there with her daughter Matilda aged twenty and her two sons, Robert aged eighteen who was working as a librarian and Frederick aged sixteen who was starting out as a photographer. The older two brothers decided on a different course. James and John chose to emigrate.

It was a major decision for the two young men. All the elements that had formed their lives governed the move. They were self-reliant and sought some purpose and direction following the events of the previous year. They wanted to explore the opportunities of an entirely new life and it was their answer to the sense of failure and the loss that had occurred. But their plans included the determination that the move would not cause the end of this close-knit family and they left with the firm intention to reunite the family at some stage. It was a dramatic moment for James. It would be a third lifestyle change in as many years. He had not yet found his future but he needed to close the past.

It was not an altogether strange move. Many young men were taking the same steps, principally emigrating to the English-speaking countries of America and Australia and South Africa. It was the time when there were great opportunities in these continents. There were territorial and economic expansions in agriculture and industry, business and commerce, enterprise of all kinds that required a range of skills. The countries required people of all abilities to fill their expansionist philosophies. America typified. The Civil War had ended in 1865 and there was a healing process and a reconstruction to be addressed. The vast west beckoned individuals like the farmers, the miners, the entrepreneurs and adventurers. The American east coast continued to industrialise and called the masses to ever expand their cities. Previous immigration was now fuelling the current wave. Many immigrants had enjoyed some kind of better life and their letters to their relatives painted an optimistic picture. Lives remained hard in many cases but there were opportunities to improve their positions. The reasons for emigration were many and varied and often as much to escape current circumstances as to better the future. Passages were relatively cheap and were sometimes assisted by organisations and often by relatives. Whilst whole families emigrated, men often went in advance. Young single males made up a substantial part of the movement. The brothers went their separate ways. John went to Canada and settled in Toronto but James eventually decided on the United States.

His practical education and subsequent work training enabled him to start as an assayer. There was an increasing demand for this service. It required a good knowledge of the basic chemistry involved and some good basic equipment. It needed a great attention to detail and the ability to process and to measure the material accurately. The business was operated in a variety of ways and locations. Some individuals simply set up office in one of the main cities or, if there was enough work, in one of the mining towns and advertised in the local newspapers. Samples were simply received, assayed and the results sent almost by return of post. Others worked on contract either for mining companies or at single mines where there might be a need to assess constantly the quality of the ore. Still others worked in company with engineers and prospectors seeking new claims.

James was sober, smart, neat and polite. He was industrious. He continued his reading and learning. All the basic characteristics of his earlier years supported his work. It was the time when James learned about mining, acquired and developed his knowledge of its engineering, metallurgy and assaying. He studied mines and their construction. He saw how they were worked. He noted where they were located. He developed his assaying and geological skills. He learned about dealing in land, in interests, in commodities. He learned about people and business. He learned that assayers and mine managers were the people to know the real value of any mine and that most of the industry was based upon pure speculation. He saw the use of company promotion and the money that was involved. His developing entrepreneurial knowledge together with his sober application, his attention to detail and engaging personality provided the basis for his steady progress.

The harsh environments of the mines and the mining camps were brutal and basic. The precious ores of gold, silver and other metals were invariably located in rugged and inhospitable territory, often hundreds of miles from any kind of settlement and transport link. As finds were made and inevitably became known, prospectors would descend on the area. Tented camps suddenly appeared, followed by makeshift shacks and huts. Often, there was little to be found and the camp was abandoned to leave a few determined to continue. However, if the discoveries increased, the population and the buildings grew. The tradesmen and businessmen would arrive and suddenly a town of several thousand was created. There was little lawlessness as such despite the often lack of legal and administrative infrastructure. Most people simply got on with their particular activity of metal prospecting, selling goods and providing services. But there were clashes occasionally with the local Indians, and occasional internal lawbreaking settled by vigilante groups.

He would recount his own adventure with the local tribe. Once, while prospecting in Idaho near the Snake River, where Native Americans were on the warpath, an Indian and his wife pitched their tents near his hut and he paid them a call. He gave the woman a plug of tobacco, an act which probably saved his life, for shortly afterwards a war party of natives came to his shanty to kill him, but the squaw who had received the tobacco induced them to leave. They proceeded down the river, and massacred three of his men. It was indicative of the circumstances then prevailing. The way of life of the prairie tribes was under severe threat from the immigration and it was often only the small groups or individuals who could be ousted by violent means.

It was a volatile time in the vast areas of the American west. There was a huge open space between the civilised eastern states of America and the Rocky Mountains. The native tribes wandered over their territories in their nomadic lifestyle. Settlements had gradually been established and major towns were beginning to emerge. Small farming towns had developed as soon as the railways had been constructed, enabling the transportation of every commodity in both directions. Farming communities frequented with their quiet reassurance and cow towns rose to prominence with their wild recklessness. On the edge of the Rocky Mountains, discoveries of precious metals, particularly gold and silver, fuelled the creation of, often, temporary settlements.

Vast numbers were pouring in from Europe to the United States and its western frontier. They came from England and Ireland, Scandinavia, central and eastern Europe, fleeing from political and religious oppression or simply economic depression. Inside America, others were escaping the aftermath of the American Civil War; those who had lost status, their livelihood or their mind. The plains offered the opportunity to begin again. Ranchers raised their cattle, farmers planted crops, tradesmen started businesses and storekeepers opened their shops. Artisans catered for the specialist requirements, everything from undertaking to dentistry. The professionals came in the form of lawyers and bankers. The entertainment people flourished with saloons, dance halls and casinos. The chancers came to get rich quickly with the prospectors and miners seeking the gold and silver. The unskilled came in their thousands to be employed in the range of labouring and menial jobs that any town required. It overwhelmed the indigenous tribes who oscillated between sporadic armed resistance and peace treaties that could never deliver what was promised. It created a marginalised group and inevitable issues of culture and attitude. There were also tensions within the new populations with the heterogeneous mix of nations, religions, cultures, individual abilities, ambitions and aspirations. It was a competition and challenging environment. Conflict and some lawlessness resulted. The life was hard and uncertain. Many prospered, mostly in a steady but unspectacular way. A few made their fortunes.

But the brutality was not confined to the local native, to the mining settlements and to the nature of the land. There was ruthlessness about the mining business itself. Its speculative nature generated greed and conflict. Fraud and deception were frequent. Claims and camps, mines and companies, appeared and disappeared rapidly as individuals sought to make their fortunes. But the entrepreneurs dominated the industry. And their principles were confined to their pockets. They had the financial clout to buy at their own price the claims and mines of initial prospectors who had little capital to develop their own find and a great deal of incentive to realise their discovery.

James took little time to understand the realities of the mining industry and that it was more profitable to deal in the industry than prospect for the ore and physically work to retrieve it from in the ground. The view led him on his commercial ventures. He worked and saved money. His work enabled him to recognise a good prospect. Eventually, he was able to buy a few shares in a mine that looked as if it would be profitable. It was only a few dollars at first. Gradually he added to his investments. He bought a mining claim outright for 500 dollars and sold a half interest in it for enough to pay back his original investment and provide working capital. The mine proved profitable, and a little later he sold his remaining half interest for a good profit. Then he did the same thing with other properties and kept doing it until he was dealing in amounts that made a profit worthwhile. He boasted that after the first 10,000 dollars was made, the rest was easy.

There were stock dealing centres in the west, typically in Denver, but the centre of business activity was the east. It was in Philadelphia that he started dealing in stock. Wright initially had limited money but he was a man who could command money. His appearance and personality enhanced his progress. He looked handsome, tall and athletic, with black hair and flashing dark eyes. He was always sober and well-dressed but not unduly dignified. He exhibited some hyperactivity and had a personal magnetism. His conversation was excellent and he made friends readily. His speech had a convincing and abnormally self-confident manner. He was prompt and fair in his business dealings and his transactions reflected credit on him. There was an honest and straightforward appearance about him. He was regarded as up-to-date in his business and shrewd. He engaged in the brokerage business dealing in grain and petroleum. He dealt in Philadelphia Oil. By 1876, Wright's career as a stockbroker was progressing.

The Philadelphia Stock Exchange traded increasingly in the securities of firms that could not meet the listing requirements of the New York Stock Exchange, such as an exchange-specified aggregate market value of publicly held shares or the minimum number of shareholders. They tended to be younger or smaller firms little known outside their local markets. In addition, individual state laws requiring registration and thereby some protection against fraud also gave exemption to firms listed on a regional exchange. Again, Philadelphia benefited. Wright grew prosperous. In the process, he gradually abandoned his first name, reducing it to a 'J', and used his middle name of Whitaker. He was now J. Whitaker Wright, a member of a Philadelphia Stock Exchange that was second only to its New York counterpart.

Philadelphia was one of the richest cities in the world. It was a vast metropolis of some 850,000 people. Its unique location on the Delaware and Schuylkill Rivers combined with excellent rail links made it a thriving trade and business centre. Monstrous wharves hugged the rivers, innumerable industries and factories lay behind them and swathes of housing predominated. The city centre was full of large and dominating administration, business and cultural buildings. Tramways served the commuting workers. It bustled and boomed. Its suburbs expanded. Whitaker Wright adapted to the city life and business in his usual confident way. He was undaunted by its size and unfazed by its activity.

The prosperity of Philadelphia had led its leading citizens to stage one of the world's leading displays. The 1876 Centennial Exposition had been a long time in the making and planning. In 1870, the Philadelphia City Council resolved to have the Centennial Exhibition in the city. After the relevant legislation had been passed in 1871, a United States Commission was established with a representative from every state and territory. Finance was raised by the Centennial Board of Finance through bond issue, loans, state grants and donations. European nations were invited to exhibit. The formal name was the International Exposition of Arts, Manufacturers, and Products of the Soil and Mine. The official theme was to celebrate the United States Centennial. It was opened on May 10$^{th}$ 1876 by Ulysses S. Grant, President of the United States, with 186,000 people attending to witness the occasion.

It was a time for a reunion. The brothers had kept very much in contact and John joined Whitaker in Philadelphia to witness the world event. John had gone to Toronto and got work as a machinist. He started making his way. In 1874, he had married Jessie Firstbrook whose father was a lumber dealer and box maker and whose brothers were machinists in their father's factory. But he was eager, as always, to improve his knowledge and understanding and himself.

John and Whitaker visited this marvel of the world in Fairmount Park. Its scale was almost unimaginable to the brothers. They travelled in the horse-drawn trolley approaching the park from the east. At the Schuylkill River crossing, they began to see the exhibition in its full glory. There were more than 200 buildings constructed within the grounds inside a perimeter fence of some three miles long. The impressive main exhibition building was prefabricated of wood, iron, glass and stone enclosing over twenty-one acres, and was the largest building in the world. They gave their fifty-cent paper script and entered.

The main hall had an interior central avenue over one mile. Exhibits dealt with mining, metallurgy, manufacturing, education and science with those from the United States at the centre and those from other nations placed around according to the country's distance from America. Exhibits included Alexander Graham Bell's telephone, the Remington typographic machine, Heinz ketchup, and the

Wallace-Farmer electric dynamo. Whitaker took particular interest in the rock collections from Canada and Norway with their examples of precious minerals.

They marvelled at range of exhibits, everything from the huge Bartholdi fountain to the latest industrial machines and plant in the machinery hall. The exhibition impacted on Whitaker. He saw the latest technology and the tremendous advances that were being made. His interest in mining was reinforced by the displays in that field. There was the agricultural hall for farm machinery and products, the horticultural hall for the plants and the memorial hall for the arts. Whitaker was especially taken with the Italian sculptures. Twenty-six US states and eleven countries had their own buildings. The two brothers inevitably orientated to the British buildings comprising what looked like extensive residential properties but containing the best the country could display. There were Minton tiles and Doulton pots, all kinds of furniture, a range of chocolate sweets, crafted items and manufactured products. There was the display of the new bicycle with tension spokes and a large front wheel nicknamed the 'penny-farthing'.

The Exposition had a significant impact on John. Although he had established himself in Toronto in his father-in-law's lumber business, he was keen to progress in the new energy of the time. He wondered at the electric dynamo in the exhibition and it stimulated him to learn about the power. He subsequently attended the lectures of Elihu Thomson and Edwin James Houston at the Philadelphia Central High School on electricity. He so impressed them that he entered into their employment where he worked on generators. He went on to help install North America's first electric-arc street lamp before returning to Toronto to further his career in that field.

Whitaker continued to prosper as a stockbroker. At age thirty-one, he claimed to be a millionaire. His wealth was rising and then his private life bloomed. He met Anna Edith Weightman in Philadelphia in 1877. She was just sixteen. Whitaker was thirty-two and not unnaturally coy about his age. She was a striking young lady with dark hair and strong eyes. Her father was Isaac Weightman who had been born in Philadelphia but spent some of his early life in Illinois before returning to the city where he became a blacksmith and married Sarah More in October 1856. They had lived in Ward 24 Precinct 5 in 1860. Anna was their third child born on 13th June 1861. At the outbreak of the Civil War, Isaac joined the 29th Pennsylvania Infantry and was killed at Pine Knob Georgia on 15th June 1864, two days after Anna's third birthday. Her brother Isaac was posthumously born in October 1864. Anna's mother remarried a labourer, Christian Eckfeldt, in October 1865. Two girls and a boy were subsequently born to the couple. By 1870, the whole family, including Anna, her sister Sarah and her brother Isaac together with their step-siblings lived in Philadelphia's District 78. It was a humble and poor background. It was basic, crowded and there was a growing conflict between her mother and step-father. Whitaker determined that she was the lady for his future.

At this time, the Wright family reunion had been completed. His mother, his sister and his two youngest brothers emigrated from England. With Whitaker's help, they settled in the city on North 46th Street. Robert started as a journeyman printer and Frederic became a stationery engineer. Not long after their arrival, his sister, Matilda, met James A. Browne. Suddenly, there were two weddings in the Wright family within a month of each other. Matilda married James Browne in April 1878 and Whitaker married Anna Weightman in May 1878. The Wright family was established in their new country.

Whitaker and his wife started their lives together at 2304 Oxford Street in Philadelphia. She immediately became pregnant and a son, Ernest Whitaker, was born in February 1879. There was a short-lived joy before Ernest died within just five weeks on 13th March of marasmus, a severe wasting of the tissue and muscles. With infant mortality rates extremely high, it was not an unusual occurrence. The parents were naturally devastated and it was a sad little ceremony when the child was buried two days later at the Mount Moriah Cemetery. It was an unhappy start to the children they both craved. The Wright family were there to support and Anna Edith was still only eighteen. They retained their optimism and intention to have a family.

As his domestic life settled, Whitaker continued his business advancement. It had not been without moments of difficulty. In June 1876, he was involved in the incorporation of the Philadelphia Woolen Manufacturing Company with Edward Saxon, W.A. Smithers, John A. McKenzie and E.S. Wheeler. The capital was to consist of $300,000 divided into 6,000 shares of $50 each. A legal requirement was that 10% of the stock had to be paid at the time of incorporation. However, the only basis for this was a cheque for $30,000 apparently loaned by a Mr. A.P. Harris but never cashed and never shown in the company books. The factory was never purchased and the whole enterprise collapsed but not before stock had been sold to Mr. Swaim Stewart, the company's book-keeper from March 1877. He maintained that he had loaned the company money and had purchased stock and had not been paid for his services. The company founders together with Harris were charged with conspiracy to defraud in October 1877 and after some initial hearings in the Magistrates' Court, a grand jury found true bills against them in February 1878. But the action never proceeded.

However, it was in mining that he found his particular interest and business advancement. He maintained a particular regard for gold and silver mining. His interest in mining was fuelled by the continued gold and silver discoveries in Colorado and other states bordering the Rocky Mountains. Various mining operations had particularly commenced in the eastern Rockies. In February 1878, rich silver ore discoveries had been made at Leadville, near Denver, Colorado. It was set high in the Rockies, over 1,000 feet higher than Denver, itself a mile high above sea level, and an arduous journey to get there. However, within four months, the place had grown beyond recognition. By August, a population exceeding 4,000 had gathered at Leadville with over 500 buildings being put up including many stores and offices, two banks and a newspaper office. There were churches, a public school and government offices including a police station. Within a few miles, there were other nearby camps of prospectors. Most got there by horse or horse and wagon or on the only stagecoach from Georgetown, near Denver, where the railroad ended.

After the initial hand prospecting and simple mining with pick and shovel, the Leadville operations soon became an affair of large capitals, of extensive machinery, and of works too onerous and expensive to be undertaken except by the co-operation of large companies. The working of isolated claims rapidly deteriorated. The silver ore was initially freighted to the railroad for shipment to Omaha and St. Louis for processing but soon this activity took place on the spot with heavy stamps to crush the ore and smelting plants to access the silver. Mining shafts became deeper and galleries longer. Great organisation was required.

Initially, local men like Horace Tabor had speculated and become fabulously rich on apparently little financial investment in the early rich claims. But as seams gave out and further exploration was necessary, funding became more hazardous. There could be no certainty that further discoveries would provide silver ore yields that warranted the capital required. Stock companies were formed but results were decidedly mixed. There was significant initial investment from St. Louis but the investors from New York and Boston were sceptical. It had been a time of great mining speculation and considerable losses.

Whitaker Wright had been watching the developments at Leadville with considerable interest. The newspapers had been full of the discoveries of ore and the expansion of the mining industry in the area. He thought the moment was right to make a move. The initial individual prospecting had given way to the commercial enterprise necessary to get the ore. The purchase of existing claims and their development by means of a company flotation was the way forward. Although, he assumed that much of the best ground had been taken it might still be possible to exploit the area. The opportunity for investment remained.

Accordingly, he travelled there in early December 1879 with Franklin Stewart and Samuel Long, representing several Philadelphia interests. It was a long and arduous journey. From Philadelphia to Denver, the railroad provided reasonable comfort. But then, it was a two-day stagecoach journey from Georgetown, the terminus of the Colorado Central Railway. They were exhausted by the trip but were greeted by a town extending by the day and an arena of activity. Philadelphia had only just begun to freeze when they left but the temperatures of Leadville had been well below freezing for some time. They found accommodation was available at a price and the three quickly settled to their task. Wright had already done some homework but he knew that there was nothing like seeing the ground. He needed to find the right site and judge the logistics and cost of the development.

Wright was surprised how well the town was laid out and the range of services. Nearly all buildings were made of wood although bricks were beginning to appear. The main streets comprised the commercial stores and offices with hotels, places to eat and drink.

The finest was Harrison Avenue which boasted gas lighting. The residential areas adjoined the commercial heart and spilled out towards the surrounding hills. There was a local government, police system, public school and churches. There were hundreds of stores and offices, a post office and many banks. An opera house had been established. The population was on the verge of 30,000. The *Leadville Times,* the *Leadville Democrat* and other newspapers provided all the local information and gossip, carrying news, advertisements for properties, mines and businesses. Silver ore was being freighted to the railroad for shipment to works at Omaha and St. Louis from where huge investment had been attracted. Mines were being worked by an army of casual labourers under the watchful eyes of mine managers anxious to serve their owners. Wright noted the enormous optimism that prevailed. The silver discoveries had continued and the prospect of direct railroad access increased the promise of money-making. Whilst there may have been some evening rowdiness outside the saloons and places of entertainment, the majority of people lived an entirely domestic existence in the many family residences. It was a comfortable place to live. It was cosmopolitan in the extreme. All nationalities and all parts of America seemed to be there, the speculator and the labourer, the skilled and the professional, the manager and the storekeeper, the single men and the families accommodated themselves in the growing town. The town itself had grown rapidly but matured in character with all the services and administration demanded by a resident population.

The altitude and the mountains and lakes had initially provided an idyllic backdrop to the mining industry and its commercial hinterland. But much of the landscape around the town had been transformed into an industrial scene. There were scores of mine shafts with numerous surface buildings and pit head towers and winches. Parts of the surrounding hills had been hacked away to leave stark outcrops of rock. Huge piles of waste rock littered the area. Large industrial plants stood against the scenery, their tall chimneys belching black smoke. Machinery and plant, stores and materials, wagons and trucks lay piled everywhere. Rough roads littered the hills. Individual gangs of workers were dwarfed by the enormous industrial enterprise. It was a landscape not unfamiliar to Whitaker Wright who recalled his days at Derby, Sheffield and Halifax. It looked a gigantic spillage of industrial working. But the essential activity lay in the financial transactions undertaken in town itself and beyond.

There was much speculation not merely relating to the location of silver seams but perhaps more to the transactions of ownership and shares, interest and investment. Ventures were readily available for sale. Bargains were advertised. Investment opportunities were promoted. The initial days of solitary prospectors had quickly been superseded by commercial arrangements involving many parties. It was clear that it had become an affair of large capital, extensive machinery, the organisation of labour, and the logistics of freight. Large capital outlays and detailed management were needed. The choice was vast. Already, large mining companies had been established. It was a time for smart men. Large sums of money were already being paid for an interest in claims, for the equipment and buildings required and for the wages for the labourers. Much of it was pure speculation. Seams of silver could vary enormously in any claim. It did not deter the men with money. Companies had been set up which were trading on the major stock exchanges. Speculation and sharp practice was rife. The 'salting' of the mine to provide the samples that would induce purchase no doubt occurred, as did the practice of 'freezing out', the mine manager who was pessimistic about the mine under his control but then reluctantly takes the shares at a low price only to discover the richness of the venture. With the usual crop of unscrupulous frauds, it was the ability to assay the quality and quantity of the ore that could be economically extracted from the ground that became the skill to possess.

The prize sites on Fryer Hill were well established and controlled by Horace Tabor. The initial New Discovery claim made in April 1878 had proved rich and had been quickly followed by the Chrysolite, the Robert E. Lee and the Little Pittsburg. But there was distrust that the silver ore seam extended to the western slope of the adjacent Yankee Hill. Wright walked over the freezing and windswept area. He carefully examined the formation of Fryer Hill and studied the dip of the ore vein and its formation. The central issue was obvious. The ore vein extended over Fryer Hill from the Chrysolite to the Robert E. Lee mine. But he had to decide if that vein extended beyond those boundaries. The claims that were available for purchase lay adjacent to the Robert E. Lee. He walked over and over the snow-covered sites. He knew that the Denver City mine had been worked for some two years but had not produced any spectacular results. The samples from the available site seemed to indicate a good silver yield. But they were only samples and veins could give out just as easily as they became plentiful. Wright pondered and his instinct rose in him. He became convinced that there was a real prospect.

There was the issue of price. Negotiations took a week or two but the Denver City mine was purchased in late December and a little later, the two further claims of the Shamus O' Brien and the Quadrilateral acquired. The substantial sum of $325,000 was the price. It was a bold calculation and a considerable amount of money rode on the decision. It was to be a significant gamble for him and his colleagues and he returned to Philadelphia to sort out the consequential business. The arrangements for the investors and his own financial contribution had to be considered. The establishment of the relevant company, its board, share price and launch gave him considerable thought.

He knew that the Leadville project would require much of his time and energy if it was to succeed. It was the largest project that he had tackled. He had to be single-minded and focus the whole of his attention on the matter. He would have to spend time away from home and devote the best part of his energies to the task. He wanted no distractions. His wife was again pregnant and he wanted to have his home life settled. After the early death of his son, Whitaker wanted every comfort and facility provided for his lady. He set out to provide the accommodation that their position warranted both on a domestic and business basis. It had to be somewhere smart and well located to enable business associates to be entertained and his wife afforded position. On 10$^{th}$ March 1880, he bought a four-storey brick and stone house at the north-west corner of 36$^{th}$ and Locust Streets. The property was located in heart of Philadelphia. He paid $12,000 but with a mortgage of $10,000. He wisely put the property into his wife's name. Two servants were engaged on a permanent basis. Their daughter, Mabel, was born there in the April. It was a delight for the whole family.

He could now turn his full attention to Leadville, the launch and development of the company and the mines that had been acquired. He was determined that the enterprise should succeed. As a man of comfortable means and no little wealth, he wanted the venture to represent a major step forward in his business life and his financial position. He wanted the recognition.

# CHAPTER 3

# Making the American Fortune

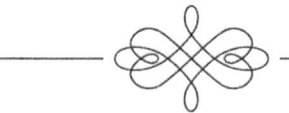

He needed little tutoring in the process of making his enterprise work. He had seen many companies succeed and fail on the Philadelphia Stock Exchange. He knew the mechanics.

The financiers had to be recruited. Those that would form the board and those that would support the initial share issue. Their money needed to be assured. The company would require a name that would sell the shares and the Denver City Consolidated Silver Mining Company was born. Its name contained all the right ingredients. It reflected the name of one of the mines on the property holding, it appeared as the leading company of the capital of Colorado and it gave the reassurance of being substantial and solid. The capital issue of the company had to be determined and the number and price of the share settled. He wanted it to be big. The prospectus needed careful composition. He knew the value of presentation and the need to deliver optimism. There was plenty of competition from the host of other companies operating in the same Leadville area and the market was full of mining companies that fuelled the inordinate speculation. His company needed to harness the fever.

He needed to establish a sound financial basis and he needed to make the attraction large. He raised the money for the Denver City mine purchase from his own resources and from those he had canvassed before visiting Leadville. His status on the Philadelphia Exchange was enough to attract the necessary finance and he set about launching the company. The Denver City Consolidated Silver Mining Company was incorporated in Denver Colorado in the spring of 1880 with 500,000 shares being issued at $10 each to give the company a capital of $5 million. Whitaker Wright became the president and George Smedley the secretary. He promoted the shares in Denver, Philadelphia and New York. The first receipts of the sales enabled the company to purchase of the mining property from Wright and his partners for cash and shares thus achieving immediate reward for the company founders.

Wright was aware that he had to show some early intent of the company. He wanted to demonstrate that the company was not a theoretical speculation but a practical enterprise based upon the extraction of quality ore from the mines. Accordingly, the development of the mine workings was a priority and Wright spent part of the summer of 1880 in Leadville. He displayed perseverance and energy. He worked with Mr. W.G. Shedd who had assisted him in obtaining control of the mine and whom he appointed as manager and financial agent. The work was steadily prosecuted. Four shafts were sunk. As little quality ore was found, drilling was started in the Denver City mine in order to see what was there. An immense body of iron, forty feet in thickness, was passed through and iron carbonate found. Interspersed were crystals carrying about them chlorides of silver of some value. Surface machinery in the form of a pump and a fine double engine were installed. By the end of the year, the ore returns were being made of an apparent value for the enterprise to pay its way. The Quadrilateral mine was also worked but not the Shamus O'Brien mine. Wright kept the newspapers informed of the apparent progress and the discoveries that had been made. He knew that good publicity fostered the standing of the company and fuelled the value of the shares.

Accordingly at the first meeting of the company on 26$^{th}$ February 1881, Wright as president was able to give an optimistic report. The directors elected were Edward Cope, William Smedley, Samuel Collins, Henry Stiles, Louis Ladner and Charles Johnson. All were leading men on the mining and financial scene. All had been carefully selected. The sale of the Denver City shares had gone well, particularly benefiting from the dividends paid by the rival company holding the adjacent Little Pittsburg on Fryers Hill mine. Several properties, covering in all twenty acres, had been consolidated under that name and formed into a joint stock company of $20 million. The company's initial reports considered the yield to be unlimited. The shareholders were inclined to think that the value of their property had not been overestimated when $100,000 was distributed among them monthly.

But it was not his only enterprise in Leadville. The Chippewa Consolidated Mining Company was incorporated on 1st January 1881 with a capital stock of $2,500,000 divided into 250,000 shares of $10 each. He was the president of the company with the board comprising Charles L. Wright of New York and the rest from Leadville. It controlled six claims south of the Breece Iron Mine. All comprised low-grade mineral but the company proposed to sink one deep shaft. The company basked in the apparent success of Denver City Consolidated.

His business status in Philadelphia was further enhanced that year. He was elected to the American Institute of Mining on 15th February and on 27th April, Wright was elected President of the Philadelphia Mining Stock Exchange. It was the culmination of his steady rise and the reward for his business acumen. He was achieving the recognition he desired and he was acquiring the capital wealth he wanted. He was the man to know.

Wright's involvement in mining projects was not confined to Leadville. There was nothing that passed by Wright and his knowledge of what was happening in the mining stock market and the new discoveries of silver ore. His attention was diverted to Lake Valley in New Mexico. The mining camp lay in the foothills of the Black Range. It was a barren and windswept area with little rainfall and accordingly little vegetation. It was very hot in summer and correspondingly cold in the winter. There were few inhabitants, ranches for some cattle farmers and a number of small settlements for pioneers. It was also the stronghold of Apaches occasionally joined by outlaws from Texas, Arizona and Mexico. Raids were brutal and defence almost impossible. There was little to take except the cattle and the occasional life. Silver had been found in the 1870s by local farmers and naturally some prospectors followed. But despite the apparent attractions of the silver, many were deterred by the local conditions and dangers. Indeed, prospecting was, at best, intermittent.

However, soon after the Atchison, Topeka & Santa Fe railroad made connection with the Southern Pacific at Deming in February 1881, John A. Miller of Silver City brought the attention of the New York and Philadelphia mining capitalists to the Lake Valley properties. The railway was now within a few miles of Lake Valley. Wright reacted immediately and George Daly was sent by Wright and George D. Roberts to evaluate these claims. George Daly was a mining engineer and operator of national reputation and then manager of the Robinson mine at Kokomo, Colorado. Daly thought that the ore lay between two dissimilar lime strata, a white and a blue lime, which had opened during rock eruptions allowing mineral solutions to flow and deposit ore.

On the basis of this initial assessment, Wright visited in the April. As with the Leadville project, he wanted to see for himself. He wanted to make his own assessment and judgment. He thoroughly inspected the area and the potential. There was certainly silver but the quantity, quality and accessibility of the deposits, as usual, were the determining factors. There were also the local conditions and logistics of shipment. It was a major gamble but he took it. And he gambled hugely. He decided that a total purchase of all of the relevant area was required comprising all of the 'outcrop' visible in the district measuring some 5,000 feet in length and virtually all of the ore deposits. A consortium was established; Wright represented the Philadelphia parties and George D. Roberts represented the New York parties. The price of $300,000 was agreed and divided between the owners with John A. Miller receiving $100,000 and McEverts, Lufkin and the other owners getting the balance. It was a bold and decisive move with a huge commitment of capital and personal reputation.

Bernard MacDonald, then manager of the Iowa Gulch Mine in Leadville was engaged by George Daly to manage the Lake Valley project from April 1881. Work progressed. Daly's belief that the silver ore deposits lay in strata was actually incorrect and it turned out the ore-bodies lay in channels of very limited depth. Nevertheless, the initial developments showed 'pay' ore in greater or lesser quantities in most of the openings which were traceable for a distance of some 3,000 feet along the outcrop. It was a good prospect. Wright and his confederates were determined to exploit it. Again the organisation of the company flotation was critical.

Wright and Roberts, assisted by Daly, formed separate companies to hold each of the mining areas. The Sierra Apache comprised ninety acres on the east side including the Kohinoor, Surprise, Crescent and Grace Darling properties; the Sierra Bella encompassed the claims immediately to the west and principally comprising the Columbia, Comstock and Last Chance claims; the Sierra Plata comprised some 100 acres including the Golden Gate, Crown Point, Silver Reef, Arizona and Stanton mines; the Sierra Grande consisted of fifty acres including the Lincoln, Emporia No.1 and Sumpter mines. The capital stock of these companies was divided into 200,000 shares at $25 per share. Over $20 million in capital was being raised. It was a launch of significance. The companies were floated on the Philadelphia Stock Exchange in the summer of 1881.

There was criticism that the venture was not operated by one company instead of the mines and interests being divided between several companies. Clearly, there was more money to be raised by the launch of several companies. Equally, the launch of many companies at the same time may not have been successful and the whole business a disaster. Speculation in mining shares was hazardous as few companies proved to be very successful. By launching several companies, it meant that most speculators would risk some money in each company rather than a larger sum in just one company. It was a matter of judgment. In the event, the launch of the enterprise had been a resounding success. Wright received some $500,000 within about two weeks. Money poured in from all over America.

Wright knew that the mines at Lake Valley needed as much credibility as possible if the promotion of the companies was to succeed. Wright used Edward Cope who was already a director of Denver City Mining. Wright and Daly took samples of the fossils from the limestone outcrop to him. As a leading American palaeontologist, Cope identified them as the same fossils found in the limestone of some famous Mexican silver mines. Wright talked Cope into investing much of his fortune in the Lake Valley mines and into being President of the Sierra Apache Company and positions with the other three companies.

Development was begun on the Sierra Grande and Sierra Bella properties as these showed the most favourable indications. Shafts were sunk but the ore was not found in the expected form. The results were mixed. Accordingly, the old-fashioned method of simply following the ore seam was pursued. The results produced some reasonable finds of silver ore in the blue lime. Other areas were also explored with apparently better results. Then on 7$^{th}$ August, Daly gave his first, intended to be weekly, report on the Sierra Plata Mining Company and an apparent strike of great importance. He wrote to Wright that over 100 shafts had been sunk near the foot of the hill designed to cut the vein of ore. They then had commenced exploring the Stanton claim and, to their astonishment, found the entire side of the hill apparently a mass of extremely rich ore, cropping through the wall of limestone in a series of fissures, very close together and running east and west across the 600 feet of the Stanton and on the Crown Point claim for a considerable distance. Daly estimated that the ore covered a width of 200 to 250 feet, north and south, and ran entirely across the mine. He assessed the ore to be of a wonderful richness. He intended to extend a shaft into the seam.

It was Daly's last communication with Wright. A group of Apaches, led by the seventy-year-old Nana, had left their reservation and begun raiding ranches including one to the north of Lake Valley. One ranch owner returned to find his home burned down and his wife and children missing. He rode into Lake Valley for help which was forthcoming from Daly, about twenty miners and a small squad of the 9$^{th}$ Cavalry comprising African-American troopers. Next morning, 18$^{th}$ August, they followed the Apaches who ambushed them in a canyon. Lieutenant Smith, leading the cavalry, and Daly were killed and a number of miners wounded. A black sergeant took command and held out for the rest of the day but there were more killed and wounded. Eventually, the Apaches withdrew and the force went back to Lake Valley. The wife and children of the rancher were later discovered alive after hiding during the original Apache raid. It was a reminder of the local dangers and the human cost of prospecting in this remote area. The death of Daly was a great loss to Wright. He had been a friend and someone to be trusted in developing the project. Wright thought that the enterprise was in some jeopardy.

Fortunately, the prospects at Lake Valley suddenly increased with the discovery of a huge find on the Sierra Grande and Sierra Plata properties. Ironically, it was made on the day Daly had been killed by Apaches. A drift was started as an open cut in the ore and was driven parallel with the outcrop but from twenty-five to thirty-five feet below it for a distance of some 800 feet. The larger deposits of silver ore were found as the drift was extended. It was decided to sink a shaft some 100 feet in advance of the drift on the dividing line between the Sierra Grande and Sierra Plata properties. Some twenty-four feet down, the joint shaft revealed rich deposits and a continuation the deposits of the outcrop drift. MacDonald named the ore deposit 'the bridal chamber' because the sparkling light reflected by the myriads of crystals of cerargyrite and calcite that studded the roof of the open space over the chloride streak. The ore was very rich. Daly's legacy enabled Wright to make his fortune.

Wright had also sought other mining ventures. In the middle of 1881, the North Horn Silver Mining Company was launched with an issue of 400,000 shares at $25 giving a capital sum of $10 million. The mines were at Frisco in Utah. There were familiar faces on the board with Edward D. Cope as president, Wright as vice-president, William Smedley as treasurer and George L. Smedley as secretary.

Meanwhile the mines at Leadville were being developed. Some of the operations were criticised, particularly the installation of extensive buildings and machinery and the apparent confidence of potentially rich finds. Shafts were sunk and drifts run. Mr. R. Bunsen had replaced Mr. Shedd who had gone temporarily to manage the mines in Lake Valley following the death of Daly. By the end of the year, although much of the ore had been of a low grade, Bunsen gave good reports of its future quality. Indeed, he intended to move his office from the town to the site. Whilst there were apparent improvements in the ore and its shipping, the company shares declined.

Wright was disappointed with the results. In spite of his best efforts and his constant attention to the detail in the development of the Leadville venture, the outcome in the form of the production of silver was low and the expenditure had been high. Denver City Mining was not the financial success that Wright had hoped and indeed, its economic stability and mining potential was a cause for concern. Wright contemplated what to do. Denver City Mining had borrowed extensively to fund the mining works and there was now little chance that it could ever repay the amounts on the basis of its current ore production and sales.

Wright proposed a plan to deal with the problem. It was simple but creative. The property holding was to be divided into two parts. The Denver City Company retained its Discovery, Shamus O'Brien and Quadrilateral shafts together with about thirteen acres of territory. The balance of the land was transferred to the newly formed Lee Basin Mining Company for the sum of $250,000. $173,000 was used to pay the debts of the Denver City Mining and, of the balance, some $25,000 was paid to the Lee Basin Company for future development. Wright contended that Denver City Mining could be put on a sound footing with the prospect of future dividends. The Lee Basin Company, comprising the same directors as Denver City Mining, held the northern part of the territory and could be developed by the same mine shaft. The directors would be the same for each company.

On 9th January 1882, at the Merchants' Exchange on Walnut Street, Philadelphia, and on 16th January at the company office in Leadville, stockholders met to consider the radical plans. Approval was a foregone conclusion. Wright and his directors were not prepared to risk failure without knowing that they held the relevant votes. The proposals were unanimously approved by votes of 343,000 shares.

J. Whitaker Wright was initially happy. His Denver City and Lee Basin companies were in shape to yield returns. Optimism continued for the operation of Denver City. But the changes did not work. In April, the Denver City mine was shut down because of the low-grade ore and the small profit achieved by smelting. There was talk of co-operation with the Lee Basin Company and of new plant. There was a proposal to establish a stamp mill to service the ore from the mine and from other mines. However, ultimately, the venture did not succeed. It was a familiar story of the mining industry. The local newspaper told the story in its assessment of the whole of the dividends paid in respect of all of the Leadville mines for 1881. Overall, there was a dividend return of about five per cent on the capital invested of over $63 million. However, only seventeen companies actually paid any dividend and twelve of those paid over eleven per cent. The speculative nature of the business was apparent. Very few companies had struck silver ore in sufficient quantity to pay large dividends. The vast majority had not fulfilled their promise and paid no dividends. Indeed, many shareholders simply lost their capital investments. The Denver City was simply one of the many companies.

Wright also faced litigation as executor for George Daly over the original purchases of the Lake Valley interests. A man named William Wilson who was apparently one of the original negotiators for the acquisition of the mines with Daly alleged that he was due further monies from Daly but had never been paid. Litigation over mining interests was inevitably prevalent as many people were often involved and sadly dissatisfied with their returns. In many cases, litigation was too costly to pursue and arrangements were made to settle.

The work continued at Lake Valley under the management of Shedd. Wright wanted to promote the mines and display them as an investment. Accordingly, in June 1882, he arranged for a party of Philadelphian businessmen who had invested in the companies, to journey to the area to be present at the starting up of the mill that would produce silver bricks in quantities from the Sierra mines. The party included Wright and Roberts, Edward D. Cope, Samuel Smedley, Dr. Middleton, Professor Benjamin Silliman Jr. and others including press representatives. Fifty of their friends assembled at the depot to cheer them off in their Pullman palace car 'Brighton'. It was a comfortable journey with first-class sleeping accommodation, the best of food and refreshments, luxurious facilities and service. Wright added some drama to the trip. Whilst the railway station was only some twelve miles from the mines, the incident with Daly's death less than a year previously meant that every precaution was taken for the safety of the party. Wright arranged for the party to be driven to 'Sierra City' from the Nutt railway station under armed guard for fear of Apache attack. It gave a sense of adventure from the start as they were taken through the desolate, arid, mountainous landscape to the industrial complex of the mining operation. But Wright wanted to give the party something even more spectacular and a visual manifestation of the wealth he believed that the mines possessed. He took them down through the Sierra Grande mine to 'Bridal Chamber' by candlelight. The tiny globules of lead and silver sparkled in the flickering candles. The subterranean cavern was a magnificent sight. He looked like a treasure trove that was simply waiting to be exploited. They could not help but be impressed.

On the surface, he pointed to the enormous piles of ore that had been mined to demonstrate the industry of the enterprise. He showed them the new stamp mill obtained at the cost of some $100,000. It consisted of two crushes and twenty stamps with a 300 horsepower engine. He was determined to show them the technology and the sheer investment in the mines. Continually, he reiterated the riches of the mines. They were eminently satisfied. But Wright was not the person to leave anything to chance. He wanted the maximum out of the excursion and arranged to telegraph the details of the trip to leading New York newspapers to ensure maximum publicity for both the party and the mines. There were glowing reports. The fabulous nature of the discoveries was particularly emphasised. The take-up of shares naturally increased.

Prof. Silliman's presence on the excursion was crucial. Like his father, he was a professor of chemistry at Yale University and had initially made his name in the fractional distillation of petroleum as a high-quality illuminator. It fuelled the start of the oil boom in Pennsylvania. It subsequently put him in great demand as a consultant to mining companies. But his judgment in respect of silver mining had proved notoriously optimistic particularly in respect of the Emma mine in Utah where the reserves were exhausted long before his estimate. Nevertheless, his reputation remained. He produced glowing reports about the Lake Valley mines although the *Mining Journal* doubted his judgment based upon previous history. Silliman estimated that there was over $2,500,000 value alone in one ore-house. He confirmed the richness of the ore in many other locations.

The press were mixed in their views. Doubts were cast about the reputations of both Roberts and Silliman and warning given against investment in Lake Valley. However, others declared that they were good mines. Further reports indicated richness and the newspapers and journals gradually changed their views to give credit to the enterprises and to Wright and his colleagues. He was winning the battle with the doubters.

In September, Wright proposed what he might have done originally and that was to put the Sierra Plata and Sierra Grande under one company. The shareholders of Sierra Plata and Sierra Grande readily agreed to consolidate into one company with 400,000 shares at $25 dollars giving an authorised capital of $10 million. It was a major success for Wright's business acumen. It meant that the Sierra Grande Consolidated was able to be listed on the New York Stock Exchange. It was also a time for some changes in the company stock ownership. Roberts' reputation was under growing scrutiny and he sold his Lake Valley stocks in October 1882, which were taken up principally by Wright and other Philadelphia interests. And the faith of the shareholders was not misplaced. A fortune in dividends was paid. A dividend of $100,000 was paid on 1$^{st}$ November and, by April 1883, the company had paid six dividends amounting to $600,000. It was a fantastic return for those who had backed Wright. He considered that it was a vindication of his enterprise.

However, by July, there was a change in fortunes. Rumours spread that the Sierra Grande was becoming worked out and indeed Bunsen, the mine manager, was reportedly confirming this position. The share price fell. The mines continued to be worked and further investments in plant and machinery made. However, it was a losing battle. The efforts could not yield any significant income over the expensive expenditure needed to retrieve the ore. The other mining areas at Lake Valley were equally devoid of profitability. Indeed, the Sierra Apache and Sierra Bella companies had never paid any dividends. The general prospects continued to deteriorate rapidly. There were arrangements to amalgamate the entirety of the Sierra companies but to no avail. By 1886, after over two years of efforts, with debts mounting and little working, efforts were made to reorganise the companies. The Sierra Bella was bought by the Sierra Grande but it did not improve the situation. The crisis could not be averted and, by 1887, individual miners worked the claims on a lease basis. Shares had rapidly declined in value and Cope lost a major portion of his money. He had to sell his fossil collection which became the basis of the American Museum of Natural History collection. Over the period, Wright had gradually been forced out of control of the Sierra companies he had founded and correspondingly gradually disposed of his shares. Inevitably, the management of the companies, the finances and the mines were the subject of public criticism.

In Colorado he had continued to develop other mining interests but in the natural resource of coal. The Gunnison country was being exploited for its vast mineral wealth spread over several thousand square miles with the advent of railway connection. Wright determined to have his share of the action. Prior to 1882, the Gunnison Improvement Company of Colorado owned a large tract of valuable coal lands. Wright and some other stockholders conceived the idea that it would be an advantage to form an independent company in New York to purchase and hold the coal lands of the improvement company. The Gunnison Coal Company of New York was formed with a capital of 500,000 shares, 240,000 of which were given to the improvement company as the purchase price for the coal lands. The coal company reserved an option to buy back 40,000 of those shares at $1 each. Wright used the situation. In order to buy these shares, 110,000 were placed in the hands of Wright (and E.P. Moxey) to raise the $40,000. If the money was raised, they were to have the 110,000 shares and the 40,000 shares so redeemed. Wright raised about $30,000 and paid it over to the improvement company. In 1884, the Gunnison Coal Company and the Gunnison Improvement Company consolidated as the Gunnison Coal and Iron Company of Colorado. The money raised by the coal company was to patent the lands owned by the improvement company but it was never done and the money was applied to other purposes in the interest of the company.

Wright had continued with many other enterprises. Other ventures included the Security Land, Mining and Improvement Company set up to develop and sell mining land in Leadville. In June 1884, it declared its second dividend of two and half per cent on its million-dollar capital stock.

In Philadelphia itself in 1882, he was involved with an underground wire speculation.

He maintained an interest in mines and mining stocks and continued to buy and sell. He had a range of property interests. He remained prosperous and could afford a wealthy standard of living.

His home life had its share of family changes; 1881 was a particularly eventful year. On 12$^{th}$ August, his mother died from a stroke. She was buried three days later at Mount Moriah. She had seen her eldest son and her daughter married and the birth of grandchildren. She had watched Whitaker make his fortune and his brothers making their way. She had witnessed her family happily and successfully settled in America. During the same year, Whittaker's brother John returned to Toronto where his interest in generated electricity developed. Anna's mother divorced the same year although it had been coming for some time. And Wright's niece, Florence Browne was born. 1882 marked further events. In March, another son, Jay Whitaker, was born to great delight. But tragedy was to enter his life. On 14$^{th}$

December, his only daughter, Mabel, died from acute enteritis. She was only two years and eight months old and was buried on 16$^{th}$ December. But four days later, Jay, aged only nine months, died from dysentery. He was buried beside his sister at Mount Moriah on 20$^{th}$ December. It was a very sad Christmas. Whitaker erected a gravestone in their memory. The losses did not deter Whitaker and Anna. Their son, Whitaker, was born in 1883 and his two sisters, Gladys and Edith, were born in 1887 and 1888 respectively. Anna's mother died prematurely on 25$^{th}$ August 1885.

But his continued business success enabled him to move from 3601 Locust Street to the fashionable Haverford in West Philadelphia. In 1886, he bought the well-known Eldridge house and property for which he paid $40,000. The house was the twin of that owned by Mr. George Philler of the First National Bank. Wright's home was fitted up like a palace with a host of servants to keep the place. His young and attractive wife was the charming hostess. He entertained on a lavish scale. He was in contact with some of the most distinguished financiers and promoters in Philadelphia and New York. He claimed acquaintance with A.J. Cassait, President of the Pennsylvania Railroad, with Charles T. Yerkes and Charles M. Schwab who were the leading financiers of the moment.

Whitaker Wright was able to indulge himself not only in a wealthy home life but in a few pleasures. While only just in his forties, he had grown somewhat stout and large. He was an imposing character of some confidence. However, he was not a great social animal, except when business demanded, and generally preferred his own company. His choice of recreation was therefore completely natural. He developed a passion for ocean sailing and had his own private yacht. His summer residence near Long Branch, New Jersey, enabled a preoccupation with the activity. It was a fashionable area of large estates and frequented by the notables of the day. Its location on the western edge of the Atlantic Ocean was ideal for the kind of yacht racing that he sought. His enthusiasm for the sport and his wealth led him to the expressed intention to build a yacht to compete for America's Cup. It was a challenge to him that perhaps was only paralleled in his business affairs.

He could look back on the last twenty years with immense satisfaction. He had left England in humbling circumstances and started a new life. He had worked hard and prospered. Philadelphia and its Stock Exchange had been the fertile ground for his advancement. He had begun modestly but applied all his skills to progress himself. His reputation in mining properties, promotions and shares had been outstanding. He was a broker of some reputation. His election as President of Philadelphia Mining Exchange in 1881 stood out in recognition of his skill and position. It had been a great honour for an immigrant of only ten years' standing.

His notorious involvement in the Leadville and Lake Valley companies had made him a millionaire. He continued to look for the opportunity and the challenge. It had often been a precarious business, requiring some luck, a lot of judgment and a strong determination. Every venture had been a gamble for both the investors and the promoters. Great expenditure was often incurred with little result. There were many such schemes and many promoters. It was a highly speculative field of operation. Wright had learned how to promote himself and his enterprises. He had always been so full of enthusiasm for his schemes. His convincing manner and self-assurance had developed a lifestyle both lavish and indulgent.

He continued his stock market dealings and his interest in mining enterprises. He continued to buy and sell both stock and properties. He used his great energy to deal with mine owners and mine managers, bankers and accountants, lawyers and agents. Inevitably, there were disputes and arguments, even litigation. The stock market in respect of the mining sector was fiercely competitive. It seemed never-ending.

In his early forties, he had expected to retire from business. But the days of huge capital acquisition were over, and by his standards, hard times came in the late 1880s. The value of his investments and securities shrank. He had problems with some of his companies. But he was not one to accept the position. He sought to relaunch himself on America's west coast. He had contacts with the significant mining fraternity based there. He sold his Haverford home to a golf club.

He gave his attention to the west coast, to California and Nevada, and sought to develop his mining interests there. It led him, in April 1887, to sell an interest in the Crown Point mine in Grass Valley. He continued with various business dealings. In 1890, with an office in San Francisco, he became involved in the Chloride Mining &

Reduction Company. It was floated with a capital of $1,000,000 comprising $10 shares. The principal company office was at Chloride New Mexico and its purpose was to take over idle mines and mills in the area, of which Wright had an interest.

He knew that the move did not significantly improve his financial position and the family knew nothing of the west-coast life. Wright needed to make more decisive arrangements to secure his future. It had to be somewhere acceptable to his wife and children and the family life he cherished. It had to be somewhere that would enable his entrepreneurial skills to flourish and where he could still continue to deal with his remaining American interests. He had many contacts but it seemed that only one place would meet the requirements. He resolved himself and made the major decision.

# CHAPTER 4

# Making the English Fortune

He knew that the decision would have a great effect on his wife and family. He convinced his lady that her position and life would be greatly improved. New opportunities could be taken. A new horizon beckoned and he could put aside any unwelcome business issues lingering in America. He felt that it was the right moment to change. He remained optimistic, even ambitious. He envisaged a bright future and enhancement to their social standing. His choice centred on England.

His wife would have a social position. She was only in her late twenties. She instinctively trusted his judgment. The children were young enough to adapt quickly. His son was seven years old and was right for the classical English education of preparatory school followed by a leading English public school. The two girls at two and three years were still in their infancy would know nothing of the change. They would have a governess. The family could all enjoy the trappings of English society in the leading capital of the world. He could be an English gentleman and Anna his lady. London would also provide the base for future enterprises with its renowned Stock Exchange and centre for world business contacts. Whitaker Wright moved back to England.

He had deliberately chosen England and London. After the

United States and Philadelphia, there was little other choice. The location had to be English-speaking, there had to be a financial centre of significance and there had to be an acceptable social framework. The possible English colonies of Australia and South Africa might have provided some opportunities but they were largely unknown to him except in mining terms.

Wright maintained his particular interest in mining on his return to England. He knew the mining industry on a worldwide basis. He knew assaying, geology, mine development and the relevant technology. He knew how to read the reports from the assayers, mine managers and geologists. He knew about company promotion. He knew the market. He had retained some mining interests and stock. He had some money and had the appetite to make more. He had his business contacts and associates and he could make others in the clubs of London and the financial markets.

He established himself by setting up office in Copthall Avenue in the heart of the City of London. He needed to acquire mining interests and properties if he was to use his skills in the same way as previously in America. In 1891, he took an interest in the Abaris Mining Corporation which held properties in Mexico. It was not successful and his interest in the American mining scene waned. He looked to other areas but knew that the commercial interests in South Africa were well-established and already controlled and viewed speculation in this continent with some scepticism.

But the Australian scene was somewhat reminiscent of his previous mining developments. There had been gold discoveries at Kimberley, at Southern Cross and at Coolgardie. Then in 1893, some rich findings were discovered at Mount Charlotte in Coolgardie. There was the initial influx of prospectors but the area was remote and the surface pickings soon gave out. The next step was underground mining but that required capital to finance the considerable plant and machinery, men and management needed to work the fields. A host of speculative companies were formed in London and the market began.

Western Australia had remarkable similarities to Colorado and New Mexico. The wilderness, the extreme climate and remote terrain combined to create an environment that made the logistics of mining problematical. There would be issues with the installation of plant and machinery and the recruitment of men. There would be challenges with shipping and refining the ore. There was, of course, rampant competition. As in his previous ventures, his entry onto the scene would need to be carefully timed. It was not a scenario with which he was unfamiliar. He was well experienced in these matters and proposed to adopt his usual practice of acquiring mines, floating a company to whom those interests would be sold for cash and shares. He would then manage the company in whatever official capacity was required. As a leading shareholder and its manager, he would develop the company in whatever direction he considered appropriate. He would form further companies as necessary to develop particular mining ventures.

The formation of a company would be based in the purchase of interests in some mines and a compelling prospectus to induce subscription in the shares. He busied himself and in September 1894, Wright issued the prospectus for the Western Australian Exploring and Finance Corporation. He had negotiated the acquisition of legal interests in various gold mines in the Coolgardie-Kalgoorlie district of Western Australia. The share capital was to be 200,000 of £1 shares comprising 195,000 ordinary shares with 5,000 preference shares. The company was to acquire Wright's interests in mines in Western Australia. Wright, as the founder and in exchange for the rights he had acquired at considerable expense being transferred to the company, would get the 5,000 preference shares and 45,000 ordinary shares when he called for them. The prospectus identified some of the properties as Mainland and the Last Chance described in the 'Australian Mining Standard' as the 'Bayleys of the Murchison'. They were among the best that could apparently be acquired. The prospectus referred to other undisclosed mines which were apparently potentially very rich. It emphasised their prospects as better than those in South Africa and the need for their development by modern means that required capital investment. It anticipated that companies would be formed and promoted to develop the particular mines. Western Australian Exploring Company shareholders would have the profits from any promotion and preference in the shares in these companies when they were issued. A list of similar companies was given where such companies had been promoted with their current Stock Exchange quotation. Western Australian Exploring would work in harmony with West Australian Goldfields Limited and

Western Australian Exploration Company Limited in the development of certain mines.

The press were particularly scornful and ironical of the prospectus. The London City Review considered the drawing of prospectus was not properly reckoned as one of the fine arts, yet this one should rank very high in the scale of professions for seldom had they read outside the range of pure fiction anything more chaste, more subtle, more vague or more delicately suggestive. It considered that the most tender-footed director need fear no responsibility for this document and, in fact, might be proud to see his name appended to it, as thereby he constituted himself, as it were, a joint author in a very pretty piece of fiction. It asserted that the prospectus of Law's Mississippi scheme or of the South Sea Bubble might have been drawn on similar lines. It reminded the writer of later productions say of the Emma mine or the Zoedone Company and he could almost fancy the light and graceful touch of the master Baron Grant. For who could suggest so much and affirm so little? How deftly the reader is carried from Australia to South Africa and back again – from the *Times* to the Melbourne *Argus* and the *Australian Mining Standard* while such high personages as the Premier of Western Australia and Sir Malcolm Fraser, the Agent General, are referred to with great familiarity as he might mention Mr. Burjoyce, the newspaper's printer, or Mr. Guinea Pigg, its director. The article considered that it might well become the model of all future prospectus.

It went into a detailed statement-by-statement critique. It was extremely snide about what the prospectus actually said. The company was formed to carry on the 'usual objects', that is all but a very big 'all'. The prospectus had stated that very few persons except those who had followed the important gold discoveries in Western Australia have any conception of the enormous mineral wealth which until lately had been dormant in the colony. The newspaper did not quite understand for the mineral wealth lay dormant still and would remain dormant until somebody dug it out. The company had stated that it was to act as the medium between investors in England and the owners of sound undertakings in Western Australia. The newspaper article derided the simplicity of the statement.

It then attacked Wright as 'founder' for his payment in the form of the 5,000 preference and 45,000 ordinary shares. It called the arrangement a novel feature and mentioned how little was apparently given for such grand profits. It did concede that two leases were being transferred. However, it was not the value of the properties that was questioned but the artistic nature of the prospectus. There was no crude, coarse and brutal assay of specimens, no assertion that the mine had been cut into and surveyed by the eminent mining engineer Mr. Tenstamp Mint. Everything was left to the imagination. It concluded in continuing irony that it admired the prospectus as the height of the draughtsman's art. In fact, the author was reminded of the work of Rabelais where on the Island of Bells, men engaged in apparently impossible tasks, such as making rope out of sand and other things too numerous to mention, as the auction catalogue put it. It encouraged the student of prospectus drafting to study that of the West Australian Exploring and Finance Corporation and become a perfect master.

There was further general criticism in the *London Statist* in October. It referred to the announcements of more West Australian companies being established with pretty well every promoter having one or more schemes in his pocket, all of them, of course, represented to be of gilt-edged character, even though Tom, Dick or Harry are button-holed in the street and asked to subscribe to this, that or other syndicate. It was feared that in the rush to promote companies, good business was being injured. It urged the public not to respond to each and every appeal to them to unbutton their pockets. It promulgated the policy to wait for proof of a valuable property and its good management before selecting an investment. It supposed that it was always the case that in such times of excitement, the greedy and unscrupulous promoter was in evidence. It recognised that West Australia as a goldfield but feared the overcapitalisation that had previously occurred in regard to the Queensland mines. They set out a list of the companies numbering well over fifty that had been formed during 1893 and 1894.

Despite the barbed newspaper criticisms of the prospectus, the Western Australian Exploring and Finance Company subscription went well. Very few had apparently taken any notice of the advice emanating from the journals. On the issue of the shares, there had been only 800 subscribers but eventually 5,000 were achieved. The three largest shareholders were stockbrokers – Hardie and Turnbull with 7,600 shares, Murray Griffiths with 5,030 and Arthur Young with 5,000. During the following year, Murray Griffiths became the single biggest shareholder with nearly 15,000 shares. However, there were significantly a considerable number of individuals with relatively small shareholdings.

Wright proceeded with his plans. The company acquired, through him, five gold mining leases then known as the Mainland Consolidated situated on the borders of Lake Austin about sixteen miles from Cae in the Murchison Goldfields, Western Australia. The property included the Mainland, Last Chance, Daly's and two central blocks, comprising about thirty-six acres. It was locally considered to be the most important area. A list of experts provided a consensus as to the richness and value of the property. A new company called Mainland Consols was created with a capital of £150,000 with shares being paid five shillings on application, five shillings on allotment, five shillings on 1$^{st}$ April 1895 and five shillings on 1$^{st}$ June 1895. The capital was guaranteed by Wright's Western Australian Exploring and Finance together with West Australian Goldfields and Western Australian Exploring. The allotment of shares was made on 31$^{st}$ January 1895 with preference being given to the shareholders of the three companies. In April, Wright's company took over the Wealth of Nations mine and in July bought the Paddington group of mines at Coolgardie for £60,000.

He had still more ambitious plans. In April 1895, Wright launched the London & Globe Finance Corporation. It had a capital of £200,000 and the same directors as Western Australian and Exploring. It had a similar share arrangement for Wright with a combination of preference shares and ordinary shares on which he could call. The company had a wide variety of purposes. It would support Wright-sponsored companies by buying their shares and generally supporting them in the market. It would buy those shares not purchased in the launch of the company in order to maintain their price and confidence. It would promote and hold companies and assets. Both Western Australian Exploring and London & Globe were from their beginnings jointly run by him as managing director.

The launches of the main companies would not have worked without the directors he induced to serve. It was essential to his schemes that the companies should have directors of social standing. Their business ability and their financial acumen were irrelevant;

indeed any of those particular skills were unwelcome as it was Whitaker Wright who would provide the necessary management. And his standing was growing. He had made contacts in clubs and in established organisations. Wright aimed high. He entertained notable persons and attended the appropriate functions and gatherings. None was more impressive than the first Chairman of both Western Australian Exploring and London & Globe.

On 6$^{th}$ May 1895, he attended the banquet given at the Holborn restaurant to honour Sir William Robinson, the retiring British Governor of Western Australia. Wright had been one of the banquet committee. Sir William Robinson had enjoyed a long career in the United Kingdom Colonial Service. He had been Governor of various colonies and had a long association with Australia. He was three times Governor of Western Australia 1875 to1877, 1880 to 1883 and 1890 to 1895 and Governor of South Australia 1883 to 1889. He had presided over the transition of Western Australia from colony to self-governance. The banquet attendance was notable and included the Secretary of State for the Colonies. The addresses echoed the accepted view of the rising star of Western Australia.

Sir William eloquently commenced his speech with a reference to the May sunshine shedding its golden rays on the goldfields of Coolgardie. He talked of the vast areas of the goldfields extending over 100,000 miles where 20,000 men were scattered in all directions. He referred to the work of the Government and private companies in addressing the issue of the scarcity of water in the area. He thought that some £13 million of British capital had been invested in the mines. Whilst there were both good and bad mines, he had complete faith in the wealth and magnitude of the mineral resources. He said that to say more on the subject would be improper in his official capacity but to say less would be disloyal to the colony and his faith in its future development. He mentioned that the export of gold had been valued at over three-quarters of a million during the last year and was estimated to exceed one and a half million the next year. He balanced his speech with references to other matters but gold had been the thrust. Indeed, later in the proceedings, the mining industry was toasted and Mr. F.A. Thompson responded with a eulogy on the colony's mineral wealth and the development of the region to secure the riches.

Wright succeeded in persuading Sir William Robinson to become chairman of both his companies. It was a major coup. Critical to his successful launch of the companies had been the selection of directors. Wright not only wanted a figurehead but aristocracy throughout the boards. Those induced to serve were highly placed personages of impeccable character and connection but without either business or financial acumen or with any considerable wealth of their own. It was their reputation and standing that was important to the enterprises. Lord Edward Pelham-Clinton was the fifty-eight-year-old son of the Duke of Newcastle and after a brief period as a Liberal M.P., had become a member of the Royal Household in 1881 and recently appointed as its Master. Lord Loch was sixty-seven when he joined Wright's companies. He had a distinguished military career in India, in the Crimean War and in China where he had a near fatal incarceration. His diplomatic career had seen him rise steadily to become Governor of Victoria in Australia in 1884 and then Governor of Cape Colony and High Commissioner for Southern Africa in 1889 until 1895 when he resigned when he was raised to the peerage. S.J. Gough-Calthorpe, 7th Baron Calthorpe, was a great landowner who had served as A.D.C. to Lord Raglan in the Crimean War and presided over the newly formed Isle of Wight County Council as its chairman.

These were the men who commanded respect and who provided the appearance of integrity. They had social standing and were part of the home and colonial establishment. They held positions of authority and were household names in the eminent social circles of the country. They were beyond reproach. They stood for solidity and permanence, for acceptability and position, for probity and value. Behind the façade, they were all interested in making money which they needed to varying degrees. Their previous positions had not been particularly wealth-making and their resultant skills did not lend themselves necessarily to improving that situation. They were open to opportunity. They were available for hire. Directorships involved little or no work particularly where the managing director got on with the job. There was scant company regulation that required any active role by a director. The directors worked seriously to perform their duties of simply turning up to nod through business at the board meetings and the annual meetings, signing the relevant papers and share certificates, saying the right words at the club when asked about the company fortunes and taking the relevant remuneration, dividend or share profit when appropriate. Whitaker Wright did not encourage any other approach except to have complete faith in his abilities as their managing director. Everything could be left safely in his hands.

As long as, of course, the company did not fail. Mining companies were particularly speculative. But it was the time of the Westralians. There were a vast number of companies being promoted. Some did fail but not in any immediate or large-scale way and some seemed to prosper. After all, everyone knew that there were precious metals to be mined in the colonies, notably Australia. Failure was put down to bad luck rather than any lack of judgment. And some enterprises were more profitable than others. Portfolios of shares were spread to cover risks and investments diversified to reap rewards. It was a financial gold rush. A fever had developed.

Over one hundred companies were registered with a variety of share capitals amounting collectively to many millions of pounds. There was significant overcapitalisation. The market competition to secure investors was naturally fierce. The Wright companies prospered through several key elements. Wright selected some of the best mines with apparently good potential as the basic holdings of his companies. He had a gift for writing the prospectus that would induce investment. He persuaded notable persons to serve as directors. He ensured a good share take-up by arranging for the buying any surplus shares. He maintained confidence in his companies and their shares using a variety of methods, not least the press.

He had quickly learned the obvious in his American enterprises that the newspapers swayed public opinion in general and financial investment in particular. Their expressed views could significantly affect the fortunes of a company. He had always ensured that the press had good copy by issuing statements that could easily be inserted without editing into the relevant newspaper and he was never slow to give an interview. He would also entertain the appropriate members of the fraternity be they plain reporter or top editor. However, it was financial inducement that ensured the most favourable coverage of company launches and meetings, significant mining developments and potential returns.

Wright established the practice of 'press calls'. A block of shares was set aside at any company issue for the purpose of what Wright described as making a market. These shares went to favoured individuals, such as people on financial journals including the *Financial Times*, the *Financial News*, some of the Australian papers and *The Citizen*, incidentally owned by the editor of *The Truth*, another financial paper. Shares were usually and quickly repurchased by the particular Wright company at an enhanced price and were often then sold on in the market at no loss to the company. Wright also ensured that company meetings were thus well covered and publicised. The printing agent responsible for the issue of any company publication was given a sum to ensure that the relevant newspaper reporters attended. Anything from five to twenty guineas would be paid to the leading men.

It was not only newspaper men who benefited from the largesse of shares. When some of the individual companies were launched, those directly involved in directorships of the company benefited. They were often given the relevant number of shares that they were required to own as part of their qualification as a director. Some were not in a financial position to fund their share allocation. It became part of their package of remuneration and incidentally ensured take-up of the subscription.

His company promotion continued with the formation on 22nd August 1895 of the Austin Friars Syndicate registered at 15 Austin Friars. It was a link-up with Arthur Young who was a financial agent and with Murray Griffiths who was a stockjobber, both with substantial shareholdings in the main Wright enterprises. It was basically a financing company but with some mining assets.

Those who had faith in Whitaker Wright were soon vindicated by company results. At the annual meeting of Western Australian and Exploration on 30th December 1895, Sir William Robinson was able to lead the congratulations. He outlined the company's achievements. A profit of 200 per cent had been made on the paid-up capital. There had been 5,000 names who had held shares in the company with the number rising to 12,000 to include the subsidiary companies. The company's share holding in other companies stood at £287,802 in the balance sheet and was readily realisable. All the preliminary expenses connected with the formation of the company and other items had been written off and all the expenses in Australia had been extinguished having been deducted from the profits made on mining properties which had been purchased, developed and resold. There was a company profit of £320,554. An interim dividend of 10% had already been paid and it was now recommended that a further dividend of 25% on ordinary shares and a dividend of nearly £10 per share on the deferred shares. Shareholders were delighted and were not prepared to support any challenge that Wright should not benefit. Despite questions raised by the auditors and solicitors, 45,000 ordinary shares had been allotted to Wright on 30th November and a dividend paid on them. The board and its shareholders felt strongly that their managing director was equitably entitled to the dividend on the basis that the transfer of Wright's original properties and his subsequent personal management of the company had chiefly made the company's profits. The speakers at the meeting overwhelmingly supported this view. The report and the dividends were unanimously approved. Wright received his dues.

The board clearly believed in supporting and rewarding Wright. They had done little to foster the company other than lend their names and take up some of the share capital for which they had been richly rewarded. The success of the enterprise had been entirely due to the work and efforts of Wright and they were not slow to recognise that without him at the helm, the continued fortunes would be at risk. Accordingly, the misgivings of the auditors and lawyers were summarily dismissed. The niceties of accountancy and law were not to prevail over the realities of financial return and continued prosperity. In any event, the board had neither the ability nor the interest to challenge its leading figure. Wright was unassailable.

But he needed to continue to work hard in the promotion of the companies. Wright continued to give encouraging reports to the boards and to the press about the Western Australian mines under his control. Whilst there had been some delay in the crushing at the Mainland Consol's mine, Wright relayed that the engineers reported that the property was steadily increasing in value and that he was confident that the shares would rise when the crushings commenced. He also referred to the marvellous developments at the Golden Crown mines and predicted a rise in their share price. Rapid progress had also been made with the development of the Wealth of Nations and the Paddington mines and again share increases were predicted. Wright knew that confidence was everything in the precarious world of gold mining and share prices. He wanted to say nothing that would affect the confidence in the company and its share price.

Wright wanted to further his Australian enterprises. Globe's representative in Australia was Charles Kaufmann, a mining surveyor, whom Wright had known from his American ventures. He had already secured the Wealth of Nations, Mainland Consols, Golden Crown, Wealth of Nations Extended, Hannans Golden Crown, Hannans Golden Treasure, Hannans Golden Dream and the Duke, although these ventures were not proving particularly lucrative. In early 1896, he took the bull by the horns and negotiated the purchase, on behalf of Globe, of the Lake View and Boulder East, then held by an Adelaide Company which had only paid £5,000 in dividends. In May of that year Wright was able to start the Lake View Consols company with a share capital of 250,000 shares of £1 each. Wright used the name 'Consols' to give the company, as he had others like Paddington Consols, the same kind of reassuring confidence of their namesake which were issued by the Government to obtain loans as Consolidated Stock or 'Consols'. Wright paid the Adelaide Company 160,000 Lake View shares to obtain the relevant mine leases and a working capital of £30,000 was provided. The shares were allotted on 24$^{th}$ August. It meant that significantly over half of the shares were not within his immediate control and therefore neither was the company. Wright knew that the mine was very rich and that there was an enormous reserve. It was very frustrating for him not to be entitled to more of the wealth that he anticipated would result. About this time, Wright also secured a large interest in the Golden Horseshoe mine with Kaufmann joining the board of that company.

His promotion of companies was furthered with Victoria Gold which was registered in July 1896 with its prospectus published November 1896. A capital of 350,000 £1 shares was subsequently issued. The basic mines of this company were held in Victoria, Australia. As usual, the take-up of shares was excellent with the shareholders of Wright's existing companies receiving preference and the whole launch virtually underwritten by his group of companies.

A considerable amount of money was now being made from the initial launch of these and other companies and from the subsequent increase in the share values together with the dividends and directors' remunerations. Money was also to be made from the dealings in the shares. Wright determined to maintain control over these companies and to foster the market price of the relevant shares. For these purposes, he required significant capital to enable large quantities of shares to be bought and sold in the market. However, he was sufficiently astute and experienced to know that the market was constantly the subject of manipulation. The rapid establishment of his various companies and the need to ensure their initial success with a good share subscription together with his inherent optimism meant that Wright was a natural 'bull' favouring an increase in share value rather than its decline. He always speculated and helped to determine that the market would rise so far as his companies were concerned. His existing methods had helped to secure these objectives. He had astutely bought the relevant mining properties. He had launched each company with care. He had issued optimistic prospectus. He had ensured a good subscription when shares were initially issued.

Whilst his existing companies and contacts would buy up any surplus stock, it remained critical to ensure sufficient financial backing for his enterprises. He needed permanent financial support for any market endeavours. But he wanted to go much further. He required a financial basis to allow him to enter the stock market on an effective, perhaps overwhelming basis. It would be a significant departure from then simple acquisition of mining interests and their exploitation by company flotation. It would involve market dealing in the range of mining enterprises. Wright needed another vehicle to further his aspirations.

He set his plans. He determined that he would make such an impact on the mining market that he would become its leading figure.

# CHAPTER 5

# Making the Name

His scheme was to create a company that was unassailable in the market, one that was deliberately designed and particularly operated to have a speculative arm to deal in the shares and affairs of other companies. Significantly, it would provide capital for Wright enterprises either directly or by its ability to obtain money. His plan was to amalgamate his two main companies into a larger one for the purposes of achieving his various objectives.

On 18th November 1896, Wright sent a circular to the shareholders of both the Western Australian Exploring and London & Globe Finance Companies from his office at 15 Austin Friars just around the corner from Copthall Avenue. He started by referring to the wave of depression passing over the financial markets and to the enquiries that had been made about the date of shareholders' meetings. Last year, he stated, the accounts of Western Australian Exploring had been closed on 30th November with the annual general meeting held on 30th December. It had been the intention of London & Globe to close its books at the same date. Owing to the fact that both companies had large transactions in Lake View shares and some delay by the Stock Exchange, the directors of both companies had decided to close the books at 31st December instead of 30th November to enable all the transactions to be included in the current year accounts. He anticipated a meeting in January. He was able to reassure them that the assets of the two companies were one million pounds each, five times the total capital of their respective companies. The assets included a controlling interest in the Lake View Consols company. Based upon the engineer's reports, Wright considered that allowing for costs of producing the gold ore, the Lake View shares were worth £10. He detailed the assay reports that had been received. He went on to inform shareholders that the two main companies had already been trading on a joint account for many months, enabling them to carry through undertakings that neither could have done separately. It was therefore proposed to hold their annual meetings on the same day and to consolidate the two corporations under a new company named the London and Globe Finance Corporation. He promised that the company would be second to none in the City of London. It was a bold and creative move.

The two companies' annual meetings were held together at the Cannon Street Hotel on 9th February 1897. Sir William Robinson presided and addressed the shareholders. He referred to the co-operation between the two companies, particularly over the Lake View Company. The profits for both companies had been nearly £1,000,000 each for the last year and their assets were valued at over £1,000,000 each. Both had substantial cash balances of and sound loans that could be called in at any time. An interim dividend of 10% had already been paid and it was now recommended that a further dividend of 40% be paid, giving a total of 50% on ordinary shares. It was also recommended to pay dividends of over £15 on the deferred shares in each company. The cost of the dividends would absorb £156,000 in each company and after deducting money for a reserve fund, there would remain a combined balance of £1,200,000. The joint assets were put at £1,600,000. It was proposed to dispose of these assets to the new consolidated company for this amount in fully paid shares to be distributed to the shareholders of the two companies.

A discussion followed. A larger dividend was proposed and there was some objection to the dividend for the deferred shares. There was also some objection to the amalgamation. Wright knew how to deal with the situation. He told the meeting that the articles of the company did not allow for a greater dividend than proposed by the directors. On the amalgamation, he stated that the directors did not care a straw about the matter one way or the other, although they believed that the consolidation and the liquidation of the deferred shares would be in the interest of the shareholders. He said that the only reason for bringing the matter forward was the hundreds of letters received from shareholders on the subject. He told them that in accordance with the companies' memoranda, on liquidation, the ordinary shareholders should first receive a return of their capital and that all surplus profits should be divided equally between the two classes of shareholder, the ordinary and the deferred. There had to be a unanimous vote of the shareholders numbering between 7,000 and 8,000. He said that the stock would not be watered down by the amalgamation and the issue of the 400,000 shares would be at not less than a pound premium. He told them that the directors and their friends would be willing to take the whole 400,000 at £2 each. Votes were then held which resulted in the unanimous approval of the board's recommendations. The directors of the new company were Lord Loch, Lord Edward Pelham-Clinton, Lt-Gen Gough-Calthorpe and Whitaker Wright as managing director. They were to receive a substantial remuneration of 5% of all dividends distributed with the chairman receiving 50% more than any other director.

At the first ordinary meeting of the London & Globe Finance on 29th June 1897, Wright reassured shareholders about the assets of the company. He declared that they owned the cream of the Hannan District with interests in seven or eight groups of mines there including the Lake View company whose control was in their hands. They also had mines in Victoria and New Zealand. They had also acquired a group of copper and nickel mines in the French colony of New Caledonia. The directors believed that by the end of the year, they would be in a position to control the world's nickel supply. They had entered into a contract to build the Baker Street and Waterloo underground railway. They were investing the reserve fund in freehold property in the city. He announced that the 400,000 company shares would shortly be issued and those not taken up by shareholders in the two previous companies would be placed on the open market. These reassurances had been necessary as on 2nd May 1897, Sir William Robinson had died and Wright knew that confidence in a company chairman was paramount. Wright had to look for a successor chairman of London & Globe Finance.

He persuaded Lord Dufferin to take the post. The Marquis of Dufferin and Ava had a similar diplomatic career to Sir William

Robinson but of a much more distinguished character. Among his posts were as Governor General of Canada and as Viceroy of India. He had been ambassador to Russia and finally to France. He had always lived beyond his means and had heavily mortgaged his estates to fund his lifestyle and improve the estates. He had, at one stage, to sell substantial parts of his lands. He faced the same financial problems on his retirement in 1896. Accordingly, he received various offers from financial speculators to use his reputation to encourage investment in their new companies. He declined them all because he felt that the investing public might attach more importance to his name than it deserved and they might be inclined to risk their money merely on the strength of his association with an enterprise, the success of which he had no peculiar power of guaranteeing. However, he considered that the offer from London & Globe was different because it was a going concern, its affairs were in full operation, all its capital had been subscribed and the late Sir William Robinson and Lord Loch were personal friends. He did not understand the mysteries of the stock market and his decision was based on the reassurance that the financial interests of the company would be in the hands of Wright as managing director. As with the other directors, it was his name and reputation that was the key element he brought to the company. He accepted the company chairmanship on 19$^{th}$ August 1897. It was another coup for Wright.

Wright's company promotion continued in October 1897 with the establishment of Ivanhoe Gold Corporation; 150,000 of its 200,000 £5 shares were offered only to London & Globe shareholders with the remaining 50,000 shares being the payment to the Melbourne Company for the mining leases. Wright, in with his usual acumen, had been following the development of the relevant mine for some time. The property had been acquired by Charles Kaufmann for Globe from the Melbourne Company. The purchase price was £50,000 in fully paid shares and over £500,000 in cash, the biggest price ever paid for a gold mine up to that date. It was to be Charles Kaufmann's last work for Wright and they parted company that year when Kaufmann left to join the rival Bottomley Group. It was an unwelcome blow to Wright as he had come to rely heavily on Kaufmann to pursue the Australian interests. However, they had fallen out over the financial rewards that Kaufmann was to receive for his work.

In December 1897, Wright took a major step in an area that had suddenly seen the start of another gold rush. The British America Company was formed by Wright with the same directors as London & Globe. The company was designed to exploit the growing and apparently lucrative mines of Rossland, British Columbia, Canada. It was launched with the same Whitaker Wright care. His prospectus set out a schedule of mining properties that had apparently been, with one exception, either acquired or had options to purchase through Wright's negotiations. Wright had recruited C.N. Mackintosh, recently British Lieutenant-Governor of the North-West Territories of Canada to assist. The new company had its own mining interests in British Columbia but was designed to co-operate with London & Globe to float, support and promote companies for individual mining properties. It was the same Wright formula. The take-up of shares in British America was well-supported with the assistance of the new London & Globe.

But there was a problem with the exceptional interest. This was the Le Roi mine. It was owned by American interests and was producing an income of £10,000 per month. It was an important element in the valuation of British America and its shares. The wrangling went on for months. There were difficulties and delays. There was some uncertainty about the actual ownership of the mines. But eventually settlement was reached. British America acquired the Le Roi mines by buying the shares in the existing company and three-quarters of the interest in the smelting works. It eventually acquired the whole interest. Accordingly, the floatation of Le Roi Mining of 200,000 £5 shares in December 1898 was subsequently undertaken with, of course, priority being given to London & Globe and British America shareholders.

On 20$^{th}$ September 1898, London & Globe held its annual meeting at Winchester House at 2 p.m. It was crowded as usual. Lord Dufferin was recovering from a bout of pneumonia and was cheered as he entered. It was his first meeting as chairman. He reviewed his reasons for accepting the post and was totally open about his lack of financial abilities. He told them that he had become one of the largest stockholders in London & Globe and British America. He paraded his naivety as honesty. He confessed that he did not understand the stock market and the subterranean machinations of the bulls and bears and their effect on the value of shares. He wanted them to understand that he and other directors could not hold themselves responsible for the fluctuations in the market. He reminded them that mining was a speculative business and those who received 15% or more on their investments must know that they deliberately ran greater risk than their less enterprising fellow subjects who were content with 2%. He reminded the audience that the most experienced mining expert could not see into the bowels of the earth but maintained that with the increase in the mining industry, engineers had acquired increased experience and the chances of miscalculation had been very much reduced. The company had adopted a policy of spreading their operations and by not putting all their eggs in one basket, they had minimised the chance of disappointment without sensibly deteriorating their expectations of success. At this point, Lord Dufferin was unable to continue and Lord Loch took over the statement which, in any event, had been prepared by Wright. The chairman's commercial innocence combined appropriately with his apparent sincerity of purpose had been particularly highlighted, as was the speculative nature of the business. It was designed to enhance the acumen of Wright without mentioning his name.

Lord Loch referred to the amalgamation to form the new London & Globe and that the shareholders of the original two companies had received a return of over 200% without counting the 15% dividend for the past year in the present company. Lord Loch stated that the last balance sheet of old Globe had shown profits of £952,605 made in the 'booming' times. The current balance sheet of the new company disclosed still larger profits of £989,679 made during a period of great financial depression arising from political complications and other causes. The directors had deducted from the current profit a sum of £500,000 as a reserve against future depreciation. The balance was to pay the interim of 10% and a further recommended figure of 5% together with a sum of nearly £250,000 to be carried forward.

Lord Loch referred to the many advantageous windfalls that had accrued to shareholders such as Lake View, Ivanhoes and very desirable ones, for example, several Le Roi mines, Victoria Deep Leads, and others, would shortly be forthcoming. In future, allotments to applicants would be made on a pro-rata basis with their company holdings and any surplus would be open to the public. He drew attention to the company's investments and the prospects of which he spoke in sanguine terms in Western Australia, New Zealand, New Caledonia and British America. He referred to the share interest of Le Roi acquired by British America and London & Globe and the legal difficulties that had been experienced. He mentioned the company's financial commitment in the construction of the Baker Street & Waterloo Railway and that it would be a valuable asset.

It was Wright who answered questions from the floor. Mr. Ford referred to the auditors who had not expressed an opinion that there was an adequate reserve. Wright maintained that they did not need to keep more than £100,000 at the bank and if they had to pay £300,000 next week, the sum could be obtained using their book assets. In response to pleas for details about the company's shareholding in other companies, Wright was emphatically not prepared to state in the books the company's particular shareholding in any other company unless it was the wish of the shareholders. It would disclose their hand to competitors. With reference to the proposed launch of the Standard Exploration Company, £250,000 of 'working capital' was guaranteed by London & Globe and it had advanced £60,000 or £70,000 to Standard to continue its operations. Standard's shares would be issued in the near future. Wright declared that London & Globe would take any part of the capital to which the public did not subscribe. The meeting adopted the company report.

The Baker Street & Waterloo Railway investment by London & Globe was significant. It was something that Lord Loch had engineered as chairman of the railway company. Wright considered that it absorbed too much of the company capital that he had earmarked for other projects. It was not the type of venture with which Wright was familiar and the management of the enterprise was not within his control. The railway company needed huge sums to progress the construction of the underground line and there was to be no return on the capital investment until the passenger income commenced. It was a very long-term commitment and there was no immediate return. Nevertheless, Wright acquiesced in order to keep Lord Loch content.

In April 1899, Wright moved his office to 43 Lothbury which became the operation centre for his main companies of London &

Globe and British America together with his other interests and the array of other companies. The same large team of clerks dealt with the administration of the affairs and dealings of this considerable operation. His chief accountant, Arthur Worters, was a trusted employee. Administration was required for the vast array of companies, the almost daily acquisition or disposal or issue of company shares and the extensive correspondence, record-keeping and property dealings.

Wright had another set of matters to resolve largely relating to the Australian enterprises that had not been progressed. His creativity and business acumen combined to create an entity that would encompass this range of largely dormant and probably unprofitable companies and interests. In May 1899, Wright launched the long-awaited Standard Exploration Company with a share capital of £1,500,000. In fact, the company had been registered over a year before but not launched. Wright had used the time to recruit the directors who were the Earl of Donoughmore, the Australian solicitor Howard Spensley and Sinclair Macleay from South Africa, together with Lord Pelham-Clinton and Gough-Calthorpe of London & Globe and British America. One million of the £1 shares were to be used to purchase various interests previously held by West Australian Exploring and Finance including Mainland Consols, Golden Crown, Paddington Consols, Wealth of Nations, Hannan's Golden Group and Hannan's Golden Treasure together shares and interests held by the Austin Friars Syndicate and another company. These companies had a combined nominal capital of some £2,305,000 whose proprietors had apparently agreed to transfer their assets to Standard Exploration for a combined total of 1,000,000 Standard Exploration fully paid shares. They were all Wright companies though not all publicly issued. Ten companies had West Australian mining interests, three were New Zealand mining interests and the Austin Friars Syndicate was a solely financing corporation. Of the remaining 500,000 shares, 286,000 were available for purchase by the general public and the balance of 214,000 by London & Globe.

He carefully drafted the prospectus. He included the usual prospects of returns on capital. His justification for the acquisitions was that great costs had been incurred in the early development of some of these properties resulting in insufficient working capital which would now be remedied by the amalgamation of the undertakings. There would be a resultant economy of management and the new working capital ought to contribute to substantial profits. Although he was careful not to name the proposed acquisitions, he had to provide some allurement and referred to the company's apparent controlling interest in Panda Basin in the Pacific Ocean off British Columbia which he declared to be the most valuable single gold property yet discovered. The prospectus also announced that a share department had been established within the new company for the purpose of the acquisition and disposal of shares in various promising companies and that shares had already been acquired in Le Roi, Columbia, Kootenay, East Le Roi, West Le Roi, and Lake View Consols, Ivanhoe, Great Boulder, Victorian Gold Estates. He reassured the prospective investors that London & Globe and British America boards had agreed to co-operate with this new company.

At this stage, none of the acquisitions had, in fact, actually been undertaken by Standard Exploration, not least the controlling interest in Panda Basin. London & Globe held most of the interests to be acquired and would naturally transfer them on the successful launch of Standard Exploration. He did not disclose that London & Globe had agreed to transfer 5,000 deferred shares in the Austin Friars syndicate for the relevant payment. It was typical of the Wright approach. It was all about intentions and the actualities would be sorted out by him in due course. It was the master at his height. In one swoop, Wright had secured several objectives. He had parcelled up and disposed of a collection of largely unproductive and certainly undeveloped properties and companies. He had raised new capital for the avowed intention of speculation. He had made significant personal money. Others had also realised capital from shares that were unlikely to fulfil their initial promise.

Wright continued to float new companies in the confident market. In the August, he set out the prospectus for Caledonia Copper with a capital issue of 150,000 of £5 shares. In the November, he published the prospectus for the Nickel Corporation with a similar issue of 150,000 shares at £5 each. It was his slight diversification into other metals. Indeed, he avowed the purpose of the Nickel Corporation was to capture the world market of the product. As intended, British America spawned individual companies to develop particular mining properties. In June and July 1900, Le Roi No 2., Rossland Great Western, Kootenay Mining companies were established with huge share issues.

The share issue of Le Roi No. 2 was a particular triumph for Wright. The take-up of shares was initially very weak and London & Globe and British America were forced to buy the outstanding balance in order to support the market price. Indeed, Wright went further. The 'bear' market speculators were selling stock on the basis that the share price would fall, that they would not have to buy shares to fulfil their obligations and that purchasers such as Wright would be forced to pay them the price difference to relieve themselves of the contract to purchase. The reverse occurred. The bears had contracted to purchase more shares than were available. Wright had cornered the market and, to fulfil their contracts, bears were forced to purchase the shares at inflated prices. London & Globe sold part of its holdings at a profit of over £100,000. Wright himself made a colossal sum in the process.

The last five years had surpassed his American exploits. The share values of his companies had grown. High dividends had been paid. London & Globe shares invariably traded at well above their face value and dividends had been excellent. Lake View shares paid dividends in three years equivalent to four and a half of any capital investment. It had paid dividends of £125,000 in 1897 and 1898, and £625,000 in 1899. Its £1 shares rose to £15. Ivanhoe paid dividends of £50,000 in 1899, and £200,000 in 1899; eventually it returned of 50% on the company's capital. Other Wright companies seemed to enjoy favourable trading.

All of his success was against the background of Great Britain in its supreme national confidence. Its white colonies of Canada, South Africa and Australia were maturing into lands of importance, allied in trade and business to their mother country, producing trade, mineral wealth and opportunity for individuals to prosper. Its eastern empire centred on India but extending into a vast area of colonies providing raw materials for British factories and consumers for the resulting manufactured products. Its army and navy were the largest in the world and generally went unchallenged. It was the leading industrial power in the world. This self-assurance, self-interest and at times, euphoria, not only characterised the London financial centre but the country itself. Money could buy absolutely anything. Property, position and people were available for sale.

Whitaker Wright epitomised that British self-assurance and apparent command of the world. He was at the top of the pile of self-made men. His reputation for the creation of wealth was renowned. He was one of the multi-millionaires of the time. His name was everywhere in the financial press. His ability to spot the venture and make it lucrative appeared unassailable. He was called 'Monte Cristo' after the hero of Alexandre Dumas' book who finds the vast treasure trove. It was an accolade that epitomised the man and the moment. He characterised the age and the time.

# CHAPTER 6

## Making the Home

In parallel with and inexorably linked to Wright's business ambitions was his desire to reinforce his social position. In America, he and his family had enjoyed a lifestyle commensurate with his great wealth. He was determined that England should provide an even better situation for them. He made millions of pounds from his financial dealings and he determined to use the money in the same spectacular manner. He had used his homes in America to entertain socially and to foster his business contacts. His principal ambition in England was to create both town and country residences to reinforce the status and position to which he aspired. He wanted to be and be recognised as a gentleman, and he wanted his wife to be a lady. He wanted to ensure that his wife and family would have the best. They had known a luxurious lifestyle in America and he wanted England to provide them with even better comfort and status. He travelled back and forth between America and England in late 1890 and in 1891 to explore the property possibilities and to make the arrangements for the change.

Initially, he settled in London at 3 West Bolton Gardens, South Kensington. It was a modestly fashionable part of the city. The property was a four-storey terraced house with a basement and sufficient for his immediate family, for guest visitors and for some entertainment. Wright could take a short and simple journey to his office in the business part of the capital. He intended it to be a temporary base while he developed his interests and secured the kind of residences he wanted.

He set his sights on an estate in Surrey centred on Lea Park at Witley. It was at the very south-west of the county near its border with Hampshire. It was an entirely rural location. There were the small nearby towns of Godalming and Haslemere and a host of tiny villages like Witley set in the gently undulating landscape of fields and woodland. There were extensive views from the lands northwards to the line of the North Downs running from Guildford to Farnham and southwards to Gibbet Hill on Hindhead Common and across the open heaths growing on the sandstone terrain. The lands were intersected by the main Godalming to Haslemere road and a series of rural lanes bordered by trees and hedges. The farm cottages and outbuildings were scattered in the fields and by the side of the lanes. It was idyllic but accessible to London by railway in somewhat less than an hour.

The lands were extensive, comprising farms and hamlets. Bowlhead Green Farm and Brook Farm were about 100 acres each in extent, Winkford and Parsonage Farms comprised over 300 acres combined, and Lower Roke Farm was about eighty acres. There was additional farmland, woodland and plots of several hundred more acres. The farms were a mixture of arable for cereal crops and pasture accommodating cattle and sheep. There were over twenty cottages and houses, a blacksmith's forge, a post office and a local dancing and concert room. The numerous residences were situated in the two hamlets of Brook and Bowlhead Green and on the various farms with most properties being occupied by local farm workers and their families.

What Wright really wanted was Lea Park itself, with its house and grounds then owned by W.H. Stone who, at one time, had been Liberal MP for Portsmouth, but was now retired with his family. The house itself was of good size sufficient to accommodate Stone, his wife and daughter, three or four guests and eight servants. It had an immediate area of formal gardens, sizeable parkland, several large ponds and woods extended over some several hundred acres and including several large outbuildings. The originally Elizabethan house had been extended in the Georgian period and later times.

The property had originally been advertised for auction in July 1893 and Wright completed the purchase at the beginning of 1894 for £60,000. He could now establish the kind of country residence of which he had dreamed. It would need a significant amount of money. Wright planned huge changes to the existing and already substantial house. It was large enough to accommodate the Wright family in some comfort but his plan was to increase its size radically to accommodate all the elements of an English country mansion. He wanted to be able to entertain on a lavish scale and to accommodate the English aristocracy. He wanted to feel proud of his country estate.

He engaged the architect Paxton-Watson to design the new house that he envisaged. The existing house would be partly demolished but increased in depth with two new and large wings constructed on its northern and southern sides. The northern wing was designed in the early English style in stone and half-timbered work to reflect part of the existing house. The northern parts were to be in stone and of a more palatial appearance. There was to be a tower and an observatory. Inside, it would be richly decorated and furnished. The new house was to have large rooms for both domestic and guest recreation and accommodation. The latest in technology would be used to provide comfort and service. Wright wanted to be able to have house guests for any period that was required and at an unrivalled level of quality. He wanted the aristocratic guests to be entirely comfortable and impressed. He wanted splendour and style. The best hotel would not be able to compete.

The entranceway was to be grand. Wright believed that first impressions made a statement about him. The scene was set by a new driveway of several hundred yards from a new entrance lodge where the Haslemere to Godalming road met Lea Coach Road leading through the open park landscape to a white gravel circular forecourt around an oval grassed area. The entrance lobby and outer hall panelled in oak with a rich plaster-modelled frieze led to an inner hall of oak panelling with rich carved oak pendants. There was a fireplace surround with well-proportioned marble mouldings and a kerb with firedogs in a recess. The adjacent beautifully fitted library in pollard oak boasted a magnificently carved oak mantelpiece.

The elegant main staircase to the first floor was in classic design with pilasters supporting a rich cornice and cushion frieze. The centrepiece was a magnificent ballroom on the first floor with an entrance from a wide landing through a pair of handsomely carved mahogany doors with a richly carved overdoor. It extended some eighty-one by thirty-three feet with a lantern light of stained glass as well as ceiling windows in oak and walnut. The parquetry flooring of oak and walnut matched the walls panelled in cedar wood, with carved and gilded borders, a finely carved and gilded frieze and arched ceiling for decoration by Italian artists. Sixteen Corinthian fluted columns of cedar wood with gilded capitals added the final touch. These supported a magnificent entablature of an elaborately carved frieze of scroll work and figures depicting cherubs in a variety of poses and holding musical instruments. The ballroom provided a fitted stage and dressing rooms and a minstrels' gallery adorned by a gilded grill with elaborate decorations. Two very fine ormolu and crystal electroliers and twelve chased ormolu wall lights illuminated the room. Wright would be able to hold the grandest of occasions in this room. He could provide a range of entertainment and amusement. Any social event could be accommodated. To add to the amusement and some intrigue, an observatory was constructed with access from the ballroom via stairs.

The new southern wing was extended in a gallery measuring ninety-two by forty-two feet leading to a magnificent rounded Palm House. The mosaic floor was designed with Greek Fret and Wave patterned borders. The Ionic columns accentuated the gallery and extended the vision up to two juxtaposed barrel-vaulted glass roofs with cunette shapes in painted glass and a large glass dome above the palm court. The rooms were set in a Renaissance style and fitted out with sculptures including one of the Three Graces in Carrara marble standing on large fish and supporting a large bowl of natural objects. It was intended to provide a stunning feature and complete the southern end of the house. Guests could view the landscape, the terraced gardens, the lake, the immediate rose garden, the cultivated vegetation and woodland, the hills beyond. It was to be an accommodation for the grandest of society in whatever the local weather might bring. It was a feature that few country houses could boast. Guests would be able to socialise and relax in the most stylish manner.

The plans showed nine family and guest bedrooms, each twenty-five by eighteen feet. All had the latest in personal accommodation and technology with lavatory fittings, hot and cold running water and central heating. There were to be three large bath and dressing rooms. Each could accommodate a lounge area providing a sofa and chairs. The master bedroom was L-shaped and partly decorated in a William & Mary style.

His male guests could retreat below ground for suitable recreation to the billiard room of thirty by twenty-one feet. It was to be fitted in carved oak with arched ceiling and lantern lights, a deep recessed fireplace fitted with richly tiled jambs and a richly carved mantel. Throughout, the house would have electric bells, wall lights, electric lighting and heating appliances. It would have its own water supply and own generator for the electricity supply. There would be the latest telephone installation. Wright was determined to display the latest in technical innovation.

But there was another surprise for all of his guests. It was to be an extraordinary feature. A submerged room provided access through a walkway tunnel to an island constructed in stone in the renamed Thursley Lake. The tunnel was constructed of steel and glass enabling visitors to walk under the lake water and view its contents. The small island set out in the lake provided a unique vantage point for guests to have views across the lake itself and back to the house at the top of the terraced lawns. It was designed to be wondrous. Its construction would require the newly enlarged lake to be drained.

Part of the northern wing would provide the servants' quarters and their work areas and accommodate the size of the establishment that Wright envisaged. Eight bedrooms for the maids and four for the menservants with two bathrooms together with a servants' hall of twenty-six by eighteen feet were provided. The housekeeper had a sitting room and the butler a bedroom. There was a lofty kitchen measuring about twenty-four feet square, a plate room, several larders and a still room and a strong room. There were extensive areas for wine and beer cellarage. There were brushing and cleaning rooms. In the house yard, there was a laundry, washing room, ice-making house, boiler house, game larder and three dog kennels with runs and a pigeon cote. The house was to have all of the service requirements of an English country house.

New stables were to replace the existing buildings completely and intended to be magnificent in their own right. There were three stables with eighteen loose boxes and seven stalls. Each was to have beautifully tiled walls and stone floors. Magnificent murals of hunting scenes and country pursuits would decorate the interior walls. The harness room and saddle room were fitted in teak. There were cleaning and washing rooms and a forage store. The large coach house boasted seven pairs of doors of linen-fold panelling. The coachman's house had four bedrooms, sitting room, kitchen and fitted bathroom. There were two rooms for grooms with seven cubicles, two bathrooms, groomsmen room, kitchen and two other rooms for men together with a recreation room of sixty-three by twenty feet. Even the simple accommodation of horses and conveyances was to be impressive. Even the servants were to have a level of accommodation as befitted employees of a man of wealth and enlightenment.

His plans for the grounds were equally spectacular. The immediate grounds were enclosed in a three-and-a-half-mile, eight-foot-high stone wall which defined the private space of the house and separated it from the working estate. The wall was stepped at regular intervals to reflect the subtle changes in the heights of the estate grounds and immediate countryside.

The one existing main entrance with a small lodge and gate would be replaced by five entrance lodges and new driveways through the park from the existing public roads. Each lodge marked the entrance to a separate driveway to the mansion. Their locations were eventually reflected in their names of Thursley, Milford, Witley, Brook and Lake. Each lodge was large enough to provide family accommodation for servants on the estate. They were properties in their own right. Brook Lodge was typical. It was designed by Paxton-Watson in a free Tudor style in sandstone. It was two storeys high with projecting square bays under gables and a tiled roof. Stacks rose to the front and rear. The lodge overarched the large carriage entrance which had massive double gates. Leaded casement windows were provided at first floor. It was meant to be impressive. Other lodges varied slightly in size but were similarly designed. Each depicted a Whitaker Wright 'crest' of four diamonds which divided the double W of his name and provided the date of construction.

The existing Lea House was set in grounds with woodlands to the north and west which would basically remain. Lea Park Farm and its outbuildings to the east of the house were to be demolished to provide uninterrupted views and openness to the area particularly along this main entrance drive. Where necessary, the landscape was to be moulded to give a pleasing undulation and a reflection of the wider countryside.

But the proposed changes to the existing water areas were the most spectacular features. There were three northern ponds and a western pond with a boathouse. On the northern boundary, he planned to enhance one of the ponds into Stable Lake immediately north of the new stables area. The remaining ponds would be drained to form 'The Shrubbery' comprising rhododendrons and similar planting along the side of the main entrance drive. Stable Lake was to have a bathing house for the use of guests. It had two dressing rooms and lavatories with hot and cold running water. The adjacent western pond was to be more than trebled to the size of twenty-five acres to form Thursley Lake and provide the water backdrop to his extended descending terraced gardens at the rear of the mansion. The lake would accommodate the island accessed by the submerged tunnel. The centre of the existing and extensive south-western woodland was to be filled with the southern part of this lake. At the bottom of the terraces, there was to be a magnificent fountain of seahorses and nymphs. A boathouse designed by the young architect Edward Lutyens was to be provided to enable guests to take boats onto the water. Finally, at the southern end of the grounds, the new Upper Lake would be carved out of the existing woodland.

The three lakes were interconnected with a sluice from the Upper to Thursley and a weir from Stable Lake to Thursley Lake with a pump house to recycle the water. The water drained from Thursley Lake eventually into the nearby River Wey. Upper and Stable Lakes were connected by a vast underground pipe to enable the water level in Stable Lake to be maintained. It was to be a visual transformation of the areas immediately adjacent to the house. Visitors would marvel at the sight and at the engineering required to achieve it.

Driveways and walkways were constructed throughout the grounds and around the lakes to provide views, interest and recreation for guests. The intention was to give an ambiance of pleasure gardens. The wide grass terraces down to Thursley Lake would give an impression of grandeur. The rose garden by the palm house, the walled kitchen garden, the old garden, the vinery and peach house would generate an atmosphere of the aristocratic residence. Other buildings were designed to provide diversion in the landscape like the octagonal spring house with its black marble walls, marble basin and sculptured mural tablet. There were sculptured stone bridges and a temple set up high in the pine woods. The temple was a monstrous building of four columned entrances supporting arches over. It provided magnificent views over the Surrey countryside. There was to be a tea house for summer afternoons. Wright wanted the residence to be leisured, cultured and splendid.

The works to the house were to take several years. The labour involved was immense. A wide range of skills was required including engineers and surveyors, stonemasons and bricklayers, plasterers and carpenters, painters, decorators, gardeners, craftsman of all kinds. Large bodies of labourers would be employed to assist on the extensive changes and the new wings to the house. Specialists were engaged to undertake the finishing grandeur.

Landscaping work required an army of navvies to dig everything by hand. It was the same breed and kind of men who had been engaged on the great Victorian projects of the roads and railways, the sewers and water pipes, and recently the new underground railway projects. Vast earthworks were undertaken by these gangs of individuals. It was sheer physical effort with no respite for weather or danger and virtually no machinery. It meant much casual employment for local people although the sheer scale of the enterprises required much recruitment from outside the immediate area. Two temporary bothys were maintained for the use of the casual labour force. These provided little more than a fire and very basic sleeping accommodation for the use of single men. Simple tents were often set up to give overnight shelter.

Wright planned to pepper the grounds with Italian statuary and he contacted Ozario Andreoni in Rome. On one of the lower terraces of the garden and immediately adjacent to Thursley Lake, Wright placed a most magnificent fountain. Its central feature was a boy on a dolphin sculptured by O. Spalmach from the Rome studio of Andreoni. Below and surrounding this statue, there were four nymphs riding sea horses within the stoned container. Within the lake was a statue of Neptune some fifteen feet high, appearing to stand on the surface of the water. A dolphin's head in marble was acquired. Its transportation was a feat in itself. It was sent from Italy but at Southampton the railway company could not transport it because of its width and weight of some thirty tons. Wright hired a traction engine and even lowered a road to get it under a bridge. Its location was to provide the outlet in Stable Lake for the underground pipe from Upper Lake. Another sculpture was an Oceanid riding two horses with eight Oceanids below. They were of Italian design and came from Carrara. Several blocks weighed five tons. Originally, some of the ladies were holding pearls suggesting pearl fishers, Pegasus, Naiads and the Birth of Venus as well as the Oceanids. He imported a larger set of statues of two naked ladies, one helping the other up. Wright intended that these huge sculptures should show his taste and refinement and, not least, his wealth and patronage of the arts. At various points were representative figures of humans, animals and mythical creatures.

The house itself was ostentatiously decorated. Italian craftsmen were particularly used. Whitaker Wright wanted the latest styles but the inclusion of his own tastes. He also liked to have his personal mark displayed. The monogram WW was embossed extensively on everything from stationery items in his study to the walls of the lodges. The rooms were gradually furnished with a dominance of either original or expensive copies of French furniture of the Louis Quatorze, Louis Quinze and Louis Seize periods. Persian carpets would adorn the floors. Paintings and sculptures would feature. He strove to acquire treasures to enhance the corridors and main rooms. He had a pipe organ put in the ballroom and the latest telescope installed in the observatory.

In October 1897, Charles Burgess sold him significant additional areas of land to the north and south of the Lea Park Estate. To the north, the land comprised Witley Common, about 235 acres of woodland and ideal for shooting. The purchase also included some further agricultural fields and seven cottages. To the south, Hindhead Common comprised nearly 800 acres, again, ideal for shooting. Hindhead Common was an upland area, itself a magnificent sight with commanding views of its own across Surrey. Significantly, with the purchase he acquired the ancient rights of the Manor of Witley and was entitled to call himself Lord of the Manor and to hold court to deal with manorial issues. It was a title that he was not slow to use in various directory entries. The sales also included the manorial rights over the much smaller areas of Grayswood Common and Shepherds Hill at Haslemere.

The household staff reflected the size of the house and the kind of entertainment he envisaged. Living at the house was the cook with two kitchen maids to assist her. His wife had a lady's maid and he had a butler who headed the establishment. There were six housemaids and two footmen to undertake all of the chores about the house. His daughters' governess also lived in the house to look after them. Some other staff from families living on the estate would attend on a daily basis for the regular menial housework and, as necessary, staff were engaged for particular functions.

His farms were run by his bailiff, Matthew Mansell, who lived at Winkford farmhouse with his wife and growing family that reached eight by 1901. Wright and Mansell would discuss and plan the development of the farms and livestock and attend and show at agricultural events. Wright's shepherd, Tom Day, who lived at Parsonage farmhouse with his wife and three children, was a key worker responsible for the flock of Southdown sheep of which Wright was particularly proud to the extent of winning the occasional prize at agricultural shows. His gamekeepers, Henry Ransom who lived at Brook Farm with his wife and four children and John Salmon who lived at Witley Lodge with his wife and two children, became increasingly essential to the estate particularly when the additional sporting areas were purchased in 1897. Harry Smith, foreman for the pleasure grounds, lived at Lea Park Lodge with his wife and three children and the coachman, Herbert Thomas, lived at the coach house at Lea Park Stables with his wife and three children and two other relatives. His building foreman, John Morris, lived with his wife and three children in one of the cottages at Lea Park. Many members of these families worked for the estate and household as farm labourers, gardeners, grooms and housemaids. Seven or eight of the men who were grooms and servants lived at Lea Park Stables. Other house and estate employees and farm workers lived in the various cottages encompassed by Wright's estate. It was an army of people who were glad of their positions, their dignity and their relative security of employment. The families felt a great belonging to the estate. Like many estates of the era, it operated as an extended family but with a strict hierarchy of position and power.

Wright took an interest in his estate and the management of his land. He had excellent relationships with all his staff and workers. His tenure was marked by constant acts of generosity and events such as great lunches, bazaars for charities, entertainments for friendly societies and working men's clubs. He was instrumental in the foundation of Milford Workmen's Club and helped to maintain the Lemon Hall which served as accommodation for local dances and other entertainment. His own kindness lay with those far less fortunate. He had a particular liking for children with treats and the occasional pennies thrown from his carriage. Most of all he provided constant and significant employment in the locality. His alterations to the landscape and his rebuilding of the wall provided particular relief in winter when there was little other casual employment.

He revelled in the local pretentious activities and slight arrogance of the role of the Lord of the Manor but used the basically ceremonial position to give generously to the ordinary people and their families. Although there was a great social side to his residence, it was, primarily, his great economic contribution to the local area that made its mark. There were a host of both permanent and casual jobs for local people both directly on his estates or farms and indirectly in the provision of occasional services that were required for his local holdings. Suppliers of goods and services from the local towns particularly benefited from the requirements of the House.

He surveyed his colossal venture on many evenings when he had returned home from London and his business dealings. His journey was only an hour door to door. He never took a hansom cab from his office. If he could not get one of the horse-drawn carriages known as a growler, he walked part of the way and then took the omnibus. But he did have a first-class compartment from Waterloo station and within forty minutes, he could arrive at Witley station. The station master was always there for a word. He could have virtually walked home across his own land such was its extent but his own carriage invariably served for the journey.

The building concept slowly became a reality. The ambitious project had taken some years and there were still some outstanding aspects. Much of the house was finished apart from the first floor above the palm court comprising the southern wing. The entrance lodges were completed or nearing completion. The reconstructed sections of perimeter wall were finished. Much of the immediate landscape was settled and beginning to accommodate its new planting schemes. He had spent many hundreds of thousands of pounds on the project.

Before dinner, he often walked over part of the house grounds. There was often much evening activity. Contractors were paid only for the work that was completed and their workers grafted as long as required. Work was often hard to come by and labourers valued sustained employment. Woodland was being uprooted and timber carried away. Hills were being moved in great cartloads. New lakes had been dug out and former ponds refilled. The land looked like a vast quarry with extensive earthworks being undertaken for some time during these years. Sections of the house were often building sites. There would be legions of men and piles of materials everywhere.

He strode out, a large man of some sixteen stones. His large head and somewhat small eyes adorned as always by his gold-framed prince-nez, were raised in confident manner. His receding forehead and chin and great bulky neck swelled over his high-necked collar. He stroked his newly styled beard. He loved to change his facial hair style. As usual, his clothes were unassuming, almost severe in their simplicity. He liked to wear a black frock coat cut in the American style when in London but was otherwise unassuming in his dress. Apart from the gold watch and chain that sparkled from his ample waistcoat, he wore no items of jewellery. He cut a cultivated and suave figure. His appearance was not unlike the Prince of Wales and they were of similar ages.

But he was not an overtly social man except in the interests of his business or self-advancement. He therefore greatly enjoyed these moments at home when he could be private. In his walk, he took a hand in supervising the works, enjoying some banter with the labourers. He liked to judge a man by his face and did not care what other people might say about them. There was directness in talking to these working men. He recounted his apparent early labours in the mining industry of America and encouraged their back-breaking work. He revelled in their response that he had been digging for something more valuable. The workers hoped that he was there to respond to more suggestions from his guests to move again some of the landscaped areas as it would mean extended employment. He was famed for his ironic humour. He told friends that after the cares of the city were left behind, his greatest delight was to go home and listen to the rooks in the elms about his estate.

His evening walk brought him back to the house and dinner. He often entertained and usually John Eyre from local Enton was waiting for him. He was a valued and close friend. They would enjoy the meal with their respective wives and then retire for a good cigar and a game of billiards. Later, after his guests' departure, he would sit in his library with one of his favourite Bret Harte stories. They told of the Californian gold rush exploits of the ordinary prospectors. The narrative romantically recounted the hard life and grim reality of those days of the 1840s. The overt violence and frequent disputes were painted with a superficial sense of justice. Shameless greed and dubious characters were benignly portrayed. A sense of gentle irony was given to the most ludicrous of events. He liked the story of 'Luck of the Roaring Camp'. The stories always fuelled his sense of those days and reinforced his own rehearsed memories of his own apparent adventures. He did not know that Wright's hero, the author, was living barely ten miles away in almost shabby gentility.

Underpinning his life was his wife and his family. She had emerged from humble origins and learned to become the young and elegant hostess. She was very attractive with her brown hair and elegant face with a slim figure that remained despite the birth of six children. She was always adorned in the latest fashions with the best silk dresses and jewellery. Although only in her thirties, she had the confidence of many years of household management and entertaining. Her American style, not least her accent and manner, endeared her to guests. She had charm and sophistication. She was the woman behind the great man.

She was devoted to Whitaker and her children. The earlier losses of their two sons, Ernest and Jay and their daughter, Mabel, were well behind them. Neither of them now had any living parents and their siblings were all living in America. Their personal focus was entirely directed to their three children. Their son, Whitaker, had attended Eton School since 1895 when he was thirteen. He was being prepared for life. Magdalen College at Oxford University followed. The two girls, Gladys and Edith, had a German governess, Miss Schenerle, who lived with the family at Witley Park. Anna ran the house and the dozen or so servants. The promises that Whitaker had made on their embarkation for England had been fulfilled. She implicitly trusted him.

And their London address was similarly grand. Location was the key. On 31$^{st}$ December 1895, Whitaker Wright took an assignment of the lease of 18 Park Lane, Hanover Square, London. He paid Ellinor Arbuthnot £4,200 for the remaining lease period which had been granted in 1886 for twenty-one years at a rent of £550 per year. He wanted to make changes to the property and undertake improvements. Accordingly, on 11$^{th}$ August 1896, he surrendered the existing lease and signed an agreement for a new lease for eighty years to start from 24$^{th}$ June 1896 at annual rent of £600. He agreed to carry out his improvements by 24$^{th}$ June 1898 at a minimum cost of £5,000.

The properties in Park Lane were imposing and extensive. They were some of the most fashionable in the capital and close enough to the heart of the city. It was a large house with extensive views through its large windows across Hyde Park. On the ground floor, there was an ample entrance hall leading to four reception rooms of two front and two rear drawing rooms with a study and dining room. On the upper floors, there were ten or so bedrooms, many with adjacent dressing rooms, several lavatories and bathrooms and small rooms. The basement comprised extensive servants' quarters and accommodation, kitchen and scullery, storerooms and larders.

It was to be the place to exhibit Wright's affluent lifestyle and city reputation. He could entertain the highest in his business and social circles. It was extensively and fashionable furnished. The centrepiece of the main drawing room was a replica, made at great expense, of the Cabinet des Rois of Louis XV, the original of which was in the Louvre. Throughout was his favourite French furniture and some of his favourite Italian sculptures. It was demonstrably grand and richly impressive if somewhat ostentatious in character. His valet, Joseph Butler, together with his wife Mary and a housemaid, looked after the property and brought in additional help when required. Essentially, it was opened for Wright and his lady when either were in any lengthy residence in town or holding a particular function for honoured guests. He used the study for some of his business work. It was complete with a telephone carrying his business number of Gerrard 5579.

Whilst Lea Park had been established as the country residence and Park Lane as the town house, there was the flat at 3 Whitehall Court which had been constructed in the mid-1880s just off Whitehall. It accommodated many notable persons. Wright and his wife used the flat simply to stay in London without the expense of opening his Park Lane property.

He travelled extensively, principally alone but sometimes with his family. There were many trips to Paris which was the stylish place to visit and excursions to Rome and Florence particularly for the sculptures. He enjoyed the winter sun of Nice where Christmas was spent in both 1896 and 1897. His passion for yachting took him to the relevant events in both England and abroad where he sailed the Mediterranean in particular.

His yachting interest had been initiated and developed in America and continued in England. He joined the prestigious Royal Temple Yacht Club which was headed, as commodore, by Baron Ferdinand de Rothchild and patronised by the Prince of Wales. Wright became a member of the club management committee. He gave valuable prizes for various races and competitions organised by British and Riviera Yacht Clubs. At Easter 1896, Wright with the French and Austrian Consuls, arranged a regatta in Malta where he donated a cup and prize money for the race from Nice to the island. In August 1896, it was Wright's prizes for an event sponsored by the Royal Victoria Yacht Club. At the March 1897 Nice International Regatta, he donated the White Heather Cup, named after his own yacht, for the match for yachts above forty tons. It was to be an annual prize. He became a member of other clubs including the Royal Cinque Ports, Royal Dorset, Royal Thames and Royal Victoria. In 1899, he was elected Rear Commodore of the Portsmouth Corinthian Yacht Club.

In 1897, he acquired a steam yacht from Martin Rucker in exchange for shares in Lake View Consols then trading at £4 each. The boat had originally been constructed at Barrow for Lord Ashburton who named her *Venetia*. The vessel was some 924 tons. Rucker had been gifted the yacht by his business partner, Hooley, who had paid £50,000 to Lily Langtree for the vessel. Wright named the yacht *Sybarite*, aptly named for it meant 'one devoted to luxury'. He sailed her to the Mediterranean in company with yachts of similar size and own by dignitaries. But he wanted more from this pastime.

He wanted something that would beat all comers. In 1900, he commissioned a Clyde yard to build a yacht based on the designs of George L. Watson and rigged as a yawl of some 214 tons. There was bold experimentation with the hull of the lightest materials. She was called *Sybarita*. He raced the yacht at annual regattas like the one at Ryde, Isle of Wight, run by the Royal Victoria Yacht Club. She was raced against the best and, on one occasion beat the Kaiser's Meteor.

There was a considerable social side to the yachting fraternity. There were banquets, parties and cruises in addition to the racing. Wright regularly attended such functions. In 1900, the Royal Temple Yacht Club hosted its annual dinner at the Hotel Cecil with an attendance of some 2,000 people. Baron de Rothchild was the commodore and was accompanied by his close friend the Prince of Wales. Wright used his yachts to accommodate dignitaries. In February 1896, he hired a special Pullman train to run his guests from London down to Southampton and then for a cruise on *White Heather* which he had bought from the German Emperor. Those in the party included his company directors Sir William and Lady Robinson, Lord Pelham-Clinton, Lt-General Gough-Calthorpe, together with business associates like Herbert Trower, Arthur Young and Murray Griffiths. In August of the same year, Wright entertained the Prince of Wales and a range of dignitaries, including again some of his fellow company directors on *White Heather* during Cowes week and then for sailing to Trouville in France. He did the same during the week of Goodwood Races.

It was particularly founded to foster Anglo-American relations. Although he was not overtly political, he was appointed as a member of the British Empire League Committee in December 1897. Its aim was to foster trade and other links with the colonies, something that was close to Whitaker Wright's heart. Wright cultivated people but principally for the purpose of his business pursuits. The personages who were to become the directors of his companies were generously entertained in various forms and on many occasions. Many were not only seduced by his wealth and the possibility of increasing their own income but also by the maintenance of their own social standings. Other notables were entertained simply because of their position, including Sir James Reid, the personal physician of Queen Victoria.

With the wealth, the assets and the properties, Wright was able to entertain the highest in the land. His London house, his country mansion and estate and his yacht provided the lavish accommodation and recreation. He could host the Prince of Wales, the next in line to the throne. He could look forward to patronage and he could expect to be honoured on some suitable occasion. He could mix with the aristocracy and the wealthy on virtually equal terms. The horizons were bright and the prospects for his future advancement were clear. His life had never been brighter.

He freely gave to charity both personally and through his companies. It was often associated with support for relief and other enterprises in the British colonies. He was an exponent of the British Empire. He donated to the London Lord Mayor's Funds like the Indian Relief Fund. He gave to the Gordon Memorial College in Khartoum sponsored by Lord Kitchener. He subscribed to the Relief of Transvaal Refugees occasioned by the Boer War. His gentle sense of humour was typically shown in one donation. In July 1899, he arranged for a doll to be raffled and it sold for £300. The purchaser was only later aware that in the doll's pocket was a free call for 500 Le Roi shares worth some two thousand pounds. The notoriety of the incident did Wright's reputation no harm at all.

Locally, he was in his element and he used the magnificence and space of Lea Park to accommodate events. Not untypical was the fundraising day held on 1st September 1900 by the Peper Harow and Godalming Habitations of the Primrose League. The organisation had been established in 1883, after the death of Conservative Prime Minister Disraeli and named to denote his favourite flower, to promote Conservative principles and the virtues of free enterprise. By this time, it had over 1,000,000 members with a substantial ladies' section. It held meetings in a series of local branches and often held events to raise funds for its organisation. Wright's agent, Y.H. Knowles, worked hard with the local League members in arranging and carrying out various details connected with the gathering.

There was an enormous attendance of over 5,000 people. Every public vehicle seemed to have been requisitioned for the purpose of conveyance to the park and, swelled by large numbers of private carriages and hundreds of bicycles, the various roads leading to Whitaker Wright's beautiful domain presented the appearance somewhat of the Epsom road on Derby Day. An ample and substantial tea was provided in two spacious tents for some 2,000 persons, ably undertaken the experienced supervision of the local League members. All the fun of the fair was provided by roundabouts, swings, cocoanut shies, etc. with the music provided by the Godalming brass band.

An open-air stage had been constructed, proudly displaying the banner of Habitation No. 590 of the League. Two hours' entertainment was given by Mr. Edward Longstaffe's variety combination including ventriloquial displays, a comic-sketching sketch, 'Hindoo' magic in native costume, and comic sketches, which afforded endless amusement to the crowds. At six-thirty, the formality of the day was inserted before the captive audience with addresses being given by Mr. John Ryde as chairman for the day, by Viscount Middleton and the Rt. Hon. St. John Brodrick, surrounded on the platform by national and local dignitaries. There was the usual speech concerning the virtues of Conservative values and, of course, generous vote of thanks to Whitaker Wright. At a quarter to nine a brilliant display of fireworks was given by Messrs. Brook & Co of Crystal Palace and mostly paid for by Whitaker Wright. It was a grand finale to a memorable day at Lea Park. A good day out was had by all.

In London, there was an entirely different scene to his rural retreat. His businesses were the subject of continual newspaper gossip. It was par for the course. The speculative nature of the mining company promotion was good copy for the newspaper industry. It provided endless columns of news about the highs and lows of share prices and company results. There were both criticisms for the methods and plaudits for the wealth created. Wright was in no different position from his rivals in the game. There were jealousies and snobberies about his acquired wealth and lavish lifestyle. Wright was ever vigilant to protect his reputation. His business methods were often the subject of veiled criticism and his company launches and his particular spat with the *Pall Mall Gazette* highlighted the sensitivity of the issues.

The publication sought to expose his payments for favourable newspaper coverage of his company launches. In 1898, following the death of their City Editor, Batrick Baker, the *Pall Mall Gazette* had uncovered cheques of several hundred pounds paid to him by London & Globe. They linked the money with testimony by Hooley, the entrepreneur then being investigated, that Baker blackmailed companies to secure favourable reports in his column. There had also been an apparently private conversation between Wright and a representative of the *Gazette* about Baker's activities with an assurance that it was entirely confidential. There was also a note to Baker in Wright's handwriting. Their article posed poignant questions on the integrity of Wright and his involvement with the payments. Wright was furious about the exposure and the effect on his and his companies' reputations. He wrote emphatically that he had not paid one penny to the *Pall Mall Gazette* or any other newspaper. He denied making accusations about Baker quoting the Latin phrase 'de mortuis nil nisi bonum'. The *Gazette* would not retract. Wright was forced, with the compliance of his company board, to issue an explanation to his shareholders. But it was a contrived story maintaining that Wright had only given share tips to Baker out of his own good nature and to get him out of the office. Wright's statement further maintained that Globe had sold Baker's shares for him in the normal course of business. Some of the press believed the story whilst others remained entirely sceptical.

The incident highlighted the nature of the uneasy relationship between the entrepreneurs and the newspapers. Both had reputations to preserve. But it served to demonstrate the kind of practice that was used to promote business ventures and the kind of accountability that was absent. However, Wright remained largely unscathed. It was his financial results that attracted attention, not his methods. His continued successful ventures and accumulated wealth bought association, bred acquiescence and instilled huge deference.

In Witley and Godalming, there was no such pretension. Respect was given because of what an individual had achieved. Everyone locally had the highest regard for him and his family. No one really knew his background but it could be seen that he had no title and that his wealth was the result of his own efforts. His Lea Park home was everything he had ever wanted. There was his wife and family and close friends. There was peace and it was security. But it was maintained at an enormous cost. His business acumen ensured that there was a constant supply of both capital and income. His wealth was enormous and his position unassailable.

# CHAPTER 7

# Making the Losses

As the century came to an end, Wright looked over his business empire with confidence and satisfaction. He had been twenty-five years in the business of stock dealing. His three colossal main companies of London & Globe, Standard Exploration and British America together with a host of mining companies spread across the mining market of the London Stock Exchange. The main companies had been set up for a variety of purposes but not least to give Wright power in the mining market. London & Globe was the particular vehicle to enable him to speculate in the market, something he had only previously been able to attempt in a much more modest way. The success of the company lent considerable weight to his financial reputation and his ability to command money and support for his businesses and dealings. Wright had been involved in some very competitive environments and the London Stock Exchange was at the extreme.

London was the world centre of finance. Commerce and industry, trade and services constantly needed money to continue. Accordingly, monstrous sums of money were advanced by banks, funding institutions, governments, groups and individuals. Money was set to work and either it earned from a particular investment or it would find somewhere that would give a return. The competition was fierce. Although the state of share prices and company standings were reported daily and the market apparently an open book, there was little regulation and little enforcement of what there was. Behind the scenes, unscrupulous men manipulated the market. The use of rumour, the engineered newspaper report, the subtle shift of money and the word in the club could dictate the fortunes of any company.

The actual business of dealing in shares was relatively straightforward. The share market at the London Stock Exchange worked on the basis of agreements to buy and sell shares at a fixed price in any listed company. The purchase money and the shares would not change hands until the end of each relevant fortnight depending on the commodity of the share being transacted. At the end of each fortnight, called 'carry-over' day, the buyer and seller had options. The transaction could be concluded with the money being paid and the share scrip being delivered. Alternatively, the shares could be carried over for the next fortnight and the money and shares were not exchanged. However, a new price for the share scrip would necessarily have to be fixed and payment made by the relevant party for the difference between the price originally agreed and the new price. On this day, carry-over prices were determined by the interaction of the buyers and sellers. More desire to carry-over than to complete the transactions meant that the price of the share in any particular company would tend to rise and the reverse meant a tendency for market value to fall. The speculation was based upon the view of what was going to happen to the share price during the following fortnight and beyond.

The anticipation, sometimes expectation, usually speculation of what was going to happen to the price of a particular share could be influenced by many factors. The news, often simply rumours, about the state of the company, its profits and its assets could change the view of an investor. Whole markets might be governed by external factors like international conflict, changes of government or the broad national economic position. Individual sectors could rise or decline on the availability and demand for its products. It was an uncertain world.

In many instances, of course, it was as much about the determination and, indeed, financial resources and backing of those engaged in the dealing. It could mean constantly paying either for shares or simply to keep an interest in the shares even without any acquisition. It could mean the commitment of considerable financial resources to acquire the relevant number of shares that would change the market situation. The 'bulls' speculated for an increase in share values and the 'bears' for their decrease. Each group played the market either by buying or by selling at critical moments to induce the price changes. Others who were not directly involved would tend to follow the trends of the price, buying when there was an upward movement and selling when there was downward movement. Many share investors did not rapidly buy and sell but simply invested for the dividend and long-term value of the share. Battles between bulls and bears were usually of short duration and limited to particular shares.

The dealings could only be undertaken by members of the Stock Exchange either on their own account but more usually on behalf of third parties. Brokers had to meet the financial obligations of the contracts they had made for share dealings or face the consequence of removal from the market. Accordingly, they would want guarantees of payment from their clients when receiving instructions to deal. Regular investors were usually backed by banks. Heavy investment required the specific backing of a specific financial institution. Large companies could trade on their reputations by a history of meeting obligations and current stability. Reputation was the key. The mining market was a particularly speculative area. Given the launch of his many new companies and the need to support them in the market, Wright was a natural 'bull'. The ultimately successful launch of Le Roi No. 2 had been notable for his activity and success.

There was one company that Wright had set his heart on controlling. Since the formation of the Lake View Consols, he had been frustrated. The payment of a substantial part of the initial issue of company shares for the acquisition of the interests had meant that so many of the shares were not held by one of his main companies. The richness of the mines and accordingly the repeated size of the dividends meant that a lucrative income evaded him. He also felt that it was his enterprise that had made the company.

During 1899 and 1900, he made huge attempts to acquire these shares. London & Globe spent considerable sums in the speculations. Wright had gone out on his own without any real knowledge on the part of his board. Not that any of the board members would have objected to the enterprise and still less understood the purpose. Wright used both company money and his personal wealth for the venture. However, it was perhaps the worst time to speculate on the market. With a few notable exceptions, mining share dividends had declined. There were various possible explanations including over-capitalisation, insufficient expenditure on mine development, poor management of mines and over-optimistic mine reports but some downright manipulations of the market could also be a cogent reason. The formal start of the Boer War in October 1899 following several false starts in the conflict brought great uncertainty and unease to the international situation. The war had a direct effect on both international and British finance. The market had already begun to decline and the war accelerated the depression. There were fluctuations but the bears were determined to exert their influence.

The full result of his speculations climaxed one morning at the beginning of October 1900 when Wright sat at his office desk at 53 Lothbury and studied the single piece of paper which his chief accountant, Arthur Worters, had left for him the evening before. It was a draft of the annual balance sheet for London & Globe made up to 30$^{th}$ September 1900. Wright could not believe the figures. He knew that financial speculations had been large and that the losses had been severe. But the balance sheet was far worse than he had expected. It showed colossal losses and very few assets. There was an apparent loss of at least one and a half million pounds. London & Globe was due to publish its balance sheet for the position at 30$^{th}$ September but Wright realised that publication in its present form would mean the end of the company. Further and without much doubt, his credibility would be lost if his flagship company were to collapse. In all probability, he would lose what was left of his own fortune. But he did not panic. He needed a strategy to deal with the situation.

He had been here before. A year earlier, he had faced a similar position. Whilst in 1896, London & Globe had floated the Lake View Consols which owned the Lake View gold mines in Kalgoorlie, Western Australia, a vast number of the shares had been used to pay for the acquisition and subsequently sold on the market. London & Globe's ownership of the shares, although substantial, was limited. The Lake View Company was very strong and its shares had been at a premium. In 1899, Wright determined to acquire these shares to enhance the assets of London & Globe. It would provide a secure income for Globe given the dividend of £4 per share that had been paid by the Lake View Company. During that year, some very large transactions had taken place with regard to these shares but London & Globe made heavy losses. Much of the speculation centred on the reports of the irregular production levels of the gold from the mines. For many months there was an apparently poor return; next came enormous production with the mine apparently producing one ton of gold per month between May and October, but then a period of moderate quantities. There were suspicions that these changes in the productive powers of the mine had occurred not in Australia but at the company office. Based upon a substantial production of gold in the first four months of 1899, the share price reached £29 by the middle of the year. Wright believed the reports and invested heavily. Suddenly, the change took place and the production level fell. The share price correspondingly fell. Wright considered that there had been misconduct by the mine manager and he was eventually dismissed. But the fall in the share price by September of the year, left London & Globe with losses of £750,000 and its sister company, Standard Exploration, with losses of £250,000. They had agreed to buy when the share price had been high and had been forced to fund the losses when the price dropped. Additionally, there had been a legal dispute with Globe's original representative in Australia, Charles Kaufmann, about the price of shares that Kaufmann had bargained to get when he had negotiated the deal for the acquisition of the Lake View company. Wright had to settle for handing some 15,000 Lake View shares at £13 each to Kaufmann. These were the very shares that Wright was so keen to acquire.

The London & Globe balance sheet had to be published to show the position on 30th September 1899. Some means in the balance sheet would have to be devised to allow for these losses and present the company as a sound financial concern. A figure of £500,000 was detailed as depreciation from the profit and loss account but to make the situation look more comfortable for the company, a figure of £534,455 was shown as 'cash at bankers'. Whilst the statement was actually true, it disguised the nature and source of the money. A set of 'contrived' transactions involving the two sister companies of London & Globe were undertaken. On 28th September, London & Globe only had £80,000 at the bank. On 29th and 30th September, London & Globe paid into its bank cheques signed by Wright and drawn on

Standard Exploration for nearly £360,000. During the same period of two days, Standard Exploration paid into its own account some £113,000 consisting of three cheques signed by Wright and drawn on British America. Standard Exploration also borrowed £100,000 from its bankers based on a letter sent by Wright. Various shares were transferred to support the payments from these two companies. Some 6,800 Lake View shares were transferred from London & Globe to Standard Exploration although some 3,000 shares actually belonged to Wright himself. The shares were priced at not quite three times their value on the market. Indeed, Wright had personally to borrow £50,000 of short-term money to pay into Standard Exploration. He had previously sold or agreed to sell nearly all of his 100,000 shares in London & Globe leaving him with only 2,500 shares. This was the minimum number he was required to keep a director's interest in the company. He used some 40,000 of these shares, then not yet transferred to the purchaser, to secure the personal bank loan. Some 80,000 shares in the Nickel Corporation and 30,000 Victoria Gold shares were apparently sold by London & Globe to Standard Exploration. Effectively Standard Exploration and British American and Wright himself had provided the cash in the bank shown in London & Globe's balance sheet shortly before 30th September based upon the sale of the shares between the three companies.

After the preparation of the balance sheet, its authentication by the auditors and its publication on 9th October 1899, the relevant transactions were simply reversed. Bank loans were repaid by Standard Exploration in early October to the bank and to Wright himself. The relevant shares came back to London & Globe in October and November. On 7th October, London & Globe repaid Standard Exploration £105,000 which Standard Exploration repaid to its bank. On 6th October, Standard Exploration gave Wright a cheque for £40,085 in settlement of the personal loan of £40,000 given to company. The 80,000 Nickel Corporation shares were sold at eighteen shillings by London & Globe and bought back for twenty shillings. The difference in price simply paid for the provision of the loan.

The company chairman, Lord Dufferin, on the basis of a long letter dated 19th October from Wright, was able at the annual general meeting on 24th October that year to state that whilst it would have been possible to declare a dividend of 25%, a figure of 10% was more prudent. Wright was able to say at the meeting that the shareholders could feel perfectly easy in their minds. He said that the cash balance was the best evidence of the prosperity of the company. It had the desired effect of maintaining confidence in London & Globe. A crisis at the 1899 London & Globe annual general meeting had been averted. Of course, the underlying absence of assets in the company needed to be addressed and Wright continued the strategy of the acquisition of Lake View shares in an attempt to restore the company's wealth. However, further losses were sustained in October and November 1899 as a result of this further speculation by London & Globe in the Lake View shares. Wright's accountant told him that unless money could be put into the company, it would have to be suspended. Accordingly, Wright arranged with the company's broker to transfer £300,000 of his own Government Consols to his chief accountant, Mr. Worters, who put it into the books in one form or another. Wright also got a loan of £85,000 on trust securities and handed them to London & Globe. It was money that he had proposed to set aside for settlement on his children. Effectively, he put his own money into the company with the sole intention of preventing a collapse in the market of London & Globe's shares. It was a successful, if costly, move. The transfer denuded him of immediate, private, realisable assets. However, to him, it was an entirely legitimate object. Again, Wright had dealt with a financial crisis in the company.

So, a year later, in October 1900, the same scenario ensued but the scale of the situation was even more disastrous. London & Globe's starting financial position in October 1899 had been perilous despite its contrived balance sheet. The speculations in the October and November 1899 followed by further speculation in 1900 had resulted in losses of some £1.6 million before the end of London & Globe's financial year at 30$^{th}$ September 1900. Wright needed to give the company a credible status to prevent the alarm of either the shareholders or the market at the company annual meeting and avoid any speculation that would lead to a collapse of confidence. He also needed to claw the company back to some kind of financial stability. The alternative was virtually to put London & Globe into some kind of voluntary administration and arrange for some kind of reconstruction. Whilst his own financial interest in London & Globe was relatively small, he knew that if the company failed, British American and Standard Exploration would also be likely to fail and a host of other companies would probably go under. He would lose whatever business fortune he possessed together with his future financial credibility. His whole business and social standing would disappear. Further, even a voluntary administration might put the company beyond his control and would probably reveal his speculative ventures about which the board knew very little.

He had fought before and he would fight again. He had been down in wealth and he had risen up in prosperity. He had an arrogance in his own ability fuelled by the confidence that others had placed in him over the last few years. He also possessed an unbounded optimism. He knew how to take risks. He could take further risks. He reflected that his life had been based upon taking the chance and making his decision work. All his previous experiences supported an action to go forward, not a passivity to accept the position. It was the zenith of self-reliance. The ultimate consequence of failure was perhaps no worse than the immediate prospect he faced. There was an opportunity to retrieve the position and he decided to take it. Over the next month, he devised his strategy to deal with the situation and basically adopted the same process as in 1899. He would create a credible and acceptable balance sheet and he would mount another attempt to speculate on the Lake View shares to provide the wealth to London & Globe.

In November, he began his endeavour to recoup the losses by further speculation. In his mind, the Lake View shares still represented a colossal asset which would ensure London & Globe's future. The previous and distinct failure to capture the Lake View shares had continually rankled with him and he blamed the 'bears'. He was determined to see them off this time. He had an ambitious strategy. His aim was for London & Globe to agree to purchase about half of the issued 250,000 Lake View shares. This scheme would enable London & Globe to control enough of the relevant shares by the end of December 1900. Possession of these shares would force their purchase by 'bears' seeking to fulfil their obligations to deliver on their agreed sales and so raise the price of those shares. In effect, he would induce the 'bears' to over-commit themselves in transactions and so be forced to purchase from his company the very shares that they had agreed to sell to his company. It would result in a significant financial gain for Wright's company and put it back on a sustainable financial basis. He recognised that significant finance would be necessary to cover the anticipated dealings but he had virtually no funds of his own as he had used his personal reserves to cover the financial crisis in the previous year. He arranged to meet Herbert Trower on 15th November. Trower was a financial agent who had just returned from Australia. Wright had previously used his services in various financial transactions and, indeed, he had been a guest of Wright on several occasions including on his yacht when notables were entertained. Wright had implicit trust in the man.

Wright's concept was for a kind of syndicate to finance the purchase of these 126,000 Lake View shares for London & Globe by the end of December settlement date. He outlined his plan to Trower who immediately began buying shares on behalf of the company and himself. Trower contacted Arthur Young and Murray Griffiths, both of whom had previously allied in share dealings and had been with Wright in the Austin Friars Syndicate and had benefited from its sale to Standard Exploration. Both had confidence in London & Globe and in the purchase of the shares. All believed that the shares were undervalued. There was discussion about the proposed scheme. Over the next few days, Trower made substantial purchases which were divided into two accounts, one for Trower and one for the company. Wright objected to this arrangement and from 20th November instructions were given to the brokers on account of London & Globe for the end of November settlement. Young provided some of the funds to settle this account.

The buying of Lake View shares proceeded. By Monday 10th December, London & Globe had agreed to purchase some 125,000 Lake View shares but could not make arrangements to carry over some 42,000 of them on the settlement day of 11th December. It had been Wright's original intention to carry over most of the shares and make his move at the end of December settlement date. However, funds were now required by 15th December to fund the actual purchase of these 42,000 shares. Wright and Trower met to discuss the position. Funding was immediately required for the purchase although Wright also had his eye on the position later in December when a further substantial sum would be required to purchase the remaining shares carried over.

On 10th and 11th December, Trower sought out notable persons who would fund the London & Globe purchase. He contacted Young who then met Griffiths initially on Brighton seafront and then in his London office. He approached Allcard of Lack & Allcard, jobbers, and Lord Hardwicke of Basil Montgomery & Co, stockbrokers. Approaches were made to Gerald Williams, Young's brother-in-law, of Williams, de Broe & Co and to Charles Tomlin and Joseph Pollack. None of them had much hesitation in providing the relevant money. Although Trower knew the precise purpose for the funding and Young knew that some kind of syndicate had been mooted for acquiring the shares, the others had no exact knowledge of Wright's intentions. Of course, they knew he was using the money for the share acquisition as the security for the funds was the acquired Lake View shares which were to be distributed to each person proportionately according to their financial contribution at a price of £11 per share. Wright viewed the arrangement somewhat differently. The whole basis of the dealings was that enough of these shares would be held at least until after the late December settlement date to cause a rise in their price when London & Globe demanded delivery of the shares. The bears would be obliged to buy them from him and others as a sufficient number of shares would not be available on the open market. The price would rise significantly and his company would make its money. Critical to the arrangement was the retention of shares and their selling price.

However, the value of the Lake View shares continued to fall. Something had to be done to stem the decline. The directors of Lake View had sent out two circulars to shareholders extolling the value of the mines and their potential but to little avail. Wright turned to the press and issued a long letter on 11th December in an attempt to convince investors of the value of the Lake View assets. He spent much of the letter on the geological position, focusing on the apparent differences in retrieving the gold from the oxidised ores and the sulphide ores. It was an ample demonstration of his knowledge of the chemistry of the subject. He excused the inconsistency of some of the production and emphasised the long-term viability of the mining operation. It was a resounding and detailed exposition of the value of the mining enterprise. Its contents did it best to talk up the value of the shares.

Friday 14th December was the critical date to raise the money for payment on the Saturday. Trower telephoned Wright from the London & Globe office saying that Wright had immediately to sign the relevant documents he had sent over. Wright was at his Park Lane residence where he was confined to bed with a cold. Trower explained that some of those supplying the money would not act until the legal documents were executed. Trower was emphatic that the documents had to be signed immediately to enable the funds to be provided. He said that the relevant people were gathered in Young's office at 15 Austin Friars. Wright had not looked at the papers and invited Trower round.

When Trower arrived, Wright glanced at the documents quickly. They were not as he had envisaged. There was no clause relating to the division of profits between London & Globe and the group of individuals. There was no mention of the further sum of a million pounds which he required for the acquisition of the shares on the late December settlement date. There was nothing about the basic concept of retaining the shares below any price level. Trower provided vague reassurance but said the group would not have it any other way. Some mention was made that as Stock Exchange members, they could not be or be seen to be in partnership with anyone. Wright was in no position to argue. He was not especially well, the money was urgent and he trusted Trower. Wright initialled the two documents already initialled by Young and Trower. One document basically provided for the funds for the Saturday settlement and the other for the group members to have a call on the shares at the price of £11. Trower wired that the documents had been signed and then stayed to lunch with Wright. Following the signing, the syndicate advanced some £336,000 at the 15th December settlement date. The shares were delivered for their distribution within the group at a price of £11 for each share. The reassured Wright considered that the share purchase scheme was being achieved.

Whilst this Lake View share speculation was underway, he put his other strategic arm into place by reorganising the London & Globe finances. His first step was to postpone the publication of the 1900 balance sheet until a more favourable position could be shown. He could legitimately put off publication for nearly three months until late December, by which time he hoped to acquire the Lake View shares or, at least a substantial part of them. The postponement was not an uncommon occurrence and, in itself, the market and the shareholders would not necessarily assume anything unusual. The real issue that he faced was how to present the company in a favourable financial light. He set about the two major aspects to enable a different balance sheet to be presented. Firstly, he would need to show apparently valuable assets and secondly, he would need to demonstrate minimal liabilities. The actual wealth he anticipated would come from the current speculations in Lake View and would vindicate his actions. Indeed, there would be little examination of the balance sheet if the wealth of the company was evident.

The previous year, there had been the company assets and available finance of his own to provide the apparent assets for the company's balance sheet. Unfortunately, virtually everything had been used at that time to deal with the September 1899 position. Now, he had neither substantial sums nor substantial share holdings. He therefore determined that the apparent assets of London & Globe would be shown in the form of valuable shares that it held in other companies. A number of transactions were involved. He would use the other holdings in the group of companies, particularly Standard Exploration and British America, to assist.

An existing Wright company, Victorian Gold Estates which had been registered on 25th July 1896 and had some mining holdings in Victoria, Australia, was effectively converted into two new companies, namely Loddon Valley Goldfields Limited registered on 24th November 1900 and Moorlort Goldfields Limited registered on 1st December 1900. Wright arranged for Victorian Gold to sell part of its property to Loddon Valley for £750,000 and virtually the rest of its property to Moorlort for £700,000, the prices being largely paid by shares in the new companies. The remaining part of the property went to London & Globe for its work as the promoter. The value of Victorian Gold Estates had thereby been dramatically increased. Although not actually trading, the shares of these two new companies were given a value. Accordingly, the value of the shares of Victorian Gold, then worth about £350,000, had been converted to £1,450,000 apparent value in the new companies. London & Globe held 40,000 of the Victorian Gold shares at the beginning of November but a further 35,000 were transferred from Standard Exploration and a further 125,000 was received from British America, reversing a payment of £250,000 that London & Globe had made to British

America in November 1899. For the purposes of the 5th December 1900 London & Globe balance sheet, its holding in these Victorian Gold shares was now worth £564,000.

Wright then showed a further asset of some £321,000 on the London & Globe balance sheet. In June 1898, British America had formed three companies to work gold mines transferred to it by London & Globe on its formation in 1897. These were West Le Roi, East Le Roi and Columbia Kootenay with their shares being entirely owned by London & Globe and British America. Arrangements had been made during 1900 for the three companies to sell their assets to three new companies whose shares would be sold on the open market. Accordingly, Le Roi No. 2 was registered in May to succeed West Le Roi, Rossland Great Western registered in June to succeed East Le Roi and Kootenay Mining registered in July to succeed Columbia Kootenay. Additionally, on 6th November, Columbian Proprietary was registered. The nominal share capital of the four companies was £2,000,000. The concept was that the proceeds would flow to London & Globe and British America once these shares had been sold to the public. Money was transferred from these companies to London & Globe as they received cash from sales of their shares and resulted in the sum of £321,000 shown as income in London & Globe's profit and loss account. However, the shares in the three predecessor companies were shown in the assets register as if these amounts had not been made. Indeed, £150,000 was shown in London & Globe's profit and loss account as income arising from its promotion of Columbian Proprietary when none of its shares had been issued to the public by the date of the balance sheet.

There was also a problem on the liability side of the balance sheet. Significant liabilities to Stock Exchange firms were being incurred at this time to fund the Lake View speculation. By 29th November, it stood at over £1.6 million. Wright arranged for this liability to be transferred to Standard Exploration. Unfortunately, the auditor, Mr. Ford, when examining the accounts on 15th December, insisted on seeing the relevant authorisation of the two companies for this agreement. Wright quickly dictated minutes for each company to a secretary and arranged for the relevant signatures by himself and Macleay although there had been no meeting of either company. Further, none of the Stock Exchange firms had any knowledge of the change in liability between the two companies. By 28th December, when payments were due, the liability had been reversed but for the purposes of the London & Globe balance sheet of 5$^{th}$ December, the relevant liabilities did not feature.

The books required auditing before their publication on 17$^{th}$ December.

The auditor worked hard to deal with the figures. On Saturday 15$^{th}$ December, he was still at his task. At two o' clock in the morning, Henry Malcolm, Worters' successor as chief accountant, was pressing him to sign as the company's annual general meeting was to be held on the Monday. But the auditor wanted the brokers' consents to the transfer of the share speculation liability from London & Globe to Standard Exploration. Apparently, Malcolm promised that the relevant letters were available and would be forthcoming in the morning. Ford signed off the balance sheet in anticipation. The letters were never forthcoming as the brokers had no knowledge of the apparent change in the liability to them for the shares.

The final balance sheet was a triumph. It now showed an apparent profit on the year from 30$^{th}$ September 1899 to 5$^{th}$ December 1900 of £463,672. It showed assets in the form of 'shares in various companies' of £2,332,632. Debt liabilities comprising loans and sundry creditors were shown as £572,314. The balance sheet was then printed and distributed to the shareholders. It was all at the last minute and barely in time for the shareholders to have the paperwork before their meeting.

On Monday 17$^{th}$ December, the annual general meeting of London & Globe was held at Winchester House. The great hall was crowded. At the outset one shareholder complained about that he had only received the directors' report that morning and questioned the legality of the meeting but no notice was taken of him. Lord Dufferin proceeded to move the adoption of the report although there was some initial disorder in the hall. His speech had been carefully prepared by Wright. Lord Dufferin said he wished that they could have met that day under the same auspicious circumstances which characterised the last occasion when he addressed them. Since then there had been a not only a period of great public anxiety but one of severe financial depression in consequence of the war in South Africa. As was always the case, these depressing circumstances had reacted very adversely upon the financial situation and securities of every kind, even of gilt-edged class, with Consols at their head rapidly fell in value, and the decline had been going on ever since. A comparison of quotations during last year and those ruling today spoke volumes as to the cost of the war and showed the nominal expenditure of nearly one hundred million pounds was but a 'drop in the bucket' compared with the indirect losses occasioned. Their own company had not been able to escape. In the face of these difficulties, however, the board applied themselves with renewed energy to replace the company's affairs on their normal prosperous footing and, as a result, they were enabled to present a balance sheet with a very substantial sum standing to the credit of the profit and loss account. On the debit side the item of sundry creditors referred mainly to balances of accounts in regard to the company's undertakings in various parts of the world and the item of loans was principally in reference to the purchase of shares. On the credit side the shares held by them in various companies stood at £2,332,632 without taking into account their shares in the Baker Street and Waterloo Railway and this was after writing off a heavy amount for loss and depreciation. Freehold properties stood at £36,000. The item representing the Baker Street & Waterloo Railway appeared in the assets as over £750,000.

He said that in regard to this enterprise, it was important to say a few words to which they were shouts of, "Hear, hear!" It was owing to the railway that the directors were compelled to advise that no dividend be declared at the present time. As many of the shareholders had inquired why the directors entered into an enterprise of this character – which was somewhat at variance with the other purposes of the company – he might say that a few years ago, when the late Sir William Robinson, whom he succeeded, was chairman of the board, he and the late Lord Loch were strongly in favour of the company engaging in some undertaking of a different nature to the mining enterprise. In this way the building of the railway was determined upon. Although it did not strongly appeal to the managing director, whose experience lay in another direction, yet Mr. Whitaker Wright and other members of the board had acquiesced in the recommendation of their chairman and his colleague Lord Loch, and the latter had been chairman of the railway company. Nor could there be any doubt that Lord Loch was quite right in his estimate of the soundness, value, and the eventual profit to be derived from this important line which it was believed would be one of the most profitable in London when it was completed. It still, however, required a large amount of money to finish and equip it and, as the London & Globe Finance Corporation had undertaken this work, the shareholders could readily see that the directors must husband the company's resources until arrangements could be made to dispose of it under favourable conditions. Negotiations were now in progress with a syndicate to take over the company's responsibilities in regard to the railway and to reimburse them the £750,000 already expended. The directors hoped to carry out these negotiations to a successful issue.

Referring to other enterprises for which the company had been sponsors and in the success of which they were interested as shareholders, Lord Dufferin stated that from the reports which the directors had received from the engineers, the Lake View Consols appeared to be entering on a new period of prosperity. There were voices of approval from the hall. The Ivanhoe maintained its reputation and it was hoped that it would in the near future increase its production. The development of the Le Roi continued and this circumstance had led the directors to equip it on a magnificent scale. The various groups controlled by the British America Corporation had developed in a satisfactory manner, the ore of Le Roi No. 2 being of exceedingly high grade for Rossland, the average value being about twice that of the original Le Roi. A good report of the Caledonia Copper would be made at the meeting and the Nickel Corporation had exceeded their expectations. Nickel had steadily increased in price since the formation of that company and all that could be mined for a year had been sold at satisfactory prices and at a profit. After several years and the expenditure of large sums of money, the gold channel in the property of the Loddon Gold Fields had been uncovered and from this, and their Moorlort Gold Fields, the directors expected to obtain very satisfactory returns for many years. In short, they were quite satisfied with the company's mining issues.

He stated that although the board did not propose any dividend on this occasion and was quite aware of the natural disappointment such an announcement would produce, they sincerely hoped to receive the unanimous support of the meeting. It was unpleasant to pay no dividend but it was sometimes necessary and when it was necessary it was the only honest course to follow. The board would be the principal sufferers, not only as large shareholders, but as directors, for, by the articles of association, where there were no dividends, there were no fees. There was laughter in the hall. So, he continued, they would have passed through an exceedingly hard year of work with no remuneration whatever. He had offered himself for re-election but he had done so purely from a sense of duty. For some time past he had felt the strain and anxiety resulting from his connection with a company whose financial operations were on so vast a scale in excess of what his advancing years and declining health were adequate to sustain. Indeed, he said, had it not been for Lord Loch's secession from the board last year, he had been in two minds whether he should not have asked the shareholders to relieve him of his present functions. There were cries of 'no' from the hall. But he felt that the resignation at the same moment both of himself and Lord Loch might have been misinterpreted and might have had an unfortunate effect on the company's interests. There were cries of approval. At that time the condition of their affairs was so flourishing as to have justified this step at all events, as far as one of them was concerned. But, although no one could be more sanguine that he was of the general soundness of the position, he did not like to desert his post on an occasion when the directors were obliged to withhold a dividend, nor would anything induce him to shirk from sharing whatever responsibility might be considered to weigh upon the managing director and his colleagues. Moved by these considerations, he had allowed his name again to be put up for nomination but the shareholders might take quite a different view of the situation and might attribute to bad management what the directors believed to be the result of unforeseen and unfortunate circumstances and that, in offering himself for re-election, instead of endeavouring to render a service to the company, he might be doing the exact reverse. Cries of 'no' echoed. If that should be the shareholders' decision, he should bow to it with the utmost respect and should regard it neither as unreasonable nor surprising.

Whitaker Wright seconded the motion to adopt the report and expressed his readiness to answer any reasonable question which the shareholders might put. There were, he added, a few disturbers in the room, but they were not present as investors or genuine shareholders, although it was true that their names were on the register. He said that a heavy depreciation had occurred this year but nevertheless, the directors showed a large credit to the profit and loss account. He would remind the shareholders that many other companies besides their own had 'passed' their dividends this year. In the discussion which ensued, Mr. Flower complained of not having received his balance sheet until the previous morning. He maintained that a list of the company's investments should be given in the report instead of their being grouped together in one item. Mr. Seal said that a reasonable time had not been given to consider the report and he proposed an amendment adjourning the meeting to the 7$^{th}$ of January. Mr. Herbert seconded this amendment. Mr. Ellasore inquired how much had been written off the over two million pounds held by the company in the sundry companies' shares. Having said that there was a tremendous organisation in existence to smash the company, he asked Wright to confine his attention to 'issuing business' and to leave the Stock Exchange and Stock Exchange speculation alone.

In reply, Wright stated that the shareholders ought to have received the report and accounts at least a week ago as the directors had intended. The notice for the meeting was issued a month ago and the delay in forwarding the report at an earlier date was attributable to the mass of transactions during the past year that had had to be verified by the auditors. Some shareholders wanted a schedule of assets given at the end of the report but the great majority of them were absolutely opposed to the publication of such information. Their profits depended on the realisation of securities which they received on the issues they made and, if it were known to the public at large that the company were selling the shares of a particular mine, others would sell and the shares would be inordinately depreciated. A shareholder had asked how much had been written off the value of their assets since the last general meeting. Wright replied over one million pounds, and it had been no easy matter to make that up. The assets were now marked down as low as possible. As to the future of the profits made, it stood in securities of all classes and characters including the money as an asset and in the Baker Street & Waterloo Railway. Consols had fallen during the past year from 110 to 97 and how could the shareholders expect not to see depreciation in a speculative company?

The directors claimed from the beginning they had acquired more good properties for the shareholders than any similar company. A certain clique were trying to write down the company's investments on the Stock Exchange but they were not selling them. It had been nothing but a sense of duty that had kept him to his post for the last two years. He had derived not a penny of personal profit on all the issues which the company had made. There were cheers from the hall. He continued that the directors had worked harmoniously with him in the shareholders' interests and they had received no fees this year but they were only too anxious to achieve success apart from that consideration. There were cries of support. When the chairman joined the company, he had bought 5,000 of its shares for which he paid thirty shillings each and when the British America Corporation was formed he also purchased nearly 20,000 of its shares. Lord Dufferin held all these shares and had made no personal profit, either, by his directorships in these companies. If the directors could succeed in completing the arrangements by transferring the Baker Street & Waterloo railway to another syndicate and realising the capital invested in that undertaking for the purposes of the company, it would not be long before they would be able to resume a dividend-paying condition. Cheers resounded from the hall.

The report was then put to the meeting despite some cries of, "The amendment first!" and it was declared carried. The chairman had apparently not heard the demand for the amendment to be put. But the feeling of the meeting appeared to be against that course. Lord Dufferin was re-elected to his seat on the board and the proceeding terminated with a vote of thanks to the chairman and the board. The meeting had been entirely successful. The majority of shareholders had enthusiastically supported the board and the few critics had made no discernible mark on the proceedings. The lack of a dividend had not been criticised and the balance sheet had been accepted. Lord Dufferin had been re-elected chairman. One part of the strategy had worked. He now had to deliver on the other part, the delivery of wealth to London & Globe and the acquisition of the Lake View shares.

London & Globe had steadily acquired these shares principally by means of 'carry over' at the relevant dates. By the mid-November account, 42,555 shares had been carried over, 62,592 by the end of November, 124,900 by mid-December although some 42,000 had to be purchased at that time. The strategy to acquire the relevant number of shares was working but the price of the shares had barely changed. Part of the scheme necessitated a price rise to put pressure on the bears and to attract the relevant supporting finance to buy the shares at the relevant date.

Wright was extremely concerned about the lack of any movement and it appeared that some shares were being bought for the second time by his company. If this were true, it meant that some of these 42,000 shares distributed among the syndicate had been sold by one or more of its members. London & Globe had bought for the shares for between £12 and £15 each, the shares had been distributed to members at £11 and then sold at a higher price. It also meant that the number of shares to be acquired was not reducing as required if the market was to be cornered. The lack of a London & Globe dividend had almost inevitably contributed to a sudden fall in the value of both London & Globe and Lake View shares.

Wright was very unhappy about the situation and decided that some steps were required. He called a meeting of the leading figures at his Lothbury office shortly after the London & Globe's annual general meeting. Herbert Trower, Arthur Young and Murray Griffith were present. He reiterated the purpose of the arrangement and that it was in all their interests to increase their holding to raise the price. By 21$^{st}$ December, a decision would have to be made on the number of shares to be delivered and the number to be carried over. Normally this date would have been the Monday of the following week but as the Christmas holiday intervened, it had been determined by the Stock Exchange that mining shares would be dealt with on the earlier day. Payment would not have to be made until Saturday 29$^{th}$ December. Wright suggested that syndicate shares were being resold. Young admitted that he had sold 20,000 shares. Trower and Young agreed not to sell any more and would take those 20,000 shares back. Griffiths said he would take in the shares he had sold. Wright's view was that no share should be sold below a price of £17 and Trower professed he would not sell below £20. There were differing views on the best course of action. Wright spoke of cornering the bears. Young thought that carrying over stock was wrong and that they should sit tight and perhaps liquidate the whole account. It all depended on their ability to raise the capital for the late December settlement date. There were only a few days left to make the decision of what to do.

Wright believed that Trower could arrange to get the money. It was a critical decision for Wright but the earlier success of obtaining the funding for the previous purchase and the assurances from Trower, Young and the others about purchases gave him the optimism he needed. In any event, all the previous efforts and expenditure would have been wasted without the follow through for the end of December when he anticipated that the bears would meet their match and give the wealth to London & Globe and so relieve its perilous state.

Accordingly, on 21$^{st}$ December, Wright committed London & Globe to buy 167,079 Lake View shares. He then committed to delivery of nearly one million pounds' worth of them with the remainder being carried over. This action was meant to force the 'bears' to go into the market to purchase the relevant shares for the delivery. Wright thought he had enough to influence the position but again the share price did not significantly alter. However, it meant that the funding for London & Globe's purchase would have to found for Saturday 29$^{th}$ December. Wright would have to raise the sum of nearly one million pounds on that day. But the confidence in the market for Lake View shares, the price of which remained stubbornly low despite the huge commitments to purchase, and confidence in London & Globe itself, reinforced to some extent by the lack of a dividend, had dissipated. It made the prospect of raising a million pounds much more difficult. Funding for the purchase of shares was based on their value and their likely value. A rising price for the Lake View shares and rising price for London & Globe as the company seeking the finance would have helped to secure the relevant money. However, neither share price rose. It was a significant sum to raise although not beyond the bounds of some financiers.

Wright became very uneasy that funding arrangements were not being made and on Thursday 27$^{th}$ December, he saw Trower and Young at his Park Lane residence. They reported on their attempts to get the money. Young said that it would materially strengthen the position if Miller and Llewellyn who were normally 'heavy bears' would cover the account. Wright tried to telephone Miller at the Hotel Cecil but he was not there. The same day, Wright decided to go to Paris to attempt to raise money and Trower agreed to go with him. On the way down, Trower asked Wright who he was going to see. When Wright mentioned the name Reutlinger, Trower told him that Reutlinger's brother was one of the biggest bears in the market. Through his contacts, Trower had learned that Reutlinger intended to buy more shares and smash the market. Amid some acrimony and disarray, they abandoned their trip at Dover and returned to London.

The market was only going one way. The bears were able to put many thousands of Lake View shares on the market and their price plummeted. The shares closed on Thursday at £13, on Friday they were initially down to £10 then to as low as £7 before coming up to about £8 each. The possibility of finance to secure the purchase of shares at the contracted higher price was becoming unachievable. Nevertheless, on Friday 28$^{th}$ December, Trower continued his efforts to raise the money. It was not entirely hopeless and approaches were still continued during the afternoon. But by 4 p.m., it could not be done. Accordingly, London & Globe could not meet its obligations to the various brokers who had arranged the purchase of the shares. London & Globe owed some £968,000. Wright's plans had gone horribly wrong.

On Saturday 29$^{th}$ December, Young called several of the parties and brokers to his office. Lord Hardwicke, Allcard and Griffiths were present. Wyatt and Hale attended from Haggard, Hale & Pixley, one of the main brokers for London & Globe over the years. James Flower was there from the firm of Flower & Co which he ran with his brother. The failure of the company to meet its obligations was announced and Young asked them to see what could be done to save the situation. The meeting was horrified. The disbelief was palpable. It soon became evident that the sums required were beyond any of their means. It was a total shock to those present and to the others involved who quickly learned of the position. They had no time to secure any alternative finance or arrangement to alleviate their predicaments.

As a result, thirteen firms of jobbers and brokers comprising twenty-nine London Stock Exchange members were immediately 'hammered' and declared in default of their obligations to other members of the Stock Exchange. A few further members were hammered on subsequent days. Whilst some members had previously had a long association with London & Globe like Haggard, Hale & Pixley, many had no association with either Wright or the company. They had simply been trading themselves on the Stock Exchange in the relevant shares or with persons who had. The Flower brothers were particularly in this category and were incensed at the apparent lack of integrity of the whole business. The humiliation rankled with them. They learned from Young who was anxious to defend his position something of what had gone on and determined to seek some form of redress. The repercussions were also considerable as shares in Wright companies inevitably suffered. On that day, the value of London & Globe shares fell over 50% to thirty pence each, British America declined to fifty-two pence and the shares in the smaller companies of Le Roi, Rossland Great Western and Le Roi No. 2 plummeted. Ordinary shareholders saw the value of their holdings rapidly decline.

Some leading newspapers saw the debacle for what it was. There had been shameless and unbridled speculation. There had been the usual victors and vanquished albeit on a slightly more prominent scale. But it was inevitable given the nature of the share market. Many did not blame Wright. Others pointed to him as the principal architect. Private accusations were also made about the parties who had initially supported the speculation and who had then apparently withdrawn. The ineffective directors of London & Globe were targeted for their inabilities. Few knew precisely what had happened. The anticipated demise of the company was blamed on the share speculation. There was uncertainty. Opinions were freely proffered.

Wright had dealt with spectacular triumph but now he faced ultimate disaster. Only he actually knew what had led to this moment. His financial empire was on the verge of total collapse and his future in the business world close to oblivion. He had returned to England and built a colossal organisation through his own ability. He had been supreme and apparently indestructible for over five years. His reputation for making money had been untouchable. He had influence and contacts in the highest quarters. It was a moment when he had to face a choice, which had not been unusual in his life. It was a test of his character and abilities.

# CHAPTER 8

# Making the Fall

Wright faced the consequences of the situation with his characteristic blend of personal confidence, external bravado and long experience. He was familiar with the upheavals of the stock market and had seen many ventures by other people reach similar disasters. It was not an unusual occurrence particularly in the market of the time. Companies failed to meet their obligations. Stockbrokers were hammered. Shares lost value. Markets fell into confusion and uncertainty.

He felt entirely let down by those who had apparently supported his venture. He was angry. His ire was directed towards those he regarded as members of the syndicate. He thought he had been on the verge of defeating the 'bears', making money and providing a future basis for London & Globe. But the funds had ultimately not been there. He blamed those he believed were providing some of the finance. These were business associates of some long-standing. Some had been guests at his house and on his yacht. He could not accept that he had not ultimately been supported by them. He regretted that he had not himself been in command of the relevant finance and rued that the three-quarters of a million that London & Globe had put into the Baker Street & Waterloo Railway venture had not been available. His position might have been quite different.

His initial anger turned to defiance and then to determination. He displayed an arrogance to succeed in the face of adversity. He would show them and others that he was undefeated. It was always his obsessive desire to demonstrate his ability. He had his reputation and he wanted to hold his head up. This kind of sudden disaster had not previously happened to him but it steeled his resolve. The unknown was not new to him and it held few fears. He recognised that unless he maintained control over the situation, his manipulations of London & Globe's balance sheet and the paucity of the company's financial position would be revealed. In time, he could recover. But he needed to deal with the immediate and to lay the ground for the future of his financial empire. He had to justify the actions that he had taken and to placate those who turned to him in blame.

There was vast newspaper opinion about the reasons and much division about where the responsibility lay. But Wright soon realised that there remained a wealth of confidence in his ability engendered by the previous years of plenty. It was clear that the London & Globe board were incapable of dealing with the matter and still looked to him to deal with the disaster. He also knew that the average shareholder would be initially angry about their apparent loss, but they would look either for a saviour or for a culprit. There was much to use to avert complete disaster. However, he also faced some hostility in the press. Most of the serious newspapers understood what had taken place so far the share speculation was concerned and condemned the bear action. However, some sections of the industry began personal stories about him and how his wealth had been achieved. He needed to counter these allegations.

He had to devise a basic strategy and he used his usual formula of providing firm leadership and buying time with an optimistic plan of action for London & Globe. The device he used was to propose a reconstruction of the company. His argument was that only a functioning company could give the shareholders some value in their existing holdings and give the creditors hope of some payment. He also knew that only by some voluntary arrangement would there be no real external examination of the company's affairs. He also considered that some legal action against those who had let him down might provide the prospect of further assets by recovering moneys against them for the disaster and deflect the blame for its consequences to where he thought it rightfully belonged. The principal remaining asset of London & Globe was its holding in the

Baker Street & Waterloo Railway. Ironically, the asset which Wright had not wanted and which had deprived him of funds for his enterprises in the stock market, might now be the company's best asset. Correspondingly, Wright's own fortune had depreciated significantly over the last year or so. He had little personal financial interest in the London & Globe and was already borrowing money against his Lea Park Estate. He could not inject money into the company as he had previously ventured in 1899. It was down to his ability to master the crisis.

The first necessary step was to reach some financial accommodation with the many creditors. It could mean that the losses of the various parties might be ameliorated and the company could continue. The creditors would have to be convinced that some reasonable payment could be made and the shareholders recognise that such losses would have to be borne. Essentially, it had to be demonstrated that the company could continue and thus enable the creditors to be satisfied in some way. If no agreement could be reached, the company would have to be liquidated but Wright wanted this to be under his control. He wanted a voluntary liquidation. Accordingly, on his recommendation, the board called an extraordinary general meeting of London & Globe on 10$^{th}$ January 1901 to consider a resolution for the winding up of the company. The meeting was held at the Cannon Street Hotel. Shareholders had begun to arrive by ten in the morning and by noon, the hall and the galleries were crowded. The whole board attended and were greeted by cheers mixed with a few hisses. The chairman, Lord Dufferin, was warmly received. He was apologetic about the turn of events and he deeply regretted the assurances given by himself and the managing director only three weeks before at the annual general meeting. Whitaker Wright would explain the circumstances for the sudden change but he wanted to state his own personal position.

Lord Dufferin reiterated much of what he had said at the annual general meeting. He referred to his limited experience in both mining and financial matters when he had accepted the chairmanship. On taking office, he had been unprepared for the bitterness of opponents of the company and complications of Stock Exchange dealing. There was laughter when he said that no one who had not been brought up in the business could hope to master its intricacies. He had always made his limited experience clear at previous meetings but had shown his commitment by the purchase of shares in London & Globe and in British America. There were cheers. He would lose money which he could little afford but he should not regret his interests if it convinced the shareholders of his bona fides. There were more cheers. As in the previous meeting, he had expressed his desire to be relieved of the burdens of the chairmanship but the appropriate opportunity had not occurred and might have been misinterpreted. He confirmed that he had recently sent in his resignation when he had news of the serious condition of his younger son in South Africa and resolved to travel there with his wife. Nobody would put any sinister interpretation on his action. There were cries of support. Lord Dufferin went on to say that he had not anticipated the present trouble but on receiving the news in Ireland, he had resumed his post and felt that private consideration must give way. There were cheers for his undoubted courage given that his elder son had recently been killed in the Boer War. His integrity endeared him to the meeting and set the tone for what was to follow.

Lord Dufferin had been well-prepared and briefed by Wright. He put forward the three courses open to them. First, there was the official route which had been advocated in some quarters of the outside world. The company could be the subject of a winding up under an official liquidator. There were negative cries. Secondly, the company itself could voluntarily commence a voluntary winding up. Finally, a reconstruction of the company could be attempted, to which there were cries of endorsement. He felt that if the matter was left in the hands of an official liquidator, he might felt bound to sell his substantial number of shares. If the liquidation was voluntary, he would be able to nurse the assets and sell to the best advantage. He recommended this course of action and was cheered by the shareholders. He was publicly portraying the roles and realities of the company's operation. Lord Dufferin was only a figurehead. He had accepted and had remained in office to give the company credibility and confidence. He had no idea of financial matters in general and Stock Exchange dealings in particular. Apart from, perhaps, Lord Leman, the remainder of the board were in the same position and left the operations to Whitaker Wright. And they were prepared to back him, not only in the good times but now that the situation had turned bad. It was a remarkable display of loyalty and confidence. They had little choice. They knew little of what was happening and they could lose money and some reputation if the company completely collapsed. Their refuge was Whitaker Wright.

Lord Dufferin continued. Frankly, he was unaware of the transactions that had given rise to the unexpected change. But they would not permit Wright to take sole responsibility for what had occurred and shield the members of the board. There were cheers. Although there might have been errors of judgment, the board had always been honest and stood together. He had never met anyone like Whitaker Wright, more devoted to the service of the interests with which he was charged and not only to sacrifice his health but to risk the chance of fatal illness in his endeavours to rectify what may be amiss and to take over misfortune from his shareholders. There were more cheers. He said that Mr. Wright may have made mistakes but they were prompted by a keen desire to advance the shareholders' interests. He thanked the shareholders for their hearing and their generosity which would be one of the brightest souvenirs of his whole life. He sat down to loud cheers.

Wright then addressed the meeting at some length. It was one of the most important speeches he had ever had to give. But the robust and hearty atmosphere had been set by Lord Dufferin and Wright knew how to present his case and draw on the confidence in his ability. He needed to give them reassurance and an explanation. He needed to provide the optimistic way forward. He assured them that the board had practically arrived at an arrangement with its creditors. With a long pull, a strong pull and all pull together, their good ship would soon be off the rocks and sailing once more in smooth water. They cheered his nautical references, knowing his yachting interests. He hoped that by the next Monday the creditors would be paid in full and that a scheme of reconstruction would ensure prosperity and occasion, no loss to them in the long run. He used the opportunity to criticise the popular press which were carrying stories about his lifestyle and how it had been funded. He complained about certain reports in recent free journals; not in the great political and financial newspapers, he added. He referred to stories about the misuse of funds and to the description of his country seat as a 'palace of delights'. He maintained that the property had been bought before London & Globe had been registered and that he had loaned the company £250,000. Although the audience made it plain they were little interested in his personal defence, he continued to harangue the writers on the basis that they sought to undermine the company.

He took them through the history of the current London & Globe, its amalgamation from Western Australian Exploring and London & Globe Finance and the returns that those shareholders had received and the dividends received in respect of the new shares. He referred to the creation of Lake View Consols and its dividend payment of four and half times the original capital investment. He turned to the issue of the Ivanhoe Corporation and its return of 50% of the capital. He went on to Le Roi Mine which under the auspices of British America would pay future dividends and increase in value. Caledonian Copper would make large returns and the Nickel Corporation would increase in value. Loddon Valley and Moorlort should yield substantial returns. He maintained that the share value of all these companies would return to their normal level as soon as the market recovered from the recent shock. There was £750,000 value in the Baker Street & Waterloo Railway. He recited other apparent assets. He did not believe that they had 'a bad egg in the basket'. London & Globe employed thousands of people worldwide and had interests in a range of minerals. He invited the shareholders to consider whether such a business should be sacrificed, to which there was a resounding negative response.

He said that he had been looking in the very near future to liquidate the company and distribute the assets among them. He had been anxious to be relieved of the burden of responsibility. Accordingly, in order to put the company on a basis of paying steady and permanent dividends, it had been decided some eighteen months ago to acquire control of the Lake View mine. He referred to the fluctuations in the mine production and to the British defeats in South Africa which had depressed the market. The company had suffered heavy losses. It had been his own initiative and he took responsibility so far as his colleagues were concerned. He did not take responsibility for the loss but sought to explain what had happened. He explained that the company had needed capital and that he arranged with certain parties a loan of £500,000 until 31$^{st}$ March consisting of over 40,000 Lake View shares and other securities. Despite cries from the audience to identify the parties, he did not name them. He said that those shares were then sold the same day or the next day and the market had been broken by the selling of those shares by those providing the loan which had prompted other sales. London & Globe's loans were called in and the company had had a loss which would take half a million pounds to settle. He hoped that a reconstruction could be arranged. It was hoped to conclude a settlement by the following Monday. He pledged his health, his strength, his life, and as far as might be his private fortune to carry the enterprise to a successful issue.

His speech had been very well received and the resolution was put to the meeting. Mr. Seal pointed out that the loss was that of the shareholders, not the directors. He had felt assured with Lord Dufferin at the head of affairs and did not feel that Wright should take all the loss on himself but he questioned the role of the other directors. He believed that any settlement with creditors should involve the shareholders and he proposed a consultative committee. Wright responded that the whole matter could be decided at the next Monday meeting. He boldly stated that he had proposed to colleagues that they seek compulsory liquidation through the appointment of the Official Receiver. He asserted that they were not afraid of investigation. They had not a single item to cover up. Everything was open to the light of day. However, the directors had been approached by both creditors and shareholders who implored them not to take that course as the shareholders would get nothing. The meeting was then adjourned.

What Wright had said at the meeting about the loan arrangements was strongly disputed by the relevant parties. They maintained that it was clear from the documentation that they had every right to sell whenever they wanted. There never was any restriction on the date of share sale. Young, in particular, sought to defend his position. He met some of the hammered brokers like the Flower brothers who had been innocently caught in the debacle and were subsequently outraged when they saw the documents. Doubt began to be expressed about Wright's actions and statements. Wright endeavoured to negotiate with the relevant brokers. Some were inclined to settle but others like Haggard, Hale & Pixley refused particularly when the figure they would get would only be 50% and that depended on selling London & Globe's interest in the Baker Street & Waterloo Railway. They wanted to proceed with a compulsory winding-up order.

At the adjourned meeting on Monday 14$^{th}$ January, Wright told them that all except one of the creditors had agreed to a payment of £485,000. He said that the sum of £500,000 and a further sum of several hundred thousand pounds were therefore required to carry on the operations of the company. It was not the slightest use to raise the money by sacrifice with a view to reconstruction unless there was sufficient working capital to carry on operations afterwards. The directors had been negotiating the sale of assets for £500,000. The draft agreement was in the hands of solicitors and the board expected completion before the end of the day. Then it was proposed to reconstruct the company with the new shares being issued with a liability of five shillings each. It might even be possible to substitute a debenture bond for this liability.

Whilst the speech was well received, there were some voices of concern about the new issue of shares. There was also reference to an anticipated winding up of Standard Exploration. The same Mr. Seal queried the sale of the assets to raise the £485,000 and its impact on the assets shown in the balance sheet at £2,332,632. Wright said that it was taking the shares at their par or cost value but it must be understood that they had during the last fortnight materially depreciated in value on the Stock Exchange. After the present difficulty was over, they would go back to their former quotations. He reassured them that Standard Exploration was not going into liquidation. There had been no petition and that the company was alright. To laughter from the hall, it was, he regretted to say, a philanthropic institution to help the people who had suffered in the earliest days of Western Australia. This was a reference to the sweeping up of the various smaller and less economic enterprises and mines when Standard Exploration had been formed. There were now proposals to form the three properties into three groups. In response to a shareholder who referred to underhand working, Wright fuelled the speculation about conspiracies against the company. Cleverly, he dismissed any idea that the directors regarded themselves as victims of conspiracy or anything else; they were simply trying to pay the debts and get the company back on its feet. However, he mentioned that the manager of the Le Roi mine had been approached by a certain engineer to lower the mine's output in exchange for profit on the Stock Exchange. Wright would not name the individual but he had passed it on to his solicitors and legal opinion with a view to public prosecution. The meeting agreed to progress a voluntary winding up and agreed to the appointment of liquidators. Wright also got the meeting to agree his proposal that the directors be requested to assist the liquidators in arranging for the reconstruction of the company on the terms that a new company be formed to take over the assets and liabilities of the existing company. Lord Dufferin finally bowed out as chairman of London & Globe. He had done his duty and was relieved to stand down.

Negotiations continued with the creditors who had already initiated an application for compulsory winding up. Wright maintained that there were assets and, as if to show the strength of his explanation of how he had been let down, London & Globe initiated proceedings against the alleged syndicate members. Accordingly, on 21$^{st}$ January, agreement was reached with the creditors on a 50% payment of the debts. The creditors recognised that the legal process would not give them any greater sum and that only a reconstructed company could fulfil the promised payment. It meant that there would be no thorough examination of what went wrong. Leading newspapers regretted the lack of shareholder scrutiny that had led to the situation unless, it was speculated, the action by Wright to sue the relevant parties who had apparently promised the funds, should be fought in court. The next day, the press turned to a much greater event. Queen Victoria died and Edward VII became king. The event dominated the headlines.

During the next few months, little occurred either to pay the debts or to reconstruct London & Globe. And Wright's other companies were soon in trouble. As he had anticipated, the collapse of London & Globe precipitated failures in his other companies. An order for winding up Standard Exploration was made in January but no immediate steps were taken to progress it. By May, British America was unable to meet its obligations. At the meeting of British America on 3$^{rd}$ June, Wright sought to persuade shareholders to vote for its voluntary liquidation. The meeting at the Cannon Street Hotel was packed and police constables were placed on the doors to prevent any disturbance. But there was uproar and a hostile reception for Wright. He and Sinclair Macleay, the chairman, were confronted with accusations of deception and shameful conduct. The chairman maintained that the present position had not arisen from any business transactions of the company but it was the aftermath of the London & Globe default. When he seconded the motion, Wright was greeted with hisses which he said he thought some of them would regret.

Wright told them of the formation of the syndicate in December last year and of the grossest treachery in connection with it. Without the treachery, there would have been no London & Globe default and the company would have made one million pounds for its shareholders. The liquidators of the London & Globe had brought a suit against the group and he asked the meeting to withhold their judgment until the question had been investigated in court. It was currently *sub judice*. At the last meeting of London & Globe, he had hoped to bring forward a reconstruction and complete the sale of the company's interest in Baker Street & Waterloo Railway. Unfortunately, an issue of vibration of the railway had arisen and the purchasers held off. It now appeared that they were ready to proceed. One of the proposed groups of purchasers had met the company board and offered £500,000 of new working capital but the proposals had dragged on. The reconstruction proposals would be presented to London & Globe shareholders this month. The shareholders could elect a new board. Nothing would ever induce him to be a director again in any company in the city of London. He maintained that there was not a British America director who would not welcome official liquidation if shareholders desired it. Whilst the meeting agreed the route of a voluntary liquidation, creditors had already petitioned the High Court for British America's compulsory winding up. It was perhaps a slightly uncharacteristic display of anger and frustration and almost resignation to the circumstances. He knew the situation was worsening and he regretted that he had not bowed to the inevitable at some earlier date. He recognised that confidence was waning in him and that his opponents were gaining ground. The financial newspapers were now openly calling for all of Wright's companies to be dealt with in a similar way. Wright persevered with his strategy. He wanted to remain in some kind of control and not have the official scrutiny demanded.

As the various company meetings were being held to deal with the consequences of London & Globe's fall, the legal action initiated against the syndicate was progressing. Whilst the action was officially brought by the liquidators, Wright was behind the process. It was his evidence of the process that was at the heart of the claim. His allegation was that these parties had reneged on the basic agreement about when the acquired shares could be sold and at what price.

At the beginning of June, the liquidators of London & Globe reported. Some progress had been made in organising the company's affairs. Some securities had been realised and some debt paid down. But substantial sums remained outstanding and no satisfactory progress could be made towards any sustainable future. The current assets were listed but not valued. The court action against the syndicate was still pending and the heavy damages claimed might provide substantial funds but the hearing was some time away. It had not been possible to realise the company's stake in the Baker Street & Waterloo Railway. A group of purchasers in New York was interested but figures could not be agreed, there were technical and financial issues with the construction and the negotiations were hampered by distance. Many of the shares held in other companies had been pledged as security against loans, for example, the Le Roi No.2 shares. Arrangements to realise London & Globe's assets in British America and Standard Exploration had yielded some money but the current state of those companies meant that there was little prospect of any significant realisation of assets. A scheme of reconstruction could not be attempted at the present time. Accordingly, Wright's optimistic plan to save the company was coming under increasing pressure.

And soon matters were prised out of Wright's control. It began with those who wanted to have British America compulsorily wound up. They took their action to the High Court and on 14th June, Mr. Justice Wright agreed with them. The Judge considered that it was a proper case for investigation by the Official Receiver particularly in view of the allegations that had been made about large losses through speculation. By this time, the serious newspapers were supporting the formal action of the compulsory winding up of the companies. They were also calling for a Board of Trade Inquiry into all three Wright companies.

On 30th July, the Senior Official Receiver, Mr. G. S. Barnes, held the first meeting of the creditors of Standard Exploration. He had the directors' written statement before him that showed apparent total assets of £1,160,000 and liabilities of £362,000. Barnes regarded them as impossible estimates. For instance, there were fourteen mines valued at £767,000 but at present none of them were producing any income. There was a large item for machinery and plant so that it could be seen that the assets were far from liquid. The value of their share holding was based upon their takeover from the

Austin Friars Syndicate at the inception of Standard Exploration but they were pledged and were due to the liquidators of London & Globe and British America. The company had bought in exchange for its own shares a considerable number of mines and had spent some money in a very haphazard manner on the development of some of them. Some were of no value. The directors had taken little interest in the mines and had devoted themselves mainly to Stock Exchange speculations. Huge losses had been made. During 1899, £228,000 had been lost in differences on Lake View Consols and a further £250,000 in differences in Caledonia Copper. Barnes commented on the apparent lack of any detailed company authorisation for these dealings and only board minutes of a general nature. There was no book containing details of sales and purchases.

His most serious comment was on the transfer of London & Globe's speculation liabilities to Standard Exploration shortly before London & Globe's 1900 balance sheet was issued. The minute was passed at a board meeting apparently only attended by Whitaker Wright and Sinclair Macleay. The stockbrokers had no knowledge of the transfer and London & Globe had reassumed liability on 13th December. Barnes commented that whilst no damage had been done to Standard Exploration, he felt bound to reveal the position. It was a major revelation showing the entanglement of London & Globe and Standard Exploration and the transfers that concealed liabilities. During a long and desultory discussion, several shareholders spoke in strong language about these revelations and the conduct of the directors. At one point, several shareholders simultaneously rose, and, addressing some of the directors who sat in the body of the hall, referred in vehement language to the conduct of the company's business. Excited shareholders demanded to know where the money had gone and the whereabouts of the responsible persons. There was even a cry for lynching. The chairman eventually calmed the meeting and promised their protection. A committee was appointed with the Official Receiver being retained as liquidator.

It was exactly what Wright had expected and, for months, tried to avoid. The nature of his business practices were being exposed. Of course, to many, the business behaviour did not come as any shock. The nature of his companies' activities necessitated only one person being in control. But the lack of any director's control, even knowledge and perhaps restraint, was surprising. Most telling was the swap of liabilities between London & Globe and Standard Exploration in December 1900 for the speculative share dealing. It exposed the credibility in the balance sheet and the company report that had been made.

Pressure grew with these revelations and the lack of any progress for London & Globe's reconstruction. A petition for the compulsory winding up of the company was presented on 7th August although, owing to the long summer vacation of the High Court, it was not scheduled for hearing until 30th October. By the end of August, Wright was removed from the board of Le Roi Mining despite his attempt to attribute undesirable motives to the shareholders who affected the decision.

Before the London & Globe petition was heard, Wright sent shareholders of all three companies 'suggestions for reconstruction'. It was his final attempt to keep some measure of control over the destiny of the company and his future. But it was seen by many of the now disillusioned shareholders and creditors as another attempt to delay proceedings. The best part of a year had elapsed without any of Wright's apparent plans and promises being fulfilled. The order for the London & Globe compulsory liquidation was made. The Official Receiver in the form of Mr. Barnes could now deal with all three companies and the web of transactions between them.

On 16th December 1901, Barnes held the first statutory meeting of London & Globe's creditors. Barnes detailed the amounts claimed by the creditors and the estimate of company assets. Total unsecured liabilities amounted to £1,142,000 with assets at £424,000, only some of which could be realised. There had been a verbal agreement for the sale of the Baker Street & Waterloo Railway interest and some share money had been realised. He anticipated that secured creditors would be paid and most of the bank loans. He referred to the pending action for damages of one million pounds against the syndicate and after taking unanimous legal advice, he decided to continue the claim. There were cheers of relief from the meeting. It was their only likely source of payment. Barnes recounted the early company formation and history which sounded a creditable record. He then went through the more recent history and the disastrous speculations in 1899 and 1900.

Barnes turned to the draft balance sheet of 30th September 1900 which although he had not seen, he believed must have shown that London & Globe was hopelessly insolvent at that date. He considered that Wright seemed to have taken steps by the inflation of the value of the assets to render the company solvent according to its books. At the same time, Wright had embarked on a new speculation. All of Wright's arrangements were detailed by Barnes, particularly the acquisition of inflated assets and the disposal of liabilities. He added that although the operations were on an enormous scale, there was little mention of them in the company minutes. He felt quite satisfied that none of the directors knew what Wright was doing, although they ought to have known. The transfer of the financial liability for the speculation had also been examined. He had interviewed the auditor about the late transfer of this liability for the Lake View share speculation to Standard Exploration. Ford, the auditor, had told him that the accountant, Malcolm, had promised the relevant consents late on the Saturday night but Malcolm absolutely denied the story. Ford had also told him that other speculations in the Railway and in Loddon Valley Goldfields had not been in the balance sheet; apparently they were lying in an office drawer. Barnes did not blame the auditor.

However, Barnes reaffirmed the legal action against the syndicate and stated that without the success of the action, assets were insufficient to pay creditors. He also told them that the Court had made an order for the public examination before Mr. Registrar Hood of Whitaker Wright in British America and Standard Exploration and he thought that a similar order would be made in respect of London & Globe. Finally, he referred to London & Globe's habit to pay 'press calls' to promote the unsold shares which he regarded as an entirely wrong proceeding and the habit of the company to present directors of subsidiary companies it promoted with qualification shares which again, Barnes considered, was a wrong proceeding.

It was a devastating indictment. It was the first time that Wright's manipulations of company assets and liabilities, his transfers between companies and his arbitrary decision-making had been scrutinised by an experienced person in a professional capacity. Barnes had shown the nature of the business operations. Wright's business and company arrangements had been revealed. It was now all outside his control. He could only defend himself and his actions. His resolution was determined and his faith in his own behaviour remained. But he would have to try to make his own case in defence of his business activities and what he had done particularly in the presentation of London & Globe's financial position.

What had remained of his business fortune had largely disappeared with the collapse of London & Globe in December 1900. Contrary to popular belief and the speculation of the newspapers, he had virtually only personal assets left. There was no portfolio of properties, no secret bank accounts and no hidden stock of shares. However, he still had a domestic life of some style to support and legal fees to fund. He was forced to turn to his Lea Park estate to provide. In January 1901, he raised a mortgage on the estate for a total of £85,000 and in the November, he had raised a further £122,000. He stopped the building works at the house. It left the entire southern extension without any first floor and other aspects of the house unfinished. Marble sculptures ordered from Italy and destined for location in the extensive grounds lay unpacked in the driveway. The family moved to Lower House on the estate. It was much more modest in scale and required less maintenance and fewer servants. Nevertheless, his son who had just finished Eton that summer, went on to study at Magdalene College, Oxford. Whitaker Wright valued his family above everything else and determined they should have a future.

But his other treasured possessions had to be sold. In February 1901, he had put up his treasured yawl *Sybarita* and his steam yacht *Sybarite* for sale. It was perhaps one of his saddest decisions. He had valued his yacht racing and the society of the yacht clubs. It was a symbol of his position and now it had to go. In any event, Wright had neither the time, inclination or welcome to pursue his sailing. William Clark, the millionaire thread manufacturer purchased *Sybarite* and re-christened her *Cherokee*. Clark died in the August and the yacht transported his body to New York.

Over Christmas in their much smaller home, Whitaker and his wife organised their future personal finances. On 2nd January 1902, he made his Will, leaving his property to his wife. On 8th January, he transferred the estate into their joint names and, with his wife, raised a further sum of £45,000 on the property. The house and the estate were now heavily mortgaged. His Park Lane property ceased its use for lavish entertainment and was closed up. His social circle had inevitably dwindled. Any remote link with royalty and sections of the aristocracy vanished overnight. He lost business acquaintances. He was no longer in the market and he had little need of them and vice-versa. Former acquaintances sought to distance themselves from any either social or business links with him.

He retained a few close friends and close advisers. His local friend and confidant, John Eyre, together with his employees, Arthur Worters and Henry Malcolm, remained close and loyal. He had a legal team for support. But it was his wife who gave him most comfort. She remained totally devoted and loving during this critical time. He was at a low ebb both physically and mentally and he faced life with an unusually subdued equanimity. He braced himself for the year ahead. The courts would now publicly decide his future.

# CHAPTER 9

## Making the Witness

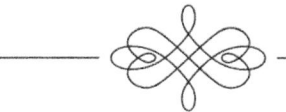

At the beginning of 1902, Wright faced three major trials connected with his collapsed businesses. Firstly and immediately, there was to be the public examination into the affairs of the three main companies. Secondly, there was the lingering case brought by a Mr. McConnell into alleged misrepresentation by Wright in the issue of the Standard Exploration prospectus. Thirdly, there was the action against the syndicate for the claim of one million pounds.

He resolved to be his usual outwardly robust self. But he had little experience of the kind of examinations that were the territory of these cases. He could stand up at public meetings of shareholders, he could deal with people individually in his office and he could talk to directors at board meetings. He could explain his actions and account for himself very well in those situations. He was not unfamiliar with the law and court actions. There had been many such situations over the years when litigation had been pursued. He was used to lawyers and judges and the whole edifice of court structure. However, he was now to be the principal witness. He would be subjected to minute and exacting scrutiny. A series of questions would inevitably lead down routes that he exposed his actions and behaviour. He could not fail to answer the question put to him as it would either be more exactingly repeated or be followed by another more telling interrogation. He could not avoid and he could not hide. His every action and dealing would be forensically examined by skilled professionals.

The public examination into his major companies was held over several days commencing in January and not concluded until the end of February. It began on 13${}^{th}$ January before Mr. Registrar Hood at Bankruptcy Buildings in Carey Street, London. There was an array of legal representation. Wright used Muir Mackenzie. Rufus Isaacs represented the Stock Exchange, one of the interested parties. The purpose was to determine whether there was sufficient evidence to send any of the directors for trial.

Wright was the first and main witness and Barnes led his examination. They went over the companies' histories and their interconnection. Wright defended their habit to support each other in the market and the mining companies that each had floated. Wright maintained that every exploration company in the city did it or, he confided, ought to do it. Wright maintained that each of the boards was independent of the other and that it was a popular fallacy to think that any of the directors were under London & Globe's control. He asserted that he had never tried to advise the directors of any of the subsidiary companies. Wright maintained that they could do as they liked. He conceded that the company secretary of each was on the staff of London & Globe.

Barnes turned to the formation of Standard Exploration. The company had been formed to absorb a large number of mainly Australian properties. Wright considered that none had proved unsuccessful but accepted that none had reached a dividend-paying stage. Barnes questioned Wright about his statement of the philanthropic nature of Standard Exploration. Wright could not remember using the phrase but confirmed that London & Globe had made no profit in its promotion nor gained anything by the absorption.

Barnes turned to London & Globe. They went over the 1899 balance sheet and the financial arrangements made shortly before its publication. In answer to Barnes' question that he had described the operation of the cash deposits at the bank as 'window dressing', Wright said that the calling in of cash at year-end was styled 'window dressing'. Wright was evasive about the cash receipts; either he could not remember without reference to the books or he simply could not remember the detail. He accepted that there had been large losses in the 1899 speculation. London & Globe and Standard Exploration had paid over one million pounds in respect of the share differences. As managing director he controlled the speculations but all of the directors knew of them. They could learn of them from the accounts of receipts and payments which were placed before the directors at fortnightly meetings. He defended the Lake View speculation as an attempt to provide London & Globe with a future income. Treachery and the South African reverses had led to the fall of the shares.

Barnes took Wright to the 1900 balance sheet and the apparent increase of value in its assets between $30^{th}$ September and $5^{th}$ December. Wright objected to Barnes' use of the word 'artificial' in increased valuation. Wright maintained that the directors did everything they could to make up the losses, they had worked hard to save the company and it was to their credit. The transfer of the one-million-pound liability from London & Globe was to hide from the stock market the extent of the operations in Lake View shares. He wanted to carry through those operations without the knowledge of persons engaged in 'bear' operations. He accepted that authority for the transfer was made after the event but all of the directors knew of the large speculation in Lake View shares.

Barnes also tackled Wright on the issue of the qualification shares given to directors of subsidiary companies. Wright said that the practice was to give reward for services and that the shares had no market value. He asserted that it would have been impossible to find persons willing to pay for them. On the matter of the so-called 'press calls' Wright said that the practice had been discontinued since 1898. He denied that he had sold blocks of shares at low prices which were then repurchased by the company at a more generous figure soon afterwards. However, Barnes confronted him with a particular transaction in November 1900 when shares in Loddon Valley had been bought and sold by London & Globe within a day at a loss of some £9,000. The contract was in the name of A.J. Benjamin, a broker, whose brother-in-law was the owner of the *Financial Times*. Wright denied knowledge and suggested that Worters be asked about the matter.

It was a silly evasion that Wright knew could not be sustained. The next day, Wright was forced to concede that the contract had taken place. He tried to explain it as a substitute for the press calls and then sought to justify the arrangement by calling it a facility to satisfy the financial press. He declared that everyone in the city knew it to be the custom and he was not going to be the scapegoat for such customs. Barnes suggested that it was done for 'puffs'. Wright asked to be preserved from puffs in the press and explained that the assistance of the press was required to print their quotations and give news of their share transactions. It was put down to advertising. He said that the loss to the company had been fictitious. The repurchased shares had been sold on the market for an increased figure. He remembered a few of the names involved. *Truth*, *Financial Times*, *Financial News* and others had all been paid. It was a famous revelation and demonstrated the nature of the business that had been involved. The editor of *Truth* resigned shortly afterwards.

Muir Mackenzie had sought an adjournment of the proceedings at the start of the day on the basis of Wright's health. He explained that Wright had not fully recovered from a severe illness. Wright had looked ill at ease when he had entered the witness box. Mr. Register Hood accepted the position and accordingly adjourned the proceedings for the day. It was not pretence. Wright was anxious to get on with the case but his health was not good. And his counsel wanted him in the best condition to deal with the allegations.

The next week, Wright faced cross-examination by the barristers representing various parties. It began with Rufus Isaacs who was representing Dr. Richardson, the official assignee of the Stock Exchange. He led Wright through the many transactions that had taken place over the relevant years. Wright's main contention was that there had been numerous dealings and that there was nothing wrong with any of his methods. He pleaded loss of memory to certain aspects and denied any knowledge of other matters. He maintained that there was nothing unusual in his business arrangements. He denied trying to make a 'corner' in Lake View shares but he maintained that it was true that a 'corner' happened as the bears were selling shares that they did not possess. His principal view was that, had the syndicate worked, London & Globe would not have failed and there would not have been the financial repercussions on the other companies. He explained that many of the share transactions had, in fact, been made on behalf of British America but he did not want the stock market to know exactly who was carrying the purchase. He put much of the accounting arrangements for the balance sheet at the door of the company accountants as well as the mistakes about the sale of shares in West Le Roi Mining between London & Globe and British America when the price which should have included the dividend incidentally increased London & Globe's apparent assets by £250,000. Wright continued to deny the effect of the so-called 'press calls' was to influence the newspaper view of his company, although he conceded that it was necessary under the conditions then prevailing and justified any expense on the grounds of promotion.

The apparent lapses of memory, the apparent fault of others and the apparent failure to identify authorities for the transactions made Wright's evidence unconvincing. Again when subsequently examined by Thomas Terrell representing shareholders, Wright was almost truculently evasive. He denied responsibility for the preparation of the balance sheet, claiming that the figures were from the books. He was not chairman, secretary, general manager, and all of the clerks and boot blacks as well. He accepted large sums had been borrowed but the arrangements were left to others. He claimed lack of knowledge about a host of arrangements. It provoked adverse comment.

Later witnesses showed the full extent of Wright's influence over and control of the companies. They revealed how the companies actually operated and the methods employed. Sinclair Macleay, chairman of British America and a director of Standard Exploration, recounted that share dealings were entirely under the control of Whitaker Wright who would inform the board that he had invested in stocks but did not give details. Macleay knew of the speculative transactions but not exact losses until after the event. He did not at the time regard the control of the managing director as part of his duty; nor did he raise any doubt as to the correctness of what the managing director was doing even though there had been minutes that he and Wright should both deal with purchases and sales of shares and another minute that a book of such transactions should be kept. Wright had apparently worried about the security of the book in the office. Only general answers were ever given to questions at board meetings. He was sorry to say that he was in ignorance on the share dealings. He stated that he had signed a board minute authorising the transfer of the Lake View liability of over one million pounds from London & Globe to Standard Exploration even though he had no recollection of attending the meeting. He maintained that as a director and, in some cases, chairman of other companies, he had gone into details of their affairs but as there was a managing director in this case, he had not exercised any discretion in the companies' affairs. Board meetings would last only fifteen or twenty minutes and simply to confirm the transactions of the managing director. In answer to a question about what he did to protect the shareholders, he responded that he never interfered with what the managing director did. Until the default of London & Globe, he had implicit confidence in Wright, in his ability in matters of finance and in his integrity. His evidence confirmed that the directors had no control over company business and that Wright was solely in charge of affairs. The directors did the little they were instructed to do.

London & Globe's chief accountant until the middle of October 1900, Arthur Worters, confirmed, to laughter at the hearing, that the directors may have only seen the outside of the company books. The directors only saw summaries of the relevant figures. He took all his instructions from Wright particularly seeing the brokers who were acting for the company. He confirmed that blocks of shares in newly promoted companies were sold to members of the financial press. There was a certain portion fixed for each journal upon which there would be a certain profit. It was generally understood that an artificial premium would be produced. The shares were sold at a certain price and then usually repurchased a day or so later by London & Globe at a higher price. He detailed the names of the financial press particularly in relation to the sale of the Le Roi No. 2 promotion. The sums set aside for the press calls were not shown in the company books but as dealings in shares. The evidence confirmed the practice that Wright had apparently denied. Later in his examination, Worters confirmed that he had shown Wright a draft balance sheet for 30th September 1900 but did not tell him that the company was insolvent. He could not remember the figures. It was not a complete one. He said that Wright had commented that certain shares relating to Rossland and Kootenay should not be shown as they belonged to British America. Worters reckoned that the balance sheet only showed a loss of not more than £100,000. He remained a faithful, if hapless, servant of Wright.

On 28th January, a letter from Lord Dufferin was read out by Barnes. Lord Dufferin was much too ill to attend but wanted to clarify his position and accept his responsibility. He gave written answers to written questions that had been posed by Barnes. He answered that directors had not taken the trouble to examine the contract notes which they left to him. They had been successful for a number of years and the directors were willing to approve any business he had negotiated. Directors knew of the large speculations in 1899 and 1900 but not the extent of it because they did not take the trouble to ascertain. Wright had not consulted him beforehand or confided in him the projects for the two operations. He queried whether Wright had acted in the way they had a right to expect or had intended them to realise the nature of his proceedings, instead of leaving them to acquire the requisite information by totting up the contract notes or signing off the cheques. Barnes had wanted to know whether they would sanction Wright for embarking in such a speculation. Lord Dufferin trusted that it was unnecessary for him to add that he should have considered himself highly criminal if he had knowingly consented to the shareholders' money being gambled away in such a manner. It was a letter from the heart. He subsequently died on 12th February at his home in Ireland.

There was direct conflict between Mr. Ford as the auditor, and Henry Malcolm, London & Globe's chief accountant who had taken over from Arthur Worters. Ford maintained that he had requested the brokers' consent for the transfer of the Lake View share speculation liability from London & Globe to Standard Exploration and that Malcolm had assured him of the relevant documentation. Only on that basis had he signed off the accounts. Malcolm denied any such meeting or request. Ford told the hearing that he had also requested minutes of the board meetings giving authorities for the share transactions. He gave a list of the relevant transactions and was given a board minute dated 13th December as authority which was after the events. As to share valuation, the auditor said that the directors and not the auditor were responsible for the figure in the balance sheet. It was not his duty to look at share prices. He had worked right up until the small hours of the Saturday morning before Globe's annual meeting on the Monday, being constantly telephoned by Wright, pressurising him to complete the task and sign the balance sheet.

Ford had added a certificate to the balance sheet stating that 'the current financial engagements of the company appear in the balance sheet at the amount expended to date thereof, and the joint transactions between this company and British America and Standard Exploration are verified by the minutes of the directors, and confirmed by the directors of allied companies; subject thereto, and to the sum written off being adequate in respect of the shares held in the allied companies and various other undertakings, we are of the opinion that the balance sheet correctly represents the position of the company's affairs as shown by the books.' Wright had asked him to take out the clause relating to the allied companies but Ford had refused. Ford maintained that the certificate unusually directly referred to transactions of a company and other companies by name. He considered his certificate was strong and ought to have set any sane man on enquiry. In his opinion, it teemed with suspicion. Ford was subjected to detailed examination about his reasons for failing to note various important transactions but he basically maintained that it was not his duty as auditor. He relied on what was basically shown to him by Malcolm.

Directors of both of London & Globe and Standard Exploration were examined. Lieutenant-General Gough-Calthorpe affably demonstrated the lack of directors' control. He admitted that he did not exercise any control over the managing director; that was the last thing he would be thinking of doing. He had absolute faith in the managing director and the board. He considered his only duty was to sign his name many hundreds of times on the share certificates. He exclaimed, to laughter, "Oh dear, no!" when asked if he guided the policy of the company in any way. He was generally aware of the speculations but not the losses. Lord Edward Pelham-Clinton, equally accepted that he exercised no independent judgment or discretion. He conceded that he did little for his director's fees. Mr. R.E. Leman had sat on the boards of London & Globe and British America initially as Lord Dufferin's legal adviser then as a director. He echoed the arrangement. He thought Wright was the proper person to see to the transactions. He ventured that had the board expressed a strong opinion that a certain thing ought not to be done, Wright would not have done it. He confirmed the process of simply confirming matters after the event. He accepted balance sheets without inquiry. The paucity of the directors' abilities and controls was amply displayed by the evidence.

On 26th February, Wright was given the opportunity to have the final word under examination from his own barrister, Muir Mackenzie. His statements were simply a bold assertion of his behaviour and were intended as a vindication of his business actions.

Millions of pounds had been made for the shareholders of London & Globe and British America. The directors had fully participated and he would not have proceeded with any acquisition if there had been any objection from any director. Full records were kept of transactions but necessarily the board could not deal with the daily share transactions. He had personally made little out of the companies. Finally, Mackenzie produced a letter dated 25$^{th}$ January 1901 from Lord Dufferin to Whitaker Wright. It expressed sympathy with Wright's troubles and commended the proposed reconstruction of London & Globe. He commended Wright's financial ability and his unremitting zeal and devotion to the interests of the shareholders. He retained perfect confidence in Wright's personal integrity. The examination concluded. The Registrar had now to consider the evidence and make his report.

The round of legal hearings and cases continued. On 24$^{th}$ April, Mr. Justice Kekewich in the High Court gave judgment in the case of McConnell v. Wright. A shareholder in Standard Exploration had brought a case alleging misrepresentations in the company prospectus prepared and issued by Wright. Evidence had been given principally by Wright. The Judge largely agreed with most of the allegations against him. Justice Kekewich described the prospectus as fascinating. It was certainly cunning and a 'tricky' prospectus. He said that it was unnecessary for the complainant to put his finger on any particular sentence. It was enough if the prospectus as a whole was the inducing cause. The main contentions that the company had acquired certain interests, particularly Panda Basin, was not borne out. There was an intention to acquire through London & Globe but the statements were deliberately false. The company had made no such acquisitions. Similarly, the Judge considered that the apparent establishment of a share department in the absence of any market was a misleading statement. He also held that a contract dated 22$^{nd}$ October 1898 between Standard Exploration and London & Globe for the transfer of 5,000 deferred shares in the Austin Friars Syndicate ought to have been disclosed in the prospectus. He found for the plaintiff and ordered an inquiry into the amount of damages. It was a not unexpected blow for Wright. It mattered little to him given the wider scenario. However, it was typical of Wright's actions that were returning to haunt him.

The case against the syndicate was next. Success in this action would put a different complexion on the financial aftermath of London & Globe's collapse. The Official Receiver had decided to proceed with this case as part of the compulsory liquidation of the company, basically on the advice of the legal team originally engaged by Wright when a voluntary liquidation of the company was being considered. The legal claim had done much to appease the creditors who viewed the prospect of a million pounds as the best prospect of securing any settlement of their outstanding money.

The civil action was taken against seven defendants. These were Basil Montgomery & Co. – essentially Lord Hardwicke, Williams de Broe & Co. – basically Gerald Williams, Murray Griffiths, Lake & Allcard, Charles Edward Tomlin & Co, Arthur Young and Herbert Trower. Five were the firms within whom the relevant individual members were involved in the arrangements to fund the Lake View share acquisition, and the other two were Young and Trower with whom Wright had dealt directly. The case started on 4th June 1902 before the Lord Chief Justice and lasted until 13th June. There was a full array of leading barristers. Sir Edward Clarke and Lawson Watson led for London & Globe. Rufus Isaacs now represented Williams de Broe and Murray Griffiths.

Wright's counsel opened with an outline of the claim. Damages were sought against the defendants. The basis of the argument was that although there were two documents prepared by Trower and signed by Wright on 14th December 1900 comprising the mortgage for the amount of half a million pounds and the call on the shares at £11, it was essential to the case that these papers did not represent the complete agreement between the parties. There were oral terms agreed relating to the price of any share sale and a division of the profits. The purpose of the syndicate was to buy and agree to buy a substantial quantity of Lake View shares such that when settlement came, they would have sufficient control over a large number of shares so that the 'bears' would have to buy from them to fulfil their obligations to sell. The syndicate would control the quantity of shares available and the share price would inevitably rise. The initial arrangement was for the mid-December account but it was contemplated that by the end-of-December settlement, a million pounds would be ready. In order for the scheme to work, the defendants were not entitled, as they had in fact done, to sell their share holding at any time. It had been agreed that no sale would take place below £17 each. The sale of the shares by certain syndicate members had ruined the scheme. The reason that most of the defendants had not signed the documents was because they were members of the Stock Exchange and could not form anything that looked like a partnership. As a result of the share dealing, London & Globe had ultimately been unable to meet its financial obligations. Trower made all the arrangements and Young was to keep the relevant accounts between the parties.

Wright went into the witness box to give the evidence to support the claim. He reiterated his version of the events and the points made by counsel in opening. Under cross-examination, Wright accepted that he had met only Young and Griffiths on one occasion. He maintained that the terms of the arrangement were verbal. He had been told by Trower that the members of the syndicate who were on the Stock Exchange had objected to signing it. About £500,000 was found for the mid-December settlement. Wright accepted that there was no mention in the documents of a limit on share price sale at £17 or the division of profits. Wright maintained that although the documents were not signed until 14th December, their terms had been acted upon since the November.

All of the defence witnesses including the actual defendants denied the additional verbal agreement. Their position was that they had simply lent sums of money to support London & Globe and had taken the shares as security. Their involvement had only started when Wright wanted money. They had been approached by Trower and Young and had agreed to join, with others, to raise the money required. The Earl of Hardwicke was contacted by Young on 10th December and agreed to see he and Trower the next day. Those two had explained that London & Globe was going to fail unless he could take some 40,000 shares in Lake View. Lord Hardwicke said that he asked for and got a commission for advancing his share of the money. Nothing was said about any limit on the right to sell the shares under £17. He never saw Whitaker Wright.

James Flower also gave evidence. He and his brother had acted as brokers for London & Globe. He gave evidence about the meeting on 29th December to try to find money to avert the collapse of London & Globe. His firm went down with the collapse. A few days later, Young produced the document which showed that he had a perfect right to sell the shares. His brother had remarked that they seemed to have turned honest men out of the house and kept the thieves in. His brother gave similar evidence. He had been cut by friends for his apparent dealing in the shares as broker for London & Globe. He had been assured by colleagues beforehand that there was no issue about the shares. Other witnesses had also been assured that they could eat their Christmas dinners in comfort as they were perfectly safe carrying over the shares. All of the defendants had lost money, position and credibility.

Only Trower had any substantial dealings with Wright and he denied any such agreement on share price. He thought that Wright may have mentioned it at a later stage. Trower, Young and Griffiths confirmed a meeting with Wright shortly after the mid-December settlement date but had different recollections. They maintained that Wright had not mentioned any 'ratting' but had made the case with which they agreed, not subsequently to sell shares with minimum prices being discussed. Trower simply maintained that he had met the various other defendants to raise money for London & Globe taking the share purchases as security. Trower had raised half a million based upon the documents but had failed to raise the further million pounds required for the end of December. He had only agreed to use his best endeavours to raise this further amount but there had been no commitment.

Evidence was inevitably given about London & Globe's financial position during this period. The defendants were able to assert that they were not responsible for the company's collapse. The company was actually in a perilous position prior to any arrangement about the Lake View shares. It was claimed that the company was absolutely and hopelessly insolvent according to its company books as at September 1900. Wright was delaying the issue and manipulating the books between the three companies so he could bring out something that looked like profit. Wright was portrayed as a desperate gambler who saw ruin staring him in the face. The whole arrangement in respect of the Lake View shares had been a dishonourable business carried on in a dishonest way. It was to be inferred that Wright had made up statements for the purpose of covering up the iniquities for which he had been responsible. The language was scathing.

On 13th June, after many days of evidence and many witnesses who had flatly contradicted Wright, Lawson Watson tried to repair some of the damage in his closing speech. It was not Wright's case but that of the liquidator of the company. He thought Wright had been treated harshly. There had been no questions that imputed that Wright had made any personal profit from the syndicate arrangement. He asked the jury to look at the whole business and to see that all parties were working together during that December for a great advantage. The documents and the conduct of the parties were entirely consistent with Wright's evidence.

The Lord Chief Justice told the jury that there was no evidence that any of the defendants had ever agreed to provide the end-of-December one million pounds. He ruled that Trower was acting on behalf of London & Globe and not the other defendants who were lending the money. Trower could not, therefore, commit them. He told them to disregard other conversations. The jury had to determine the bargain between the parties at the time the 42,000 Lake View shares were deposited with the defendants including any agreement not to sell below £17 and division of the profits of sale between London & Globe and the defendants. The jury would then have to consider the damages. He invited them to look at the company's financial position at the time. Wright could not claim damages when it might be due to other causes. Wright had gone into the market not knowing he could get the funding. It was a speculation. He referred to London & Globe's 1900 balance sheet. The jury would have to be satisfied that Globe had demonstrated the sale of shares by the defendants had entailed pecuniary loss by them.

The jury considered the matter for a mere fifteen minutes. They were of the opinion that there had been no agreement by the defendants either to sell below a certain figure or to divide the profits. It was a devastating defeat for Wright. All prospect of some large sum that would accrue to London & Globe's coffers had disappeared. Creditors would now receive little from the liquidation of the company. And there would now be a different view of the reasons for and the aftermath of the company collapse.

The Official Receiver had been endeavouring to sort out the aftermath left by the collapse of the three Wright companies. It was a very tangled web with claims by and between the main and the subsidiary companies being made. On 7th August, the interim report of the Official Receiver was given. He went through his report on the position. On the issue of the syndicate case, formal notice of an appeal on a point of law had been given on legal advice but the final decision on proceeding was left to a full meeting of creditors. On claims between the companies, the respective creditors of London & Globe and British America were considering a compromise of their respective claims against each other. On criminal proceedings, legal advice had been received that it was not at present desirable to take any action against any of the London & Globe directors for misfeasance but consideration was still being given to legal action against those who had been involved in the press calls and the directors of the subsidiary companies in respect of their qualification shares. On payments, it was anticipated that some small dividends representing about 5% of any claim would be paid to creditors. On one aspect, summonses were being issued against Wright and Leman for the recovery of some £750,000 in respect of the Loddon Valley and Moorloot share transactions conducted by London & Globe and British America. On realising assets, some sales of the properties belonging to Standard Exploration had been completed. Overall, the report highlighted the immensity and complexity of the task before the Official Receiver and gave little comfort that any kind of settlement would be accomplished within the foreseeable future.

Wright was assailed on all sides. He had lost all of the legal battles and faced more litigation and proceedings. With an estimated one hundred million pounds lost in the failures of the various Wright companies, there was a feeling in the city that further action was appropriate. A special petition circulated the Stock Exchange signed by many influential men demanding the prosecution of Whitaker Wright. Sections of the newspapers agreed. Wright was entirely dispirited by the public examination and the syndicate case. His past reputation for making money faded in the light of the means that he had employed to achieve that objective. Although his methods and business behaviour differed only by degree from other similar operators, their exposure seemed personal and direct. Any sympathy for him evaporated. He was alone and he had no company to operate. It looked like the end of his business life. But he was wrong to think that the whole affair was over. The new prospect of prosecution confronted him. He became concerned and anxious. His wife developed insomnia and a gloom hung over the family.

# CHAPTER 10

## Making the Flight

The professional men who had conducted the various hearings into the collapse of London & Globe and its allied companies had made their reports and had attributed full responsibility to Whitaker Wright. His methods and operations had been the subject of the most extreme of adverse comment. What had emerged from the report of Barnes for the Official Receiver and the public examinations under Registrar Hood fuelled the view that he had gone well beyond acceptable business behaviour. The Lord Chief Justice had described as unpleasant reading the Official Receiver's report into London & Globe when considering the case against the syndicate. And there were individuals, particularly former shareholders and creditors together with sections of the press, who considered that some further form of justice should prevail against Whitaker Wright. Some thought that a judicial inquiry was appropriate and there were hints that criminal proceedings should be pursued.

Brothers John and James Flower had been one of the firms of stockbrokers hammered as a result of the collapse of London & Globe. They had acted as brokers for London & Globe towards the end of 1900 without any knowledge of the full intentions of Wright. They had attended the meeting on 28th December 1900 when Arthur Young had told them that the money for the purchase of the Lake

View shares could not be put up and it remained for them as brokers to see what they could do. Their funds were quite inadequate and the firm of Flower & Co. went down. As expressed in the syndicate case, they were even more incensed when they learned the true facts of the case and the behaviour of Whitaker Wright. They both thought that the money for the purchase of the shares had been paid to the credit of their firm in the usual way. They had been total victims of the Wright operations at that time and were determined to retrieve their reputations and have Wright brought to some kind of justice. As creditors, the brothers had attended the various meetings concerned with the collapse of London & Globe and its allied companies.

John Flower contacted the Attorney General in an attempt to persuade him to instruct the Director of Public Prosecutions to take criminal action against Wright. However, the Attorney General considered that the law provided insufficient grounds for proceeding against those responsible for the London & Globe balance sheet and without any prospect of success. He wrote to John Flower on 20$^{th}$ December on that basis. The brothers would not let the matter rest and, with others like Arnold White, they were instrumental in a meeting held at Anderson's Hotel in Fleet Street on 16$^{th}$ January 1903 to discuss the legal position with likeminded individuals. Many had lost their investments with the collapse of the companies. They had obtained the legal view of Sir George Lewis that there was a clear case for a prosecution against Wright and the directors. There was a free discussion particularly about the reasons for the lack of criminal proceedings. There was a consideration that the individuals were sheltering behind great names and it was rumoured that a royal duke had invested his money in the corporation.

But the general view was that their motivations must not be seen as political and that it should be a simple case of justice. If the Attorney General could not see his way clear to investigating the scandal while the minor crime of tossing for halfpence in the street was taken, it turned justice into a mockery. At least, some judicial investigation ought to be initiated by the Government. Flower thought that they had been the victims of the most heartless and gigantic swindles which would have been impossible but for the company directors being dummies, the auditors careless and indifferent and the managing directors unscrupulously working in collusion with skilled accountants within the walls of his office. It was agreed to form a committee to raise the sum of £5,000 and obtain the best legal advice. The London & Globe Prosecution Fund was established. Arnold White agreed to be the prosecutor if the funds could found. At the beginning of February, a circular letter was sent to London & Globe shareholders seeking financial contributions to the fund. There was newspaper support in the form of detailing the aims of the committee.

But then it did become political. Many disgruntled shareholders had written to their Members of Parliament and there had been leading articles in the newspapers. The Attorney General's decision that there were insufficient grounds to proceed had been greeted with some scepticism by the opposition Liberal Members of Parliament who decided to act. On the evening of 19th February 1903, the House of Commons debated the matter when George Lambert, Liberal MP for South Moulton in Devon since 1891, used the procedural device of moving an amendment to the Address, "And we humbly express our regret that no prosecution has been instituted against the directors of the London & Globe Finance Corporation."

Lambert explained that he had no financial interest in the matter but it was a public question. He took members through the balance sheets, some of the share dealings and some of the basic facts. Here was a company which issued a report showing a profit of half a million pounds and twenty-eight days afterwards it collapsed and was unable to meet its liabilities. He referred to rumours that exalted people were involved. This was a reference to the Duke of Clarence, brother of Edward VII. Lambert added that it was well known that a member of the government was a sleeping partner in one of the companies connected with these transactions. This was a reference to Lord Hardwicke who was a member of the syndicate. He had been Under-Secretary of State for India and Under-Secretary of State for War for periods since 1900. Lambert asserted that he did not make any charges or suggest that it would have any influence on the Attorney General. But if a bank manager or bank clerk embezzled £100, the law swooped down on him at once. The law ought not to be stirred in the case of the poor and hesitating and doubtful in the case of the rich. There had been aristocratic gentlemen mixed up this affair. He was really very sorry that if their names had been used to the unwary investor, they must bear responsibility. Fraud and falsification had been openly alleged. He asked the Attorney General to allow twelve Britishers to decide the matter. There had been cheers throughout from the opposition benches.

The Attorney General, Sir Robert Finlay, was an experienced barrister who had been appointed to his post in 1900. Coincidentally, he had appointed as Rector of Edinburgh University in 1902 in succession to the late Lord Dufferin. Finlay refuted the suggestion that the absence of action by the Director of Public Prosecutions was due to the connection of some exalted personages with this case. He dismissed as insinuation that any member of the government was involved. Finlay did not defend the transactions. The transactions were reprehensible and deserved the severe judgment by all who were prepared to value commercial integrity and honour. But the question was not one of civil liability. The question was one of inquiry and investigation. There was all the difference in the world between a case for proper inquiry and it being proper for criminal prosecution by the Director of Public Prosecutions. The Attorney General continued that anyone could initiate a prosecution and that there should be no prejudice to any proceedings by an individual. He would not say any word on the subject in order not to prejudice any subsequent proceedings. He had studied the evidence and had invited further evidence in the form of statements which he had considered. But they did not vary his original decision.

A debate ensued. There were very strongly held opinions. Members had obviously received letters and read the newspapers. The merits of the case were argued. No one doubted the guilt of Wright. No one sought to defend him. Most poured scorn on his activities. One member said the facts were undisputed that a fraudulent balance sheet had been issued and on the faith of it credit had been obtained. He thought that there could be no worse offence. Other members spoke in similar terms. There was no argument about the merits of the case but the issue turned on the role of the Government. There was considerable discussion about the role of Attorney General. It was argued that it was for him to make the decision and not for either the Government or the House of Commons to superimpose its view. If the law was inadequate, it ought to be changed.

Eventually the Prime Minister, Arthur Balfour, who had not intended to get involved, felt obliged to speak. The sixty-three-year-old Scot had taken over the basically Conservative administration in July 1902. He had no need of this affair and wanted to put an end to it. He had listened carefully to the debate. He understood the feelings of Members that the Commons ought to take some action. He considered that no one doubted the honesty of the Attorney General. He reiterated the independence of the Attorney General. He supported the judgement of the Attorney General on the facts of the case. He accepted the feeling of deep and profound indignation at the fraudulent transactions in which Whitaker Wright had been engaged. He maintained that if the fault lay with the law it ought to be amended and he would carry that view into effect. The Government had an easy majority of fifty-one votes.

In essence, the parliamentary debate had been more about politics than justice. The Conservative Government in general and Arthur Balfour in particular, rumoured to have dealt in London & Globe shares, were anxious not to get involved in the matter. There were doubts about the success of a prosecution and the Government did not want to be involved in a failure. There was little merit in a legal action which might seem to highlight the Government's inadequacy in regulating the market. On the other side, the Liberal opposition might genuinely have had some of its Members feeling that action was required to deal with a scandal but the scope for exposing apparent Government ineptitude and secret complicity was more appealing. The session was more about the two parties than it was about Whitaker Wright who was roundly condemned by both factions.

Letters to the press followed on the legal position and approach of the Attorney General. They typified the legal views about the likely success of a prosecution. Immediately, Arnold White penned his contribution. His main criticism was reserved for the Attorney General. He cited the case of the Millwall Dock's manager recently convicted for making false entries in the company's books amounting to £30,000. The man had been sent to prison for nine months with hard labour. Interestingly, one of the now Treasury counsel had actually prosecuted in that case. The legal principle was that if you publish a false statement intending it to be acted on, you are is guilty of publishing it with intent to defraud. There was no difference, White asserted, between that case and Wright's case. There was no need for any amendment of the law as suggested by the Prime Minister. White was also keen to defend the action of the committee to prosecute by stating that it was not an attack on royalty, nor on the late Lords Dufferin and Loch, nor as a newspaper campaign and not in enmity against Wright or other directors. He invited the Government to assist the committee in taking action against a sanctimonious middle-class swindler. With the criticism, there was also some defence about the Attorney General's opinion. Another view was that Wright intended to deceive the Stock Exchange and not any shareholder or creditor as required by the criminal law. There was great argument about the relevant sections of the law, particularly the issue of any intent to deceive by Whitaker Wright. It was all very intense and kept the matter in the public eye.

Wright had been monitoring developments with increasing concern and despair. His financial position was becoming extremely difficult. In October 1902, he borrowed a further £10,000 against Lea Park with the interest on the previous borrowing being capitalised against the estate. He and his wife had moved into Sir Edgar Horne's newly built property at Tigbourne Court in nearby Hambledon. It was an impressive property designed in his own distinctive style by Edward Lutyens, although somewhat smaller than Lea Park House. Anna Wright had become extremely distressed and continued to suffer from insomnia. Whitaker Wright would often retreat to his small study in the house. On his desk were the small monogrammed stationery objects from Lea Park House. He turned to his bookshelves and liked to comfort himself in a Guy Boothby book. With perhaps some sense of quiet self-irony, he enjoyed the collection of stories in *A Prince of Swindlers* detailing the exploits of the Simon Carne character who was the likeable gentleman rogue regularly relieving the rich of their wealth.

But the wider scene continued to invade. In January 1903, his appeal against the decision in the McConnell case about the Standard Exploration prospectus had been substantially lost. The significance was that other similar cases could be brought against him. He believed that every court would rule against him. The prospect of prosecution remained a threat despite the ruling of the Attorney General. Indeed, the Government officers in the parliamentary debate had expressly viewed a private prosecution as the best way forward although its protagonists had considered cost to be inhibitive. And Wright now became aware that steps were being progressed to secure those criminal proceedings.

The committee for the prosecution had to get judicial sanction before proceeding. Application for permission to mount a private prosecution was made before Mr. Justice Buckley at the High Court on 17th February. The Judge was the leading authority on company law. Originally, an earlier application had been made in the Judges' Chambers as was usual but Mr. Justice Buckley decided that any hearing should be in open court as he considered that the accused person should have the opportunity to witness the case against him being heard. Opposition to the application came from some creditors who feared the cost of the case would leave them with less money from the company's liquidation. The case was accordingly adjourned for a hearing in open court.

The prospect of prosecution was now too close for comfort. Wright discussed the situation with his wife. He could stay and take his chances but his recent experience of judicial process and his fear about the likelihood of conviction given the adverse publicity proved too much for his usual bravado. If criminal proceedings were commenced, he believed that he had little chance of a fair trial. The whole tenor of public opinion was totally against him and a jury would be easily influenced. He could see only a conviction and a lengthy term of imprisonment. He could not see any way of avoiding the situation other than to leave the country. It was a sudden and unplanned decision. He drew £500 from his bank account and sailed with his valet, Bishop, for France on 21st February.

On 23rd February, Bishop telegraphed Wright's usual Hotel Binda at Rue La Rochelle in Paris – 'Keep the rooms for tomorrow night.' Wright and Bishop arrived with seven trunks on 24th February. He had a sitting room as well as a bedroom. He had stayed many times before with and without his family and was well known to the proprietor, Charles Bind. It was a fashionable hotel in the heart of Paris. Wright availed himself of the break. Mr. Arthur Dryon acted as his guide around the city. They motored around enjoying the sites. Wright talked fantastically about his intention of going to Norway in his own yacht. He explained that it was a cruise he had always wanted to take to escape the pressures of business. He had various callers including his solicitor, Burn, who wanted him to sign the document giving security for costs in the appeal against the decision in the syndicate case. Burn told him that Flowers was bent on the prosecution but considered that they had not a ghost of a chance.

The view contrasted with Wright's own pessimism. He was right to be concerned.

Mr. Justice Buckley heard the argument for the initiation of the prosecution on 3$^{rd}$ and 4$^{th}$ March and reserved judgment. However, the decision appeared inevitable to Wright's wife. She sent a telegram to Wright on 5$^{th}$ March from the nearby Wormley Post Office – 'Case to prosecute settled today. Everything looks bad. Telegraph Burn for result.' Wright had been thinking about the next step and had decided on his one remaining option. There was now only one destination. He would travel to America where he had family and some friends and acquaintances. He knew the country and language was no barrier.

Wright responded to his wife but in Bishop's name, stating, 'Give Florence £500. She sails tomorrow Friday evening. Will meet her Havre. Forward no more letters.' Florence Browne was Wright's niece and had lived at Lea Park for some time. Wright then got Mr. Andreone who was on a visit to Paris from Rome to help with the arrangements. Andreone, in company with Florence, booked two tickets on the SS *La Lorraine* sailing from Le Havre to New York. There was a bit of negotiation on the price and the purchase was made using money given to him by Wright. They were to have adjacent first-class cabins de lux. The bookings were in the names of Andreone and Miss Andreone. Whitaker and Florence sailed on 7$^{th}$ March.

It was not until 10$^{th}$ March that Mr. Justice Buckley made his formal decision. He decided that there was a *prima facie* case for prosecution and he exercised his discretion under the Companies Act 1862 to direct such prosecution. He considered that he ought not to allow the refusal of the Attorney General to act to influence his judgment. He had no sympathy for the creditors and made an order for costs to be met out of company assets so far as required in aid of the £1,250 already paid into court by the committee for the prosecution. Ironically, Wright was to be prosecuted with money from the company he had started. The prosecution was put in the hands of the company's Official Receiver whose Committee of Inspection had voted overwhelmingly to proceed with the matter.

Within two hours, an Information was laid before the London City Magistrate, Alderman Smallman, charging Wright under the Larceny Act with issuing a false balance sheet. A summons was issued at 6 p.m. that Tuesday evening. The next day, the police attempted to serve the summons on Wright at Tigbourne Court at Hambledon but discovered he had gone. His wife was evasive about where he had gone. She expressed the thought that he was going to Egypt for his health. A warrant was then issued for his arrest. He was described in somewhat vivid and unflattering terms: 'Aged about 50, height 5 feet 9 or 10 inches, stout build, large head, dark hair and moustache, florid complexion, small eyes, receding forehead, small chin with large fat roll beneath. Wears gold prince-nez with gold chain attached. Speaks with slight American accent. Usually dresses in frock-coat suit and silk hat.' The police were not slow to investigate Wright's whereabouts. They discovered the telegrams sent between him and his wife. They were able to trace one of Wright's one-hundred-pound banknotes to the shipping office at Le Havre. They identified the boat on which he had sailed and speedily communicated with their American colleagues.

On Sunday 15th March, New York Central Office detectives acting under directions from George McClusky arrested Wright on the pier of the Comapagnie Generale Transatlantique. Wright was taken to the Federal Building and separated from Florence. She was questioned but expressed no knowledge of Whitaker's financial matters. The tall and slender Florence had stood up well but was greatly affected by the turn of events. Reunited with Whitaker, she laid her head on his shoulder for several minutes as they sat together in Marshall Henkel's office in the Federal Building. He tried to keep up a cheerful appearance. They parted as he was taken to be kept overnight in the nearby Ludlow Street Jail which was the usual place to hold prisoners in immigration and extradition matters.

The news of his arrest spread rapidly and a large crowd followed him on his way the next day from the jail to the Federal Building. He was quick and eager to seize the opportunity to give his version of events. He told reporters that the accounts published about the Globe losses were all bosh. All dividends had been paid out of secured capital. The Boer War with its financial irregularities contributed in no small extent and was chiefly responsible for destroying the value of mining properties. The Globe Corporation would have been on its feet had it not been for the underground railway. He asserted that the Official Receiver had been over the books and the whole matter fought out in Parliament. The Attorney

General had said that he was not culpable and that he was entitled to a clean bill of health. He was an Englishman but an American citizen. His mother was buried in Philadelphia and he had an American wife and three children in England. He claimed his dealings had been honest and he proposed to return to England as soon as permitted.

In court, Wright's counsel, Maurice Untermyer, argued that Wright was willing to take the next steamship for England but owing to the advice of counsel he asked only for a few days' delay to get an idea of the exact charges against him. He opposed the proposed fortnight's adjournment requested by the British Consul's representative, Charles Fox. Of course, there was no chance that he would be released. The court was well used to this kind of case. The law did not provide for bail in extradition cases given the high prospect of the defendant absconding from the jurisdiction. It was to be the same pattern of dispute of many hearings in March and April. The prosecution side was continually seeking postponement while relevant papers were sent from England. Wright offered to return voluntarily if extradition proceedings were dropped but the request was refused. Over a month elapsed and little progress had really been made. Several applications for bail were made but rejected. The original charges were elaborated. Dispositions were presented by some relevant witnesses including Arthur Russell for the Official Receiver and John Flower for the prosecuting committee.

Wright followed the relevant press reports. Again, he took the opportunity to make his case on the basis that public opinion would speed his release. He complained to the *New York Times* about their article appearing on 16$^{th}$ April. He objected to the expressed view that the extradition was on the basis of charges of wrecking the London & Globe. He asserted that the law officers of the Crown had decided that there was no case of fraudulent intent, and stated their view to Parliament. He argued in a letter to the press that the charges were brought by one of the firms of defaulting stockbrokers and that the offences were of a technical nature. The charge did not impute that any director personally profited. He maintained that he had sacrificed his own resources in an effort to prevent the failure of the company. He accepted all the responsibility that inured on him but he wanted to see the alleged offence correctly stated, that his numerous American friends should not be misled about the issue. It was a view that Wright continued to hold. He had not tried to defraud. He never had any intention to deceive. He had tried to save the company and not run away from his responsibilities. Balance sheets were notoriously used to promote a company and not to give an accurate picture.

At home, Wright's wife was in some distress. Whitaker's flight and the desperate financial position were being exacerbated by newspaper reports that she had become estranged from her husband. She was forced to issue a statement stating that Florence Browne had accompanied Whitaker with her full knowledge and consent as she could not go with her husband because of her heart condition and the welfare of her children, and he needed someone to look after him. She added that Florence's mother, Wright's sister Matilda, was living in Surrey and was broken-hearted at the treatment of her daughter. She challenged if Mr. Wright would be as a poor as he was if he had profited by this failure. She maintained that she had been left with practically nothing, she found it difficult to meet her bills and that she had to sell some of her jewellery to defray expenses. The affair had killed her.

After over a month of imprisonment, and in consultation with his legal team, a decision was made to apply to the Circuit Court of the southern district of New York for a writ of *habeas corpus* and for bail on the basis that extradition did not lie between the United States and the United Kingdom for the alleged offences. The case was argued on 28th and 29th April. Another month went by before there was any result. Mr. Chief Justice Fuller gave his decision on 1st June. The issue was whether or not the charges against Wright were the subject of the Extradition Treaty dated 1842 between the United States and Great Britain. He went over several earlier cases. He reached the conclusion that the charges had to be substantially the same in the State of the United States to where the fugitive had resorted, and in Great Britain. Accordingly, the New York Penal Code had to have the same offence as Wright was charged with in Great Britain. He had no difficulty in ruling that Penal Code number 611 which referred to fraud by a member or officer of a company and made it an offence to publish a report that was materially false, was substantially analogous to the British offence. Absolute identity was not required, only an essential character of the transaction had to be the same. He ruled that the New York commissioner had jurisdiction to consider Wright's case. Chief Justice Fuller also considered the issue of bail. He stated that there was no United States statute that provided for the admission of bail in cases of foreign extradition.

The New York commissioner was therefore entitled to keep hold of Wright and the processes continued. Wright had spent the whole time in Ludlow Jail. It was not a large establishment, fronting some ninety feet of both Ludlow Street and Essex Market Place. It had some eighty-seven cells, each about ten feet square, enough to fit two beds, two chairs, wash basin and designed to accommodate two prisoners. The high windows provided light and ventilation and a high wall surrounded the exercise yard for daily use. Its inmates were mainly imprisoned for civil offences or, like Whitaker Wright, awaiting some legal proceedings without the benefit of bail. It was an unpleasant time. His confinement to one room was not something that he had ever experienced. His wealth and previous life had not prepared him for this situation and it became intolerable to him. He complained about the conditions although they might actually have been much worse. But his health deteriorated and he looked more ill at every court appearance. He lost weight and his face showed the strain. On 3$^{rd}$ June, he was placed in the jail hospital suffering from vertigo. It could not go on. Whitaker Wright could not fight any more. He was worn down by the confinement, the lack of any prospect of release and the inevitability of the result.

At the beginning of July, his counsel wrote to Wright's legal team in London that he agreed to waive the question of extradition and return to England. He advised that Wright was seriously ill with vertigo and it was doubtful whether he would live until the determination of the extradition question which would take six months. The battle was over. Wright had accepted that the proceedings would result in his forcible return and that incarceration would continue until that time. He could not face the prolonged imprisonment and accepted that a return to England was the only course realistically open. At least he would be removed from jail and reunited with his family, as there was a good prospect that in London he could get bail. He could live with his family and he could defend himself.

He defiantly expressed his views to the American press. He said that he had been ill since his arrival and for that reason he did not care to make the ocean voyage at that time. He believed that his return to England would result in his complete vindication. He maintained that the charges against him were all spiteful work on the part of some counsellors in England who represented the small fry. These persons thought that they had not received enough attention during the investigation of his affairs. He had no doubt that this matter would be settled in a manner favourable to him. He added that he did not run away but remained in England during an investigation of his affairs that lasted nearly two years. He said that he was greatly surprised at his arrest. He had stayed in London against the advice of his physicians. His arrest had interfered with his travel plans which he had contemplated for his health.

He was still another three weeks in jail. Over four months of incarceration had seriously affected him. His physical and mental health, not least weakened by the recent two years of wrangling, was poor. He looked forward to the voyage albeit under the auspices of the judicial system. He left for England on 29th July. He was accompanied by two detective inspectors, Willis and Phillips. A stateroom on the White Star Liner *Oceanic* had been reserved for him but he protested that it was too small and was transferred to suites 3 to 7 on the promenade deck, one section of which contained a library. He was determined to travel in style. He recovered some of his spirit on the voyage. There was the sea air and a relative freedom. There was good food and service. There was peace and relaxation. Asked to join in the shipboard entertainment that the passengers were getting up, he replied with his usual ironic good humour that he would make a short speech on the decadence of British fair play. But he did not do it and contributed to the concert fund instead. He needed the time and the space to resolve himself.

He arrived at Liverpool on the morning of 5th August in the company of the two detectives. A crowd was there to see him. The press were present in force as it was the main news of the moment. The three men left for London on the express train. He appeared at Guildhall Police Court, at just after 3 p.m. that day before the City of London magistrate, Alderman Smallman. The Old Council Chamber was used to accommodate the public and press that had gathered to see him. He was immaculately dressed in a blue suit with a brown derby hat. He looked in fairly good health albeit somewhat thinner than when he left. He sported a neatly trimmed beard. Wright sat to read the charges. The prosecution simply applied to prove the arrest of Wright and the detective inspector John Wills gave evidence about the issue of the warrant and Wright's apprehension in New York. Mr. Muir, counsel on Wright's behalf, applied for bail and sought to explain Wright's departure to America particularly to get rid of the suggestion in the baser class of newspaper that Wright had absconded and thereby confessed his guilt. He said that his client had remained in England during the whole period of the investigations which included his public and private examinations, and in the syndicate case. It was public knowledge that the Director of Public Prosecutions had declined to act in criminal proceedings. He maintained that Wright had then felt at liberty to start his business life again. His movements could be easily followed and he referred to the cheque which he cashed in his own name, to the trail of banknotes and the Paris hotel registration which had been in his own name. Wright had left for America before Mr. Justice Buckley's decision and the issue of the warrants. He explained that bail could not been granted in America in cases of extradition. Guy Stephenson for the prosecution said that he would leave it for the magistrate to decide on bail, merely referring to the various telegrams sent between Wright and his wife which had indicated a different interpretation of events. Alderman Smallman decided to grant bail in the sum of £50,000 comprising £25,000 in Wright's own bond, two sureties of £10,000 and one of £5,000. Wright was then taken to Brixton Prison. Two days later, when the bail sureties had been arranged, he was released on bail.

On the day of his release, Wright's legal team were already in the High Court alleging contempt by the editor of the *Sunday Sun* contained in an article by Arnold White which had appeared on 2nd August while Wright was on his way back to England. The article was scathing in its attack on the Attorney General and the Prime Minister for their unfulfilled promise to change the law to deal with the Wright case. It was written ostensibly to protest the possibility of bail being granted for Wright on his return. It stated that Wright had not been allowed bail in the United States. It asserted that the rich and the poor should be treated the same under the law. Reference was made to the recent convictions of Henry Golding, a labourer who had been given six months' hard labour at Colchester Sessions for stealing a pair of boots and Clara Walkley, a barmaid who had been sentenced to three months' hard labour for stealing from her employer. They had not been granted bail.

On 12th August, the court heard the opposing parties. The newspaper maintained that there was no malice and that the granting of bail was a matter of public interest. However, it was now accepted by the newspaper that it should not have been allowed to go to press; they apologised and stated that it was published in good faith without any intention of preventing a fair trial. It was maintained on behalf of the newspaper that it was simply want of care. However, the court decided that there had been contempt. There had been passages in the article that had practically commented on Mr. Wright as a guilty man and indicated that there were forces at work to prevent his case being investigated and to prevent a fair trial or to prevent his being tried at all. These had been apparently inserted in an article that was supposed to discuss the question of whether or not bail should be granted. It went far beyond legitimate comment on a matter of public interest. The Judge decided that it was difficult to understand that anyone connected with journalism could believe that they would not be in contempt of court. He ordered the newspaper editor to pay the costs. However, the Judge ruled that although Arnold White had acted very properly in taking steps to see that justice was done, the result was that he was indirectly one of the prosecutors and therefore his position was more serious. He ordered him to pay a fine of £100 and be imprisoned until it was paid.

The formal committal proceedings were heard at the Guildhall in late August and September. The lower court had to decide that there was a sufficient case to go to the Central Criminal Court for consideration. Evidence had to be produced by the prosecution in the form either of statements or the actual witnesses, if required by the defence. It gave the defence an opportunity to see the precise nature of their statements and the character of the witnesses themselves. The defence did not have to call any witnesses and the defendant did not have to give any evidence. The defence gave no evidence but gave notice that they required full access to all of London & Globe's books which were in the hands of the Official Receiver, and that considerable time would be required to examine them. There was no objection to the committal. It would have been a formality in any event. On the formal reading of the charges, Wright stated only that he declared his innocence and reserved his entire defence to the trial of the case. The representative of the prosecution fund committee kept a watching brief. However, as decided by Mr. Justice Buckley, the prosecution was now in name of the Official Receiver.

Wright spent a good part of his time with his lawyers, particularly Sir Richard Muir. They had innumerable consultations and there was a mutual liking. Muir believed that Wright had been more a victim of his own foolish vanity than that of criminal intent. Muir thought that Wright's head had been turned by unending adulation. He looked on Wright as a super-optimist. He was convinced that had Wright remained in England, he would never have been brought to trial. Wright privately conceded to him that he was a fool to have run away. Both Muir and Wright thought he had a good case but neither thought that there would be a fair trial. Muir thought him as a man who had been hounded to death for having failed. It was incontrovertible that Wright himself rendered it almost impossible to obtain an acquittal. The lavish expenditure he had indulged in and the culpability which necessarily attached to his flight so prejudiced the public mind that his condemnation was a foregone conclusion. During Wright's absence in New York, the newspapers had published accounts of his apparent lifestyle and particularly about the extravagant amount of money spent on the development of Lea Park.

Wright's legal team were concerned about the trial venue. The case had been properly committed to the Central Criminal Court, the Old Bailey, where major criminal offences were invariably held. However, there was a significant concern about any jury understanding the complex financial issues and reaching an unbiased verdict. Application was therefore made in November to move the hearing to the Crown side of the King's Bench Division. This would enable what was essentially a civil court to decide a criminal matter. It would enable a special jury to be selected, people with some education, and the trial to be held in a court with some business knowledge. The move was not opposed by the prosecution although it had some complaints about further delays. The request was granted. From Wright's perspective, there might be a better understanding of the financial intricacies and hence the stratagems employed by him and they might accept that they were legitimate. However, it was a change not without some risk. The ability of the jury to listen to the evidence and arguments might not necessarily be to Wright's advantage. They might readily realise what had occurred. Preparations continued on both sides. For the prosecution, there was the organisation of the witnesses and the relevant paperwork. A huge number of documents were involved. For the defence, it was attention to Wright's explanations about the paperwork that required rehearsal. There was complex evidence, a variety of witnesses and important legal issues to discuss. It was an intense time for both sides.

At least Whitaker Wright had his freedom and he could spend time with his family, who since the April had been living at Lower House on the Lea Park Estate. His wife was suffering the strain badly. She remained reclusive, anxious and sleepless. She regretted the return to England despite the wealth and position that he had apparently brought. Now the social scene had gone and she relied on very few close acquaintances. Life was centred on the home. Their twenty-year-old son, Whitaker, was totally supportive. But, as usual recently, there was a shortage of personal funds. In the October, Wright and his wife raised further money by mortgaging the estate property. They had no other source and no other income.

The family had Christmas together. The last three years had been devastating with the gradual loss of wealth, home, business and reputation. They had remained a family. There was loyalty, mutual respect, love and a determination to remain totally and firmly together. Their mutual feelings were a great comfort to each of them. It was to their credit that their love remained. Locally, the family were still held in the highest regard. Nothing could shake the village belief that Whitaker Wright would defy his critics and prove his innocence. It provided great comfort and some little optimism for the family. He steeled himself for the great performance that he would have to give. The stage was now set for the trial of Whitaker Wright.

# CHAPTER 11

## Making the Moment

The trial of Whitaker Wright began on Monday 11th January 1904. As determined by the High Court in November, it had been moved from the Old Bailey to the Crown side of the King's Bench Division, before a special jury and held in the law courts in the Strand. It meant that the defendant could sit with his lawyers and not alone in a dock. Wright sat in front of the lawyers in the well of the court at a table with Sir Richard Muir. Immediately in front of him was Mr. Russell, the Clerk of the Court, and his assistants and above them, on the high bench, the Judge presided. The barristers sat in ranks behind Wright. Piles of paper and boxes of documents surrounded them. To his right were the jury of the twelve men. To his left was the witness box. There was considerable newspaper interest and the reporters were there in force immediately to the side of the witness box. It was the case of the moment. They had been somewhat inhibited before the start of the trial, fearing contempt of court based upon any possibly prejudicial article. But now they could print everything that was going to be said. There were some reserved seats and many stood during the hearing.

The Judge was Mr. Justice Bigham who had been born in Liverpool in 1840 to a merchant family. After a London law degree, he was called to the bar in 1870 and became a Queen's Counsel in

1883. He was elected the Liberal Member of Parliament for Toxteth, Liverpool, in 1895 after several unsuccessful attempts. But it had been a short parliamentary career as he was appointed as a Judge in 1897. He was well experienced in commercial cases. He had a steady and deliberate approach but could be robust with witnesses. The prosecution was led by Rufus Isaacs with Horace Avory, and Guy Stephenson. Rufus Isaacs similarly came from a business family. He was born in 1870 and the son of a fruit merchant in London and initially worked in the family business. He became a jobber on the London Stock Exchange from 1880 until 1884 but financial losses turned him to study law. He had been called to bar in 1887 and became a Queen's Counsel in 1890. He had political ambitions. The Liberal Party had him earmarked for a suitable bye-election and future Government office. Whitaker Wright had the team of Lawson Walton with Richard Muir and Felix Cassell. Lawson Walton was the son of a Wesleyan missionary who in 1887 became President of the Wesleyan Conference. He was called to bar in 1877 and became a Queens Counsel in 1890. In 1892 he had become MP for Leeds South. He had a strong association with Methodist Church. He and Isaacs were colleagues. There were other legal representatives keeping watching briefs for interested persons. It was a spectacular array of the legal profession.

The prosecution and defence lawyers had previously been involved at some time or other and had represented various affected parties during the last two or three years in the aftermath of the collapse of London & Globe and its allied companies in the various cases and hearings. They were thoroughly familiar with the facts and figures, the events and the people involved. However, whilst there had been previous findings of facts, conclusions reached and reports made, the criminal proceedings meant that everything had to be freshly considered. Witnesses would have to give their evidence and the lawyers would have to present their arguments as though there had been no such previous hearing. Any conclusion could result. The criminal issues were not the same as the statutory and civil responsibilities previously at issue.

Whitaker Wright was charged with twenty-six offences under the Larceny Act 1861. Section 83 made it an offence that being a director of a public company shall, within intent to defraud, destroy, alter, mutilate or falsify any book, paper, writing, or valuable security belonging to that company, or shall make or concur in the making of any false entry, or omit or concur in the omitting of any material particular in any book of account or other document. Section 84 was the making, circulating, or publishing, or the concurring in the making, circulating or publishing, as a director of a company, of any written statement or account, knowing the same to be false in some material particular, with intent to deceive or defraud any member, shareholder, or creditor of such company. Four counts related to the 1899 balance sheet and four to his speech to the annual general meeting of 1899. Four counts related to the 1900 balance sheet and four to his speech to the annual general meeting of 1900. Other counts related to omissions in the 1900 balance sheet and to entries in the 1900 accounts referring to different brokers.

The prosecution had to prove every element of the offences beyond reasonable doubt. It also had to anticipate the likely defences. In complex cases of fraud, there was the danger that the jury or even the Judge might not be able to follow either the chain of events or the complicated transactions that had taken place. The web of dealings, the mass of figures, the arrangements between the various and many companies, the involvement of other parties including banks and brokers, shareholders and creditors was formidable. The timing of certain actions and the occurrence of particular events was crucial. All of that would have to be carefully explained. All of the witnesses would need to give their evidence to support those facts. However, the major issue was the defendant's role. What the prosecution had to show was that Wright and Wright alone intended to commit what were basically frauds and that he intended to deceive. The prosecution knew the kind of layers Wright would present in his defence. There was nothing wrong with the balance sheets. Transactions prior to their publication were entirely legitimate. The arrangement and presentation of the balance sheets were normal business practice. Any errors were not solely attributable to the managing director. The errors and mistakes had been made by various employees. His intention had been to save the company and thereby to save the value of the company for the shareholders. He had never intended to deceive. There was no criminal responsibility on his part. It was an array of issues. The prosecution had to make its case. It had to set the scene, tell the story, present the facts and deliver the witnesses.

The opening for the prosecution by Rufus Isaacs was masterful. He put the accusation simply. The charges were knowingly making and publishing false statements with intent to defraud shareholders and creditors and possible shareholders and creditors. He dealt with the immediate background that had been heavily featured in the press. He told the jury to exclude from their consideration all of the debate in the House of Commons. He dismissed the Attorney General's lack of action, anticipating that the defence would raise this issue. The prosecution had the relevant authority. He reminded the court of the huge losses of some five million pounds and the low payments to creditors.

Isaacs needed to put Wright at the centre of operations. He outlined the history of the London & Globe and said that from beginning to end, Wright was the ruling spirit. Although there was a board of directors, the whole work and responsibility lay with Wright. He signed all the cheques. Wright had also founded and was in control of British America and Standard Exploration. The sales and purchases between the companies were controlled by Wright who dispensed even with the formality of recording the transactions. They were not real transactions but enabled Wright to get rid of doubtful securities and enabled London & Globe to get rid of large blocks of shares to other companies and alter the balance sheet. By these devices, impressions were created and statements made by Wright which he knew to be false. The balance sheets showed a flourishing state of things, but there had been intentional concealment.

He carefully took the jury through the nature of the alleged offences and what had to be shown to prove guilt. It had to be shown that the statement was made in writing, that it was known to be false in a material particular by the person making it and that there must be an intent to defraud or deceive. To deceive involved an attempt to induce a state of mind, to defraud, to induce a course of action. If the statements were false to the defendant's knowledge, the conclusion was irresistible that the whole conduct was criminal. Omission to make an entry was equally fraudulent. He emphasised the enormity of the losses incurred as a result of the collapse of London & Globe and remarked that if the facts were true, it would be scandalous if they did not constitute a criminal offence.

Although he did not expressly say, he had to demonstrate that

Whitaker Wright alone was responsible as no one else had been charged. Neither the chairman nor the directors of the company nor any other member of their officers had been charged in the proceedings. He had to deal with this aspect. He had already referred to the way Wright had run the company but he emphasised that even the speeches given by Lord Dufferin as chairman were prepared by Wright. His speeches were printed and distributed among the shareholders. It did not represent the true position of the company. The boards of directors had little control.

Isaacs then took them carefully through each of the two balance sheets of 1899 and 1900. He detailed the transactions between the companies. Wright had acted in many characters, the transactions being, as it were, counters. He detailed the way shares had been transferred at different prices, how new companies had been created out of existing companies with transfer of assets, the artificial valuation of shares held by the company, the transfer of liabilities and assets on certain days and then their transfer back again days later, the hidden losses of the company and the manipulation of the accounts and balance sheet to show a different situation, the attempt to validate some transactions by minutes of boards meetings that had not taken place, and the speeches made by Wright. He highlighted the particular points and events. The sudden improvements in London & Globe's financial position immediately before each balance sheet were the key features. He gave them the figures. He told the jury about the transactions undertaken to give London & Globe apparent assets. He singled out Wright's words to shareholders giving further credibility to the false figures. London & Globe's 1900 balance sheet had shown substantial assets but within days the company had collapsed.

Isaacs concluded his opening address by referring to Wright's journey to Paris and New York and the extradition proceedings. His barb was the telegram from Wright's wife that everything looked bad. He sat down at 4.30 p.m. The opening took all of the first day. Isaacs had skilfully set the scene. He had seized the initiative. What seemed to have been a complex case had been simply but expertly presented, albeit at some length. His legal team needed to plod through the relevant evidence, slowly and surely making the case against Wright.

The following day, Tuesday 12$^{th}$ January, was typical of the detailed evidence. William Boustred, a clerk of the Joint Stock Registry at Somerset House, produced the official files on the companies involved and was taken through them by Horace Avory. The records detailed the establishment of the relevant companies and particularly the share holdings and remuneration of Wright and his powers to deal with company matters. The witness also dealt with some of the transfers between the companies.

Edgar Waterlow of Waterlow & Sons gave evidence of the printing and posting to shareholders of the balance sheet and directors' report, and the handwritten alterations made on the proof sheets for 1899 and similarly for 1900. The prosecution intent was to show Wright's hand on every aspect.

George Alexander, manager for J.W. Yickers, an advertising agency, gave evidence that on instructions and a cheque from Whitaker Wright, he arranged payments to some forty of fifty newspaper reporters for covering the annual general meetings of Globe in 1899 and 1900. There was laughter in the court when he stated that payment was in proportion to the length of their report. And even more laughter when he explained that he also got a commission from the newspapers. Again, it demonstrated Wright's involvement in every detail.

Mr. H.L. Peppercora, managing clerk to the late Lord Dufferin's solicitors, produced a letter dated 19$^{th}$ October 1899 from Wright to Lord Dufferin enclosing the substance of what was to be said at the 1899 annual meeting. He also produced the written-out speech of Lord Dufferin with alterations made in Wright's handwriting. He produced notes of a speech for the meeting on 17$^{th}$ December 1900. Again, there were alterations made in Wright's handwriting. Peppercora produced correspondence from Wright to Lord Dufferin representing the success of the company at various times. It was yet another example that Wright's hand was everywhere in the process.

Three witnesses were then produced to show that shares had been bought on the strength of the reports and statements made at the two annual meetings. Ben Nicholson of Gosport stated that following the 1899 meeting, he bought a further 1,200 shares in London & Globe. The next year, he received the annual report and read the statement made by Wright that over a million pounds had been written off for depreciation during the previous year and that the list of assets had been marked down as low as possible. He then bought a further 1,000 shares. Cross-examined, Nicholson accepted he had received a substantial dividend on the amalgamation of the first London & Globe and West Australian Exploring. He also accepted that Lord Dufferin had referred in his 1899 speech to the many contingencies that might affect the share market and the inevitably speculative character of investments that paid high dividends. The witness confirmed that he had responded to a circular sent out by Mr. Flower inviting subscription to the prosecution committee and had given written evidence in support of the application to prosecute. Mr. A.E. Flowers of Portsmouth, incidentally pointing out that he was not the same Mr. Flower who led the prosecuting committee, gave evidence of his purchase of shares after the 1899 meeting and his subscription of one guinea to the prosecution fund. Mr. J. Millard of Bromley, Kent, also stated that he had bought shares after both meetings. He confirmed that he had written to the Attorney General. Walton, on Wright's behalf, tried to elicit the witnesses' acceptance that share purchase was speculative as emphasised by Lord Dufferin in his annual speeches. However, these witnesses showed that shareholders had been induced to purchase further shares in reliance on London & Globe's annual statements and what was said at the annual meetings. Their evidence demonstrated that the intent to induce either retention or purchase of company shares had resulted in actual transactions.

Charles Bind, manager of Hotel Binda in Paris, gave evidence of Wright's stay in Paris in late February and early March 1903. He confirmed that Wright had not attempted to conceal his identity and that he and his valet, Bishop, had signed the hotel register in their correct names. Mr. Ganglofi, manager of the Paris office of the steamship line for La Lorraine confirmed the bookings in the name of Andreone but that the boat list had corrected the names of Mr. J.W. Wright and Miss F. Brown. He could not remember seeing Wright. The Judge intervened to question if he noticed the lady. It provoked laughter in the court. Walton was privately annoyed at this kind of evidence. It had little to do with the charges but was, of course, intended to paint his client in a poor light. The Judge, he felt, was not helping his client by invoking some mirth.

Finally that day, William Harding, clerk to the brokers, Bobarts, Lubbock & Co, gave details about bank credit arrangements for the purchase of shares by Standard Exploration as authorised by Whitaker Wright. It was clear from that day's evidence that the prosecution was steadily building its case particularly showing Whitaker Wright's presence in all matters.

It was continued on the morning of Wednesday 13$^{th}$ January when witnesses from several joint stock banks detailed certain transactions. All the evidence was that it was Wright who had made all the arrangements for loans, transfer of funds and the other financial aspects. But the main witness over the remainder of Wednesday and throughout much of Thursday of this first week was Arthur Russell, the senior examiner of the Official Receiver in Companies. He had charge of the London & Globe and Standard Exploration liquidations. This was the bulk of the evidence about the transactions undertaken by Whitaker Wright in and around the preparation of the two balance sheets.

Russell detailed the setting up of the companies, their directors and the balance sheets of 1899 and 1900. It was a laborious examination. All of Isaacs' ability and patience as an advocate was required. All of the documentary evidence had to be put before the court in absolute detail. The solicitors behind Isaacs were swamped in a mass of ledgers and tin boxes and documents in different states of preservation. There was a constant turning over of papers and hunting after documents. A constant buzz of reference went on while the witness gave his evidence. The sub-current of interruption was unavoidable but Isaacs remained calm and imperturbable. He threaded his way through the perplexing details, never suffering himself to be put out of stride either by the multitude of suggestions from his own side or from the interruptions of the Judge or from the challenges of the defence. Arthur Russell was also equal to the task. He knew the paperwork and he knew his job. He made an excellent and steady witness.

Russell gave evidence about the make-up of the 1899 balance sheet. He referred to the International Copper Corporation, in which London & Globe held shares, and the previous sale of their property to Caledonian Copper. The Judge asked if the witness knew what the property was and if anyone had ever seen it. This provoked a spat between the Judge and Walton. Walton objected to this as there was no complaint about this aspect of the balance sheet. The Judge said he wanted to get to the truth of the matter and Walton retorted that this was a criminal trial, not an inquiry. Walton remarked that His Lordship had already made the gravest suggestions as to International Copper which were calculated to prejudice the case. Justice Bigham considered the evidence relevant. Walton said he would ask for an adjournment if necessary and Bigham said if there was any chance of prejudice he would give Walton the opportunity for making it. It was a bad sign of the attitude of the Judge and there was little that Walton could do but complain.

Russell continued his evidence about the transactions that made up the 1899 balance sheet. The Judge asked the jury if they understood the transactions and the jury intimated they did not. It was not unexpected that they should become lost in the detail. Bigham did his best to explain. The witness detailed the share and loan arrangements that made were undertaken shortly before the date of the 1899 balance sheet and what had occurred in the days afterwards. He referred to the lack of any director involvement in the arrangements.

Isaacs then sought to show what the London & Globe's position if the 1900 balance sheet had been made up to $30^{th}$ September and not to $5^{th}$ December and to show how much more unsatisfactory it was. Russell stated that a loss of more than £1,000,000 would have been shown. He said that the balance sheet showed £2,332,000 for the shares held in other companies. However, the trading value of these shares was much lower at the time. There was great overvaluation. Isaacs gave illustrations. Standard Exploration shares were valued at over twenty shillings but trading at less than ten shillings. British America shares were valued at nearly nineteen shillings but were trading at only fourteen shillings.

The witness then dealt with London & Globe's liability to its brokers for the Lake View share speculation in December 1900, its transfer to Standard Exploration and then the retransfer to London & Globe. He referred to the apparent value of the assets held in other companies such as Victoria Gold Estates and Columbia Kootenay, although these properties had largely been sold, and the value of anticipated sums which London & Globe would have realised on the issue of shares in other companies when they were floated. The amount shown in the heading of 'depreciation' in the balance sheet had included significant losses in share dealings. The heading would imply that London & Globe still owned the shares but that they had merely depreciated in value whereas the shares had actually been sold at a loss. Isaacs contended that it was so as not to disclose to shareholders what was being done. Russell stated that the items £8,161 British American, £37,759 Nickel Corporation, £48,066 Standard Exploration and £5,416 Caledonian Copper shares were losses on share transactions which had been closed. It would make £920,000 which was loss and not depreciation. The Judge asked what Wright had said about what had been written off for depreciation. Isaacs replied that he had said over £1,000,000. It was part of the prosecution's case that Wright had omitted informing shareholders of the losses and implying only that the value of the shares had depreciated. Walton intervened to state the issue was whether, taking Wright's speech as a whole, the figure indicated depreciation or loss and depreciation.

Another spat between Bigham and Walton ensued after Russell had given details of the losses to the creditors. Walton argued that the evidence was immaterial as the assets were sold at breaking prices after the collapse of the companies. He argued that these details had nothing to do with the balance sheets or Wright's statements. But the Judge allowed the evidence. It was another example of the Judge's view and his determination that absolutely everything about the defendant's conduct would be revealed.

Next day, Walton had the opportunity to cross-examine. Russell accepted that Wright had actually been a creditor of London & Globe at its collapse and after the huge losses at the end of 1899, Wright advanced the company some £473,000 of which £100,000 had been in Consols. Russell accepted that his only challenge to the 1899 balance sheet was the £359,000 received from Standard Exploration. He accepted that Wright, as managing director, had powers to borrow money and that, given the number of share transactions, it might have been impossible to authorise every borrowing or other transaction in advance. In essence, there was little wrong with the 1899 balance sheet. There was a view that the prosecution had considered the need for its inclusion and to show its falsity in some way to demonstrate that shareholders had relied on its contents as there might be some doubt of the similar reliance of shareholders a year later, given the few days between the publication of the 1900 balance sheet and the collapse of

London & Globe. On the 1900 balance sheet, Walton raised the issue of share valuation with the witness. Another spat between Walton and the Judge followed. Walton stated the view of London & Globe was that the market value was no criterion of true value. The Judge had never heard of such a thing to which Walton considered His Lordship's experience was limited and that there were scores of companies that did it.

Walton made no attempt to discredit Russell. He sought to deflect the most telling aspects. In reality there was little to challenge. However, there could be other explanations, other reasons and accordingly other interpretations for the dealings and transactions. Russell stuck very simply to the facts. He maintained his evidence. He would not be greatly moved. He maintained, for example, that the shares in three companies ought not to have been brought into the assets. East Le Roi, West Le Roi and Columbia paid over purchase moneys to the old companies which ought to have been allotted to their shareholders but all the money was sent to London & Globe and to British America. Walton had done his best and did not want to make more of the evidence. He knew that both he and Isaacs would use it in their closing speeches, giving their different interpretations.

There was surprise recall of Nicholson who was obliged to state that he made a mistake about the time when he bought his shares. Walton sought to make some capital out of the errors particularly that he could not have relied on what Wright had said at the 1900 London & Globe annual meeting. But Isaacs countered by asking the witness to confirm that he had not sold any shares in reliance on the Wright statement. Then Frederick Davey, from the Official Receiver's office, gave evidence about British America and its dealings with London & Globe. Every fact had to be given although there was little between the parties about what had actually happened. Indeed, Walton would have readily conceded much of the evidence. Its steady delivery did the defendant no good. It was a drip, drip process. But it continued on Friday 15th January as various witnesses gave details about the share transactions. These were brokers who dealt with the relevant transactions. Dr. Richardson from the Stock Exchange gave evidence about share prices and the company secretary of London & Globe produced the company's records and minutes.

Finally, Henry Malcolm was called. He had been the London & Globe accountant who had taken over from Worters on 31$^{st}$ October 1900 and who had previously acted as Wright's clerk in his private affairs. He was the last witness of this first week and continued his evidence on the Monday of the following week. Malcolm was examined by Horace Avory. Although called by the prosecution, Malcolm's loyalty to Wright was evident from the start. So much so that Avory sought to have the Judge treat him as a hostile witness thereby allowing a different form of questioning in a more interrogatory style. But the Judge declined. Initially, he was being asked to confirm the entries for the share dealings in the company's records and the basis for the preparation of the 1900 balance sheet. But it was on the issue of Wright's involvement that the witness and the barrister significantly clashed. Avory wanted Malcolm to admit that he had acted completely on Wright's instructions in all these matters and Malcolm simply refused to concede. It was a constant battle as Avory went through each transaction and entry. Malcolm would agree to some Wright involvement but also pointed to other directors, members of staff and the auditors. Much was made of the entries concerning the valuation of the shares of the newly created Loddon Valley and Moorlort companies. Walton, in his cross-examination of the witness, was able to have someone with some sympathy but it was lost in a welter of explanations about paper transactions with the Judge frequently intervening. Two further witnesses from the accountants' department of London & Globe also gave other details. The prosecution was determined that every last fact on which they wished to rely was before the court.

To round off his case, Isaacs presented evidence about the issue of the summons and the warrant for Wright's arrest, the police work in ascertaining Wright's whereabouts together with his New York arrest. The relevant telegrams were produced. Mr. Barnes, the senior officer of the Official Receiver, also gave evidence about his role in obtaining the order to prosecute. He accepted, in answer to Walton, that he had not accepted Wright's offer to return voluntarily to England if the extradition proceedings were dropped.

The prosecution had methodically and steadily presented its case over the course of six days. Isaacs and his team had skilfully arranged for a complex case to be straightforwardly given. It had been slow and generally unspectacular but entirely thorough. As the prosecution witnesses had given their evidence, it was clear that no element had been forgotten and to Wright it sounded like a series of doors being closed. His basic layers of defence had been peeled back. Worst of all had been the attitude of the Judge. He had frequently interrupted often in a jocular manner to the apparent prejudice of the defendant. Walton had complained in vain. It was a grim picture but now it was Wright's turn.

# CHAPTER 12

## Making the Defence

Whitaker Wright had sat through the prosecution case with an unusual mixture of intensity and relaxation. He had heard virtually the same evidence at his public examination. Tedium naturally set in until the witness, or the Judge, or Isaacs would a make point that had stirred him. There would be his occasional comment with some brief, quiet but audible words cutting into the proceedings, loud enough for the Judge to hear but without seeming to interrupt. There were flurries of activity as he searched through the array of papers that covered his table. There was nothing that was new and there was nothing that came as any surprise. It was a recipe for almost indifference. He knew that his counsel would barely challenge the facts, only seek some different interpretation of them.

He would arrive early at the court and go to the room which had been set aside for his use within its precincts. It was available for his frequent legal consultations, his peace and comfort. This was the civil side of the judiciary. There were no cells here. In any event, he was on bail with complete freedom of movement. There was a legal consultation every morning before the court began and every afternoon after the court rose. He would have lunch in the room when he was largely left on his own. Each evening he dined with John Eyre usually until midnight before he retired to the flat at

Whitehall Court.

The defence strategy was based on more than an expectation for an acquittal. He and the team knew the bias that could not be avoided and the Judge was increasingly displaying an antagonistic disposition. But there was a good prospect of an undecided jury. The complexity of the case might lead to a division of opinion and a lack of unanimity. There might even be the brave view of a few that would support Wright's case. It would only take one dissenter to scupper the prosecution. All twelve jurymen needed to find guilt. Above all, the defence needed to counter the bad publicity over the losses, the wealthy lifestyle and the flight from justice. Accordingly, their evidence had to concentrate on Wright's successes and attempts to save the company and its shareholders and creditors from loss. He had to be portrayed as someone who had been equally ruined through no fault of his own. He had to be presented as someone of standing and experience who had done nothing that was not to the credit of the company or something that was not usual business practice. Plausible explanations were required to the most relevant of the transactions. It was a formidable task. Walton now had the opportunity to paint a different picture and to present an entirely different side of his client and his actions.

On Tuesday 19th January, Whitaker Wright went into the witness box. He arrayed his papers on its edge and asked for some water. Walton told the Judge that his client had been ill. The Judge arranged for a chair but Wright preferred to stand. He was composed but keen to proceed. Walton carefully took Wright through the history. He started with his foundation of Western Australian Exploring and the original London & Globe, then their amalgamation and then the creation of British America and Standard Exploration. Wright emphasised the apparent separate conduct of each company. He emphasised the successes, particularly share issues and dividends paid by Ivanhoe and Lake View. He spoke of the involvement of the directors and the roles of the accountants and auditors. It was an attempt to show that he was not solely in charge.

He went through the 1899 balance sheet. He contended that the late transactions had simply been to show the true position of the company which required its assets to be gathered together at the end of its financial year. The transactions between the various companies were simply to give effect to that objective. As to the chairman's address to the annual meeting, he confirmed that notes were given by him to Lord Dufferin but he emphasised that the chairman could make alterations and object. He believed that it was common practice in the city for the managing director to provide the information for his chairman.

In regard to the 1900 balance sheet, Wright maintained that it was prepared by the accountant and not submitted to him before it was completed. Some of Wright's instructions were carried out. The shares had been valued as in previous years. Shares bought during the year were valued at cost. As they were bought at different times, the accountant added up the totals and divided by the number of shares, giving an average price. In his large experience, this was the valuation method both in America and Europe. The auditors had accepted the method. He maintained that he had not suggested any variation in the balance sheet. Wright maintained that he was not an accountant and it was the company accountants who were responsible for the balance sheet. As to his speech at the annual meeting of 1900, he maintained that he had not intended to misrepresent the position by referring only to depreciation. The figures included losses and depreciation. The various transactions between London & Globe and Standard Exploration were because they operated one account and it was intended to conceal the speculative share operation from those who were trying to ruin the plan. There was no intention to mislead shareholders. The directors knew what was happening. He maintained that creation of the Loddon Valley and Moorloot companies was in the interests of London & Globe but that subsequently the Official Receiver got nothing like the shares were worth. He had attempted a reconstruction scheme but a hostile petition for compulsory winding up had prevented its implementation.

As to his apparent flight, he had stayed two years in the country and gave evidence in support of an action against certain jobbers and brokers. In 1903, he had gone to Paris on business and not learned of the prosecution summons until 4$^{th}$ March. He had not given a false name to travel to New York. A friend, Mr. Andreone, had simply obtained a discount as the shipping people were Germans and Italians. When in New York, he had offered to return voluntarily but it was refused. After the judgment of the United States Court, he had returned voluntarily.

It had been a confident albeit tame performance by Wright. He was not addressing a public meeting where he was at his rhetorical best and not at a board meeting where he used his persuasion, neither was he dealing with staff where his hectoring might win. It was not his usual forum and his words were necessarily limited to what he was asked. It was his version of events. He had done his best. It was what Walton wanted. He wished to present his client as a serious and sober man, as someone who had endeavoured to serve his companies and as a person of quiet resolve and integrity.

Wright's cross-examination began that afternoon. It was the critical point of the trial. The ordeal with Isaacs would present great problems for him. He knew the questions would be directed with precision and there was no room to hide. There was a contrast between the large figure of Wright apparently self-possessed and the pale, somewhat slender figure of Isaacs. Isaacs' style was of calm and almost dispassionate concentration on his task. He asked his questions courteously but incisively. He did not seek to brow-beat or antagonise the witness. The answers would either evade the issue or confirm the fact. It did not matter, therefore, that the witness refused to answer the question. It would look like evasion and provide confirmation of Isaac's contention. Either way he would succeed. The examination was relentless as Isaacs took Wright through the whole story.

Isaacs began with the departure of Wright from England on the verge of the decision to allow the prosecution. There was the timing of his trip to Paris and then to New York, there was the telegram from his wife that all appeared lost, there was the £500 via Florence Brown, there were the names for the tickets. Wright asserted that he had gone to Paris after the House of Commons debate which had indicated that a prosecution would not be undertaken. The telegram was the work of a nervous woman and he had already arranged to leave France before he had received it. The dates were a coincidence. He had not run away. Wright had fallen into the trap of being dishonest from the outset. The answers appeared obviously untruthful. Isaacs had immediately wrong-footed the defendant.

Isaacs then sought to show Wright's domination of his companies and his sole responsibility for what had occurred. Isaacs asserted that Wright had received all the money as chairman of one company, from himself as chairman of another company. Wright responded that he did not like that way of putting it and added, amid some laughter, that the money was paid by one company to another. Isaacs took him through the evidence to show that he was the man in control of the company. Wright attempted to assert that it was Lord Loch who wanted to have the liquid assets at year end and hence the need for the transactions. It looked a pathetic response and a straight attempt to shift responsibility.

He turned to the 1899 balance sheet and the entry of £500,000 in cash at the bank. Isaacs asked him if the object was to be able to say that his profits were in cash. Wright replied that it was nothing of the kind and that it was put in to show that they had good substantial liquid assets. After further questions, Wright stated that Isaacs would never get him to the crack of doom to admit that there was anything wrong with the 1899 balance sheet. Isaacs asked if he thought that the shareholders would be more impressed with the statement that the directors aimed to make the company a ten per cent dividend when they saw the balance in cash. The inference was that the dividend would not have been sustainable without the cash position in the balance sheet. Wright stated that he was not responsible for the inference that shareholders might draw.

Isaacs asked if Lord Dufferin said at the annual meeting that this policy would be appreciated by the genuine investor who would be able to sleep without thinking of the safety of his investments. There was laughter in the court. Wright said that was not the passage he wanted him to read. He asked if it was true that Wright had said at the meeting that if the market value of the shares was less than cost, they were marked down to market value. Wright said that the auditors had proposed it but it was not done. On being pressed, Wright conceded that his words were not strictly correct. He declared that if you go to any city meeting and answer a hundred questions, it was not easy to choose your words. The London & Globe profit shown was after deducting £500,000 for market value. Wright said that it was a slip of the tongue. Isaacs asked if he had written to Lord Dufferin; Wright said that it was perfectly straight and fair. Wright further accepted that the word 'market' ought not to have been used. The court adjourned for the day. Isaacs had already begun to damage Wright's credibility.

Wright arrived early the next day as usual and took his seat at his table. He was anxious to proceed. It had been a lonely time. In the middle of a cross-examination, he had been unable to consult any of his legal team or talk to anyone connected with the case. His usual morning legal consultation had been replaced by simple courtesies and greetings. On taking his seat, Mr. Justice Bigham addressed the court. He desired to say that daily, he received anonymous communications of a most abusive kind about this case. He would not have taken notice of such communications had he not reason to believe that attempts had recently been made in other directions of a more serious character to interfere with the course of justice. He desired to publicly warn that persons guilty of such conduct made themselves liable for very serious consequences. He did not elaborate but the inference was that some attempt had been made to influence the jury either by bribery or threat. It was an unsavoury turn in already tense and dramatic proceedings.

The cross-examination resumed. The maze of figures continued. The share transactions between the three companies during 1899 and 1900 were detailed to Wright, laced with the constant suggestion that they were simply to boost the apparent wealth of any one of the companies at any one time. Wright sought to give some explanations but retreated, in many cases, to an apparent ignorance. It was a matter for the accountants or the book-keepers. He could not remember the precise dates. He did not know when a transaction was really a purchase and sale, it ought to be recorded in the minutes. Ironically, he asked Isaacs if he wanted him to be chairman and secretary and everything. Isaacs responded that he thought that he was quite enough. It was a cold and incisive riposte. Isaacs was the master of any exchange with a witness.

Wright fought to give a reason for every transaction and to maintain that it was appropriate. Isaacs referred to a deal in exchange shares between Standard Exploration and British America. Wright asserted that Standard Exploration could have demanded cash but it would not have been expedient. The Judge intervened to refer to London & Globe's manipulation of the figures provoking the court again to laughter. Walton rose. The explanation was perfectly clear and not ridiculous. The Judge said that it was better that his impressions should be made known in order for Mr. Walton and Mr. Wright to meet his difficulties. Walton protested against eliciting merriment from the gallery by the Judge as it tended to prejudice the jury. The Judge explained to the jury that they were concerned with the effect produced on the London & Globe's account, not that on British America. The Judge's presence was becoming even more hostile to the defendant's cause. Wright conceded that the 1899 balance sheet had been shown to him before publication and that he had given instructions about it, and that when it had been drawn up according to those instructions he had approved it. He maintained that he was only one of the people who would consider it after it had been printed but in the only copy of the draft produced at the trial, the corrections were all in his handwriting.

The 1900 balance sheet was then at issue. Questioned about the loss of £750,000 on Lake View shares, Wright accepted that he did not wish to disclose the true state of affairs with regard to every operation of the market. Isaacs stated that there was no reference to this loss at the meeting but Wright said that it appeared in the figures. The Judge intervened to enquire about the postponement of the issue of the balance sheet from 30$^{th}$ September to 5$^{th}$ December. It appeared to him that some £1,200,000 in securities was created by London & Globe. Wright said it was issued not created. The Judge insisted that they were not in existence on 30$^{th}$ September and that in their present form they were created and a balance sheet of an extremely satisfactory appearance was produced. Wright was forced to agree. But he regarded it grossly inaccurate to accept the Judge's assertion that London & Globe had been insolvent at 30$^{th}$ September. He could not admit that there were insufficient assets at that time to meet its liabilities to creditors.

Wright accepted that he had made a speech at the 1900 annual meeting and in view of rumours about London & Globe's position, he had been anxious to put the best face on the company's affairs. He accepted that the creditors were given as £570,000 and the assets at £2,700,000 and that the largest item of that was the value of the shares at £2,332,000 in sundry companies. Isaacs put to him that Wright had said that over £1,000,000 had been written off for depreciation. He asked if that was an untrue. Wright would not admit it. He accepted that he should have said for loss and depreciation and that it was an extempore utterance. Isaacs said that, as it stood, the statement was untrue. He asked Wright to confirm his statement at the meeting that the Lake View shares had been marked down as low as possible, and therefore had they been marked down to a penny? Wright admitted that the sum of £500,000 had not been taken into account. Isaacs goaded him and asked if he had made a slip of the tongue. Wright was forced to agree but declared that he was not an accountant. The Judge said that there must be an answer. Isaacs put it to Wright that £500,000 had been put back into the assets. Wright accepted that the sum had been put back. Isaacs replied that the effect was therefore to write up the value of the assets. Wright could not admit it. The Judge again demanded an answer. Wright fell back on the assertion that they had taken the Baker Street and Waterloo at par. Isaacs then referred to the report of the meeting which Wright had edited to the extent of putting in 'hear, hears' but not correcting the slip of the tongue. Wright said his time was absorbed, that the manager or the secretary ought to have done it, that he had to do everybody's work in the company. The share valuations for the purposes of the 1900 balance sheet were attacked by Isaacs. Wright continued to maintain that the correct valuation had been given even if the price of the share was not that reflected on the Stock Market at the time. He fell back on the accountants' apparent role and his lack of knowledge. His evidence became increasingly untenable. His statements at the annual meeting were exposed as giving a different impression from the accounting realities. It was entirely damaging to Wright's defence.

The same vigour of the cross-examination continued the next morning. Isaac's son had sat in the public gallery to watch his father's brilliant and devastating performance. He likened Wright to a bewildered and angry bull. He saw as question after question went home like darts deep into his shoulder. Wright seemed to back away the front of the box with lowered head, as if to put himself out of range of his too nimble enemy. It was the almost dispassionate matador, pale and slender, continually teasing the bull with the cloak of a question only to remove it to expose the paucity of the answer. Isaacs had demolished the defence. Wright's evidence had been reduced to implausibility and evasion. Wright had wilted under the relentless questions. There had been no escape from the consequences of his actions.

Rufus Isaacs then closed his case. He spoke the rest of that Thursday and all of the Friday. He had nothing to withdraw from what he had said in opening. Nothing had been disproved. Indeed

Wright had accepted, conceded or admitted virtually every fact. He had convicted himself. It was essentially the combination of what had been contrived to present the balance sheets and what had been said at the annual meetings that had created the false nature of Wright's actions. He had admitted that the 1900 balance sheet concealed the true nature of London & Globe's affairs. Wright had been heavily engaged in share dealing from the autumn of 1899 through to December 1900 involving colossal losses, yet his manipulation of the figures appeared to show the company had significant assets over its liabilities. Within eleven days, the company had come to grief with creditors for two million pounds who got a shilling in the pound and might get another sixpence, and not a penny for the shareholders. He asserted that nothing could be more pregnant with meaning. Wright had made many misrepresentations, omissions, slips of the tongue and uncorrected statements. He portrayed Wright as the alchemist who could turn paper into gold. He used the example of the division of Victoria Gold Estates into the two companies of Loddon Valley and Moorloot Estates to illustrate the methods. Continually, he emphasised Wright's directing hand on everything that went on at London & Globe and at the related companies. Isaacs covered the whole ground, carefully retelling the history of the events and their consequences. It was his sober and masterful best. The court adjourned on the Friday afternoon, giving Lawson Walton the weekend to prepare his closing speech. He was entitled to the last word as only the defendant had given evidence. It was the last opportunity to provide any defence for Whitaker Wright.

Wright spent a quiet weekend at Lower House with his family. His wife retained a constant belief in her husband and the young Whitaker an admiration for his father. Neither would be deterred in their support. Whitaker Wright dined and read. He walked about Lea Park and around the lakes and landscapes that he had created. He looked at the virtually completed but now empty mansion he had built. He reflected on what he had accomplished and on what he had lost. He gazed away to the long, low line of the North Downs, then turned to look across the magnificent slopes of Hindhead Common with Beacon Hill standing out as an ironic reminder to his predicament. It was idyllic. It was peaceful. It was the home he had wanted. He talked to the agricultural workers going about their farming tasks. The locals overwhelmingly believed that their lord of the manor would be acquitted and had started on preparations for his triumphal return. He had been very good to all of them, many in hard times, and it was their opportunity to respond. He rested and relaxed. It was good to be with his family. And there was a gentle farewell from his wife that Sunday evening. She expressed confidence of his early return during the week after the ordeal was over. He took the train back to London. He told the Witley station master that he was as innocent as a new-born babe. It was malice on the part of competitors that had placed him in the current position. He owed no man anything and he feared no man as he had never done anyone any injury.

Lawson Watson gave his closing speech on the Monday morning. It was the last opportunity for the defence to convince the jury that Wright should be acquitted. He was as masterful as Isaacs with far less material with which to work. He started with an attack on the prosecution motives. He doubted whether he had ever met a case where the prosecution had been conducted with such marked vindictiveness. The defendant was entitled to a presumption of innocence but he had been subjected in the witness box to innuendoes of every kind of falsehood and misrepresentation. When he hesitated in order to give accurately his own state of mind he was said to be wriggling. The jury should rid themselves of these impressions. He should not have been surprised at the attitude of the prosecution if there had been charges of robbing the shareholders or that he had built up his own fortune out of the calamities of others. The prosecution ought to have remembered that they represented, not private malevolence, but the dignified and indulgent impartiality of the Crown.

Mr. Whitaker Wright had been the only one charged. He rhetorically enquired the whereabouts of the other directors. Lord Dufferin and Lord Loch were no longer alive. Had they been living, he wondered if a prosecution would have dared suggest the duplicity they had suggested on the part of Wright who was selected as a vicarious expiation to wipe out the offences that the prosecution asked them to believe had been committed against commercial morality in the City of London. He asked why the other directors and the auditor had been left out. They ought, at least, to be standing in the box as witnesses, anxious as they must have been to vindicate themselves. His client did not adopt this line on his own judgment but on that of his colleagues who collectively could not be believed to be guilty of the falsehoods charged.

The case was stale. Years had elapsed. After the collapse of London & Globe, Whitaker Wright had submitted a scheme of reconstruction but that did not commend it to some persons and the winding-up was made compulsory. The following public examination provided the information on which the prosecution was now founded. An action was brought by London & Globe against certain jobbers and he wondered, if the case had been successful, would they have ever heard of this prosecution? The Attorney General had refused sanction to prosecute at public expense. Mr. John Flower then sent circulars to induce subscription for a prosecution and asked if they had been misled. They got the evidence of three shareholders out of 10,000 and one stockbroker. It was a miserable and abortive result. He went through the witnesses alleged to have relied on Wright. Mr. Nicholson never acted on the balance sheet, Mr. Flower had said he had increased his holding because he had been promised at a meeting, not by Wright, but someone else, and the stockbroker saw nothing in the balance sheet to make him discontinue acting for London & Globe. The effort to show that some persons had been defrauded had failed. He reminded the court that the application before Mr. Justice Buckley to grant leave for a prosecution had been made on the basis of affidavits, not statements. Wright had not tried to flee from justice. No prosecution had been brought in the two years that he was in the country. A man as well-known as Whitaker Wright could be easily traced. Even if it were true, could they wonder that he almost despaired of getting justice in this country? Unguarded comments had been made in the privilege of the House of Commons. Nevertheless, Walton told them that he retained his faith in the impartiality of the British jury.

He took them through the history. Wright had founded the new London & Globe and its shareholders got their capital back five times over. British America and Standard Exploration had separate boards though one staff of clerks. The books were in the charge of Mr. Worters and had been well kept. There was not one scrap of evidence that Wright had ever interfered with the transactions. It was not Wright's duty to record the board's minutes, that was the duty of Mr. Dealtry who was an honourable man. The auditors framed the minutes for the purpose of the directors' sanctioning of certain transactions. It was not a mere formality for honourable men like

Lord Dufferin.

Wright had written to Lord Dufferin in the summer of 1900 to suggest a ten per cent dividend and a month later British America a like dividend. Wright had hoped that by that time the West Le Roi issue would have taken place. Wright had sold his shares to make provision for his family, not because he had lost faith in the company. He had made money available to the company in 1899 and had lost £300,000 or £400,000 trying to help it. That was the character of the man. He declared that the 1899 balance sheet was not substantially challenged. The item 'cash at bankers' had been attacked. It was a liquid asset designed to show that the company was in a strong position and that it could command such a sum. Banks could call in their loans for a similar purpose. The directors could write a cheque for that sum. The Judge intervened to doubt that but said that it was not material. Walton ignored him and pressed on. The operations with Standard Exploration were entirely legitimate. There were no drawbacks for either company. Lord Loch and the other directors had the means to satisfy themselves about the position.

He turned to the issue of the valuation of the shares. They were dealing in commodities of extreme fluctuations. Thus market value was out of the questions. They struck an average cost and therefore their value as a market value. It was not the market value of the day but an average over the whole period. This was the market value term that Wright had used in his letter to Lord Dufferin. As to the issue of the losses not being mentioned in respect of the depreciation, it was a slip of the tongue by Wright, an obvious blunder; neither Lord Dufferin nor the shareholders were misled.

Walton carefully went through the events leading to the 1900 balance sheet and the annual meeting of London & Globe. He maintained that Wright was entitled to postpone the meeting in the interests of both shareholders and creditors. If there were prospects of improvement, he was bound in duty to postpone it. Any intelligent shareholder would have seen it desirable first to complete certain matters of business before the meeting. There was the Baker Street & Waterloo Railway that Wright thought might be realised as an investment. There followed the establishment of the subsidiary companies of Victoria Gold Estates. The Judge intervened, commenting that they were brought into the balance sheet. Walton retorted that London & Globe was entitled to say it was worth the money. These subsidiary companies of Loddon Valley and Moorloot owned a valley rich in gold. In any event, it was the board of Victoria Gold that made the arrangements to issue the shares in the companies. In no sense was Wright responsible. Wright was justified, however, in taking these shares on their face value on the evidence. The London & Globe annual meeting was postponed for the purpose of realising outstanding assets and Wright's action was amply vindicated. It was said that London & Globe ought not to have put value on Columbian Proprietary as the shares had not been issued but it was for the prosecution to prove the worthlessness which they alleged.

Next he would investigate the genesis of the 1900 balance sheet. The witnesses had told the story of the preparation and it was clear that the managing director would not view it until it was nearly complete, but before that it came to the auditor. The defendant was no more responsible than the auditor or Mr. Malcolm or than other directors. There was no discussion or suggested alteration. What were the misrepresentations relied on? Firstly, there was no statement as to the mode of valuation of the assets. It was left out, no one knew why. Walton admitted that the expression 'securities held' was ambiguous as it gave no mention of date. But the auditors' certificate was there and it seemed they were responsible for the obscurity. The certificate showed that the word 'depreciation' was synonymous with loss. There was depreciation on the shares account in which differences were recorded whenever a loss was sustained. It was not for him to justify as a moralist all that was done in connection with the balance sheet; he only had to prove that no criminal motive or criminal liability could be affixed to the defendant. He referred to Wright's speech and maintained that the word 'depreciation' included loss. Wright had said that it had been the unpleasant duty to write off an enormous loss through depreciation. The correct figures for loss and depreciation had been given. There had been no attempt to make the balance sheet unduly favourable to the company. The conduct throughout showed a desire to do business honestly. The transfer of the speculation liability to Standard Exploration was to prevent wreckers having the knowledge that London & Globe was engaged in the operation with a syndicate to purchase Lake View shares. It was never suggested that this was not a legitimate operation. The Judge intervened to question the relevance. Walton said that if the transaction was right, it was necessary for London & Globe to do everything to make it complete and for that the transfer to Standard Exploration was necessary. The failure of London & Globe meant that assets were thrown onto the market at 'break-up' prices.

He finalised his speech with the critical issue. The main question was whether there was any intention on the part of Wright and his colleagues whom Walton declined to disassociate from him, to deceive or defraud persons whom it was their duty to serve. It was easy for a staff of accountants at the disposal of the liquidator to produce, after many months, a small sheaf of transactions, pickings from the bones of London & Globe that might form a meal for those who wished to found such a prosecution as this. He asked if anyone could conceive of a motive to defraud the shareholders. If they had not done what they did the company would have been brought down months before. If their object was to serve the shareholders, the jury could not find that their conduct was tainted with intentional fraud. Unless they could find that base motive, this huge superstructure of untruth should be brushed aside. The jury could not find conscious wickedness or intent to defraud. The defendant had been brought here by hue and cry. The jury had to decide on the evidence and not on prejudice. They should decide with independence and courage and bring in a general verdict of not guilty.

It was as much about representing Wright's feelings and beliefs as it was an attempt to secure an acquittal. It was full of explanation and emotion. It was an eloquent defence of his client's actions. Walton had represented Wright's case to the full. His purpose was to show that his client's actions had an alternative and entirely legitimate explanation and that his client had served the best interests of the company and its shareholders. He had made the defence and he waited for the Judge's summary and for the jury's verdict.

# CHAPTER 13

# Making the End

On Tuesday 26th January and the twelfth day of the trial, Mr. Justice Bigham proceeded with his summing up of the case. He congratulated the jury on having reached the final stage of an intricate and wearisome case. He thanked both counsels and said that he had not listened to speeches of more eloquence. He did not agree with Mr. Walton when he complained of the vindictiveness of the prosecution. He thought both sides had been conducted in a fair, proper and straightforward matter. He had been pestered with anonymous and ill-considered letters. He had been told that the jury had been subject to like impertinences but they should cast them out of their minds and consider the evidence.

The charge was in substance that of having issued two false and fraudulent balance sheets. He asked the jury to give a general verdict on the basis he would go through all of the twenty-six counts. In expressing his opinion he only wanted to guide their judgment. They must not let what he said over master their better judgment. It was for the prosecution to bring home the guilt of the defendant clearly and plainly. These were serious charges and they ought not to find the defendant guilty unless their minds were free from reasonable doubt. They must bring common sense to bear on the facts.

It had been said by Mr. Walton that a verdict of guilty would involve a similar verdict against Lord Loch and the late Lord Dufferin. It would do nothing of the kind. Their conduct was consistent with having made mistakes and been negligent in matters in which they were not as conversant as Mr. Whitaker Wright. It was said as a reproach to the prosecution that they had not called Mr. Leman, Mr. Macleay, General Gough. But it was open to the defence to call those witnesses. It had been said that the charge was stale but the criminal system imposed no fixed time a man could not be vexed by a prosecution. These were serious swipes at several of the defence arguments.

He went through the counts which dealt with each of the balance sheets and the speeches given at each of the annual meetings. The jury would have to consider if the defendant published the material, whether it was false, whether the defendant knew it was false, and did he publish it with the intent to deceive or defraud? He went through the evidence. He ploughed his diligent way through the two balance sheets, the innumerable transactions and the annual speeches. It was thorough, somewhat boring, but designed to indicate the full extent of the financial manipulations. Nowhere did he highlight any of the explanations or interruptions given by either side. It was pure facts. He ensured that the summing up was incapable of any appeal on the grounds of misdirection of the jury.

The Judge said that if a man committed fraud, motive was of no importance; only the character of the act was to be considered. The main argument of Whitaker Wright had been that he had no intention to defraud, only to save the company. The Judge was legally and correctly determined to ensure that the jury would not allow that route of escape. It was his actions, not his motive that proved intent. Nor was any regard to be paid to the defendant's social position. He was living in fine style and was a great man in the eyes of the world. The defendant had told them that when the company came to its end he found himself stranded with a mass of unmarketable securities. He meant, His Lordship supposed, that if the company had kept on its legs he would have been a rich man; but that was not a matter for consideration. He had deprived Wright of one of his principal and perhaps final arguments that he had acted for the best of reasons and not with any fraudulent intention. It also served to remind the jury of Wright's former wealth.

He referred to the decision of the Attorney General and to the subsequent decision of Mr. Justice Buckley to order the prosecution. He then referred to the defendant's visit to Paris and the telegrams. It might be said that the defendant's conduct was consistent with innocence and a desire to get rid of proceedings which in any case would be a terrible trial and anxiety. He would leave the jury to form their own opinion. He told them that where there was fair reason to doubt let them give the defendant the benefit of it.

Good, sound common sense said that a man must be proved guilty; but if the evidence brought home guilt let them not hesitate to say so, for it was important that commercial frauds should be exposed and punished. The trading reputation as a nation was of value and it would be a lamentable thing if frauds when exposed were not punished. If they said that he was not guilty, there was an end to the matter but if they found a verdict of guilty, he would like them to say whether there were any counts on which the evidence had not satisfied them. They should disregard counts nine and eighteen. They should retire and consider their verdict. It was midday.

It was a scrupulous summing up of the evidence but undertaken in such a manner that indicated the correct course for the jury. It was evident to Wright. His face had paled and palled during the address. His demeanour shifted to the ghastly and the pathetic with a shadow of doom plainly in his face. Throughout the Judge's summary, Wright had scribbled on a pad of paper in front of him. At the top were endless 'W's, underneath the Roman character 'VII' appeared over half the page and centred in the middle was the word 'intent' in capital letters. The rest of the pad was littered with large scrawled and black images. Walton had told him he faced seven years and he feared the worst. It loomed so large in his mind that his only outlet was to scrawl out the number developed from his own initials.

The jury retired and the court adjourned for lunch. After speaking to his counsel, Wright went down to the room reserved for his use. He had his lunch with his solicitor, George Lewis. Wright told Lewis that he hoped the jury might find a verdict of 'not guilty' and, if they did not do that, he certainly believed that they would disagree. It was all over bar the verdict. There was only the tension of waiting. And suddenly, they were told to return to the courtroom.

After lunch and then only sixty minutes of consideration, the jury indicated to the court official that they reached their verdict. It was a major surprise but an indicator of the likely result. At just after 3 p.m., the court re-convened. Lewis went back into court with Wright who asked him to come back to the consultation room with him afterwards. The jury returned and gave a verdict of guilty on all counts except the two the Judge had told them to disregard. They intimated that they desired to express an opinion. The Judge asked them if it was with reference to the verdict and the foreman replied that it was not. A paper was handed to the Judge who said that it was not necessary to refer to it. He handed it to Walton, saying he might affect what he was going to say.

Wright's counsel rose on behalf of his client. Walton first requested a stay of execution. Although he knew that it would not be granted, he said that it was his duty to make the application. He then put in mitigation on Wright's behalf. He said that Wright had a reputation as an honourable man. It was not suggested that he was actuated by motives of personal gain. He was a creditor of the Globe for £50,000 and had sustained serious losses. He asked His Lordship to accept an argument that perhaps had no strict relation to criminality. Though Wright wished to save the company he might still be within the section, but if his line of action was adopted to serve the interests of the company, the moral view of his conduct was very much moderated. His pleas were in vain.

Bigham told Wright that in his opinion the jury could have arrived at no other opinion than that which they had expressed in their verdict. He confessed that he could see nothing that in any way excused the crime of which he had been found guilty and he could not conceive a worse case than his under the sections of the Act of Parliament which defined the offence. He did not think that he had an option but to visit him with the severest punishment that Act permitted and that is that he should go into penal servitude for seven years. Wright stood cool and firm with his hands behind his back. All he could say was that he was innocent of any intent to deceive anyone. Wright listened attentively as the Judge thanked the jury and regretted that it was not in his power to remunerate them. He did relieve them of further jury service for the next seven years. Wright was then taken charge of by the tipstaff, Mr. John Dixon, and left the courtroom by a small door below the bench. It was a humiliation that he bore fortunately without any of his family being present.

Wright was taken by the tipstaff back to the consultation room where he was joined by his solicitor George Lewis, his great friend John Eyre, his former chief accountant George Worters and the assistant superintendent of the Royal courts of Justice, Mr. Smith. Wright then walked with Smith to the lavatory which was almost immediately opposite his room. He turned on the light and put his hand on the door. He said that he would not be a moment and Smith said he would wait.

Whitaker had always faced the immediate circumstances in his life. His determination had enabled him to be in control and allowed him to make his choices. He was tired and care-worn from the immediate case and the last few years. The exhilaration of his earlier years and the prosperity of his later ones had given way to remorseless and interminable efforts simply to exist. The recent years had been wasted time with little ultimately to show for all the strain and determination. His apparently advancing age, deteriorating health and limited financial resources gave little prospect of any quality of life that he relished. He knew that any appeal would not succeed. He knew that he would not survive much of the seven years imprisonment. The four months in Ludlow Street Jail had been intolerable. He had vowed never to serve one day of any sentence. There was only one alternative and he had already decided on that course.

He had prepared in his usual assiduous manner. He checked the revolver in his hip pocket. It was fully loaded. He cocked it and returned it to his pocket. It provided the added insurance of finality. The moment had come. There would not be another opportunity. He took out the small piece of folded paper from his waistcoat pocket and tipped the tiny amount of the crystal contents onto his tongue. He threw the paper into the bowl and pulled the lavatory chain. He went back with Smith into the consultation room.

When Smith and the tipstaff had left the room, Whitaker expressed amazement at the result. He asked if this was British justice. He repeated several times that he had never intentionally done anything wrong at all. He said that he was absolutely innocent of what had been charged against him. There was a silence in the room as his colleagues struggled to express any words. They were uneasy. A little later, he told them that he really thought that he was the most composed of all of them. He talked for a few minutes in regard to the question of an application for a new trial which they had previously decided should be made in the event of an adverse verdict. The basis was to be that there were issues about whether or not he had assented. He had agreed to do as he was advised.

He then thanked them for all that they had done for him. He moved towards the fire and added that everything that could have been done had been done. The table had not been cleared since lunch and Whitaker picked up a glass of whisky and water as he talked. He drank a little and smoked a cigar. John Eyre asked him if he should telephone Mrs. Wright but Whitaker told him that there was plenty of time for doing that. He took out his watch and chain and handed it to Eyre, saying that he had no use for them where he was going and that he should keep them for him. Eyre promised to keep them until they met again.

Whitaker walked to the armchair on the other side of the room. He asked Worters to give him another cigar. This was handed to him from his case on the table together with a lighted match. Whitaker took the match but then threw it to the ground, asking Worters to stamp it out. He breathed heavily and Lewis thought it was a reaction to the strain of the proceedings. The potassium cyanide had remained on his tongue and in his throat the whole time. He had been unable to swallow it all completely and the poison had only just begun to work. Whitaker slumped back into the armchair and appeared ill. Lewis went to the door to ask the tipstaff to get a doctor.

Mr. Oliver Atkey, the acting house physician at King's College Hospital, came within a few minutes. He saw him in the armchair, with a very dusky colour, breathing heavily and in a serious condition. Dr. Atkey smelled spirits on his breath. On the doctor's instructions, Whitaker was laid on the ground, his clothes loosened and the windows opened. The doctor initially thought that he was having a fit and told them that he had only moments to live. He died some fifteen minutes later without saying another word. It was 3.55 p.m.

At 4 p.m. Eyre telegraphed Wright's home and the news of his conviction was received by the son who had to tell his mother. She had loyally believed in his innocence. She cried that it was a gross injustice and fainted. She knew the implications. About an hour and half later, the news of his death was similarly conveyed. In the meantime, she had composed herself sufficiently to anticipate what had subsequently happened. She thanked God that he had escaped imprisonment. She had seen the devastating results in the health and well-being of her husband on his return from America and his period of incarceration. He had confided to her his dread of any further imprisonment. She regretted that they had ever seen England.

The news spread rapidly. His death was included in the late editions of the newspapers. It was a sensational end to the case that had gripped the public. Most believed that it was the strain of the proceedings that had caused his demise. But other suggestions were canvassed. It overshadowed the verdict itself. At 7.30 p.m. that evening, in the presence of PC Veale, Wright's servant, William Baxter from Whitehall Court, found the fully loaded and cocked revolver in his right-hand hip pocket. The significance was obvious. He carried a few other items including a signet ring, a purse containing some money and a tabloid. Wright's body was removed at 9 p.m. through the door that faced Clements Inn and taken to the Westminster mortuary. The next day, a post-mortem examination was undertaken.

The inquest was held on Thursday 28th January by Mr. J. Troutbeck, the Coroner for Westminster at the Horseferry Road Court. He sat with a jury. There was much public interest although given the size of the court, there was little space for them allowing for the attendance of those connected with the proceedings and the press. Muir represented the Wright family. The jury viewed the body in the mortuary attached to the court. Wright's son, Whitaker, of Lower House, Witley, identified his father and confirmed his father's age at fifty-eight years. He said he was a mining engineer and a mining chemist. He had last seen him on the Sunday.

George Lewis and John Eyre gave an account of Wright's actions and statements in the consultation room on the Tuesday afternoon. None had the slightest inkling of what Wright had intended to do. They spoke of his composure. During the trial they confirmed that Wright had never suggested doing anything to himself in the event of an adverse verdict. The court staff gave evidence. They had had no instructions to search him and the defendant had therefore not been searched. It was essentially a civil court with no system as they had in criminal courts. Even after conviction, the convicted man would not be searched until he reached prison. They never considered that the prisoner would harm himself. Muir commented that it was a civil court where such arrangements were not normally made. The personal items found on him were produced – a signet ring, a purse of money containing five sovereigns, a tabloid and the revolver. His son could not identify the gun but said that his father kept several pistols. It looked to be of American make. Dr. Atkey told the court of his attendance and stated that he had been unable to form an opinion as to the cause of death. His initial view was that Wright was having some kind of fit and a heart attack. He had not smelled any poison.

Dr. Froyberger, pathologist to the London County Council, gave evidence of his post-mortem examination carried out the day following Wright's death. The body was well nourished and the brain perfectly healthy. But both lungs were much engorged and enlarged. The heart was twice the normal size and very fatty. Every organ seemed to give off a penetrating smell of prussic acid. This was most marked in the stomach. He did not find in the contents of the stomach the residue of any capsule or tabloid. At the back of the tongue, there was a place where the mucous membrane was more corroded than in any other place and this suggested that the poisonous substance which was taken had remained there for some time before it was swallowed. In his opinion, the cause of death was suffocation in consequence of swallowing cyanide of potassium. Dr. Froyberger stated that potassium cyanide was not put up in tabloids like the one found in the tabloid case on Wright but was a poison with which a mining chemist would be well acquainted. It was used in photography and there would be no difficulty getting it. From what he had heard, he concluded that a period of a quarter of an hour must have elapsed between the swallowing of the poison and the actual occurrence of death. He thought that the poison must have been held on the tongue for some time and that, after he had come back from the lavatory, Wright must have drunk it down. Death was as a result of poisoning.

The coroner briefly summed up the case which he said was perfectly simple and free from doubt on the facts. There was no suggestion that Wright was out of his mind. On the contrary, it had been shown that he had thoroughly understood the position he was in right up to the last moment he remained conscious. It was also extremely significant, in the circumstances, that he should have gone to court with a revolver, fully loaded in all chambers and cocked. It was certain beyond doubt that he had taken his own life and it was clear that he knew exactly what he was doing. There was no suggestion of insanity but there was an extremely strong motive explaining why he acted as he did. There was evidence to show that it must have come to his knowledge that there might be an adverse verdict which would ruin him and he then went into court prepared to take certain steps if such a verdict were given. The jury immediately returned a simple verdict of suicide.

The verdict spread immediately. The late editions of the newspapers reported the suicide in the most vivid of terms. It was another sensational twist in an already major story. Rufus Isaacs confided that he had initially feared that the strain of the cross-examination had contributed to the death and was relieved by the information. Wright had chosen his own way.

The body of Whitaker Wright was removed from the Westminster mortuary between 5 and 6 p.m. that Thursday evening and taken to Waterloo Station where it was placed in the brake van attached to the 6.20 p.m. train for Witley. Mr. T.P. King, the station superintendent, received the body on behalf of the railway company. A small crowd was present and they removed their hats as the coffin was placed in the van. His son knelt before the coffin and placed two wreaths on it. The inscription on the coffin simply gave his name and dates of birth and death. Wright's son was accompanied by John Eyre and they travelled by the same train which reached Witley Station at 7.58 p.m. Although the time of arrival had not been made known, a large number of people gathered around the station. Several policemen attended to preserve order.

Mr. Milton, the Witley undertaker, conveyed the oak coffin in a car draw by two black horses to the Witley estate. Small groups of locals grouped together at various places along the route. His local support remained. There had been plans for a great homecoming with the Mouse Hill band, a torchlight procession and the intention for villagers to draw his carriage home in triumph. But all this was abandoned on news of his death. On the arrival of the body at Lea Park, it was placed in the fine hall of the now deserted mansion which had been converted into a kind of *chapelle ardente* with a wealth of beautiful palms and flowers, the coffin being watched day and night by people from the estate.

The interment was timed for 1.30 on the Saturday afternoon, 30$^{th}$ January 1904. An hour earlier, an open hearse containing the coffin and the family flowers left Lea Park followed by several carriages in which were the immediate mourners. Signs of mourning were evident in Witley in drawn blinds and partly closed shops, and many persons wore bunches of violets, a brisk sale for which was found by several hawkers. As the cortege went along in the drenching downpour of rain which fell almost incessantly the whole day, its progress was watched by a goodly number of the residents. The police comprising Superintendent Collis, Sergeants Pyke and Baker and thirteen constables attended to deal with the large but orderly crowd. The roads were lined with local people, heads bowed in respect.

On arriving at the entrance to the churchyard, the coffin was met by the Rev. E.J. Seymour, Vicar of Witley, and the Rev. J.E. Eddis, Vicar of Great Barton, Suffolk, and the former Vicar of Witley. The coffin was not taken into the church and the service conducted at the graveside. Rev. Eddis read the opening sentences as the coffin was wheeled on a hand-bier direct to the grave which was situated in consecrated ground on the north side of the church and which had been lined with moss and ferns, and previous to the burial, covered with tarpaulin in order to prevent flooding. Around the grave stood the deceased's son, Whitaker, and his daughters, Gladys and Edith, the indomitable John Eyre and George Lewis. The widow was prostrate through her terrible loss and totally unable to attend. Immediate friends swelled the family group including Mr. Yalden, H. Knowles J.P., Mr. M.J. Burn – at one time solicitor to Wright, Mrs. Burn, Dr. Hall, Wright's medical attendant, Mr. Watkins – civil engineer formerly in charge of the Lea Park Estate, Mrs. Watkins. His faithful employees, Malcolm and Worters, stood nearby. The servants from Lea Park and Lower House gathered behind. The great and the good showed their respect in attendance. The mourners included Murray Griffiths, Henry Trower, several members of the Stock Exchange, local dignitaries, tradesmen and residents from Godalming and many of the poorer inhabitants from Witley and Milford.

The service was conducted in conformity with the Burial Act 1882 which made it possible in the case of those who 'have laid violent hands upon themselves' to receive burial in a special form with the Church of England, prepared by the Bishop of Winchester. The ceremony omitted the committal prayer and the two collects following in the Book of Common Prayer. The words 'forasmuch as it hath pleased Almighty God of his great mercy' were specifically excluded. Rev. Seymour chose the several collects to reflect the situation and the deceased's life. The words of Psalm 143 were used. 'O lord give hear to my supplications and enter not into judgment with thy servant for in thy sight shall no man living be justified.' He concluded with a blessing.

The wreaths epitomised the sympathy and the regard for the man. Three wreaths covered the coffin. The first comprised lilies of the valley and other white blooms with the inscription 'from his broken-hearted widow'. The second was 'from his loving children'. The third 'mourning the best of brothers' was from his sister, Matilda. Other wreaths and inscriptions reflected the widespread regard and sentiments. The wreath 'in memory of a true friend – at last at peace' was from the Burns, with 'deepest sympathy' from the inhabitants of Park Lane, Brook and Witley, and 'a last token of truest friendship' from John Eyre. Others were from his late farm employees, from Milford Workmen's Club, from the Columbia Lodge, from Sinclair Mcleay, from Milford tradesmen, from his house servants. The inscription on the wreath from Moffat Ford probably reflected what many thought: 'To a great and exceedingly brave man who certainly did not realise that he was doing wrong but chose to suffer death rather than dishonour, who courted death a superb courage passing the wit of man to understand.' Subsequently, over one thousand letters of sympathy were received by his widow from all over the world and many from people she did not know. She could not respond to them all but, through the newspapers, she thanked them on 9$^{th}$ February. It would have been Whitaker's 58$^{th}$ birthday.

The verdict, the suicide, the funeral gave the newspapers the opportunity to recount his history, detail and marvel about his lifestyle and rehearse the arguments about his moral standing. The reporting was worldwide, America to Australia, England to China. There was great division about all of the issues. His death served only to exacerbate the disparate views and opinions.

He had left his own version and view of his life and the newspapers printed the stories that he had given the American press during the extradition proceedings. He was keen to emphasise his humble beginning and his rise to wealth through his own endeavour.

He maintained that he was a poor boy from Cheshire and crossed the Atlantic in his youth to seek his fortune. In some accounts, he said that his father had given a good education; in other versions, it was a practical education. He had early interest in inorganic chemistry and started work in America as an assayer. He had no capital and worked hard to achieve his first $10,000 (£2,000) but after that it was easy though his insight into human nature, his clear head and absolute integrity. His early dealings in mining interests and his later speculation on the New York Stock Exchange had made him a dollar millionaire at thirty-one. He had returned to England at forty-three expecting to retire from business. His apparently moderate fortune enabled him to begin operations on the London Stock Exchange in 1891 but it was not until 1894 with the advent of the West Australian Goldfields that his opportunity came.

He was candid about the part luck played in mining operations. Not one in a hundred mines paid. It was speculation. He castigated those in the public who risked their money for rich reward but regarded their investments as deposits in a savings bank. He said that waves of prosperity advanced like waves of an incoming tide and nothing could stop the prices from advancing but nor could human power check the recession of the wave when prices tumbled. He said shrewd men with insight into the causes were the ones who made millions. He could not stem the tide of depression that followed the South African War. He had failed to accomplish the impossible. It was a mixture of usual bravado maintaining his own efforts and integrity against forces beyond his control. It was entirely the character of the man that he had conveyed and was left as his own obituary.

The newspapers across America were full of anecdotes about Wright's past, their accuracy tempered by the fact that their main sources had been the man himself. There was much condemnation of the 'get rich quick' schemes by which he was characterised but as much reprobation for the investors as for the promoters. The American press were inclined to express some sympathy with the man. The *New York Times* considered that during the last few years not a few collapses of speculation had occurred in their country differing but slightly in degree and not all in kind from those in which Whitaker Wright was engaged. Some had involved men and station comparable to those of Wright. *The Tribune* wanted the exponents of speculation to reflect that if they were under the jurisdiction of the

English courts, there might be dolorous days ahead for them. It was a reproach to American lawmakers that they had left it comparatively easy for such grasp at riches in utter disregard of the misery they inflicted, whether they succeed or fail, to escape their just deserts. *The Evening Post* thought that in point of morality the Wright case differed in no respect from the promoters of the Shipbuilding Trust. *The Trust*, like Globe, relied on the names of men supposed to embody high commercial ideals. It went on that there was one vast difference between Wright and some of the leaders of high finance. Wright was amenable to the severe English company law, he transgressed it and he paid the penalty. Their transgressors of the same moral law walked in free air, were lavish with their philanthropies and were lauded from the pulpits as examples to the youth.

British press were divided. There was criticism of the Government by its known critics. *The Westminster Gazette* wrote that the handling of the matter had reflected more discredit on the government than its other mistakes with even greater consequences. Distinguished people were involved and some of them had had happy escapes. It was alleged that Wright might have made disclosures which would have seriously discomforted some people but it declared that Wright had been loyal as well as courageous and that he had carried his secrets to his grave. Other papers carried some thinly veiled criticism of Mr. Justice Bigham and his conduct of the case, citing his apparent humour and clashes with Lawson Walton as prejudice against Wright.

The serious newspapers centred on the enormity of the financial losses and the responsibility for them. Someone perhaps had to pay for the greedy speculation. The role of some of the financial papers was reviewed. Many had only printed information when they were paid leading to accusations of prejudice. Many had also actively promoted investment in the Wright companies. However, some of the newspaper and magazine articles reflected the growing morality about behaviour. The March issue of *Blackwood's Magazine* was particularly scathing. It recounted Wright's business history and methods highlighting his apparent personal greed. It set his dealings in the context of the times and equally condemned the unscrupulous and the gullible, the government and the financial market.

The public mood was shifting away from some of the previous values. It was not enough to be self-made. There was a wider duty to others, a recognition that the ordinary citizen had a right to protection from excesses by whoever. The mood was changing to accept greater social responsibility for the individual to be reflected in government legislation and judicial pronouncements holding individuals and bodies accountable for damage caused by their actions.

The popular press did not hesitate in their condemnation. The conviction and the suicide meant that anything could be said about him. The excesses of his lifestyle were the particular subject of vilification. It was his Lea Park house and estate that coloured much of their views. The huge costs, the lavishness of the decoration and artefacts, the enormous scale of the construction of the house and grounds enabled the stench of greed to be effortlessly laid at his door. The charge was that the splendour had been acquired at the expense of the public. He had used the money of others to support his lifestyle. The growing morality about inequality was evident in their language. The portrayal of the wealth being obtained by apparent dishonesty fuelled the debate. Wright's name as a fraudster began. The epithet was constantly repeated and used in articles and cartoons to attack those considered to be of a similar ilk. The size of the enterprises and the corresponding losses weighed heavily in the condemnation.

Once the immediate furore had settled, there remained other aspects to be concluded. The case appeared in various parliamentary debates. The Government had to pay the costs of bringing Wright before the courts and a reimbursement of the private prosecution after some wrangles with Flower. The Attorney General was naturally the subject of attack through his lack of action given the ultimate result. Disparaging attempts by opposition Members were made to make him personally pay. The Official Receiver slowly proceeded with the winding up of companies, the recovery and distribution of assets to creditors. The shareholders in the main companies received nothing. Some of the smaller companies went under and some prospered. There were reconstructions. But the Wright Empire had effectively gone. The wealth he had made and then lost was never recovered.

The holders of the mortgages on Lea Park now proceeded to seek its sale and recover the huge sums that Wright had borrowed during the three years since the London & Globe crash. A court order was obtained on 31st March 1905 appointing a Receiver to deal with the estate and on 18th April an order for foreclosure was made. The estate was put on the market but there were no buyers and accordingly on 27th October 1905, it was put up in fifty lots for auction at the Borough Hall in Godalming, Surrey. There was great interest. The auctioneer was Mr. Holland Peck from Hampton & Sons in conjunction with F.A and A.W. Mellersh, local solicitors and financiers.

Peck announced that the Master in Chancery had set such low reserves that he had no doubt that nearly all the lots would be sold. He answered questions about manorial and shooting rights from the audience. He went on to say that it would be carrying coals to Newcastle if he were to tell them anything about the beautiful neighbourhood and the healthfulness of their own district and the choice lots available. Over £50,000 was realised from forty-four lots. There were numerous cottages, residences and building land. Substantial areas were not sold. Bowlhead Green Farm was withdrawn from sale with bidding at £5,860, as was the Winkford and Parsonage Farms at £11,600. Lower House, where the family were living, was also withdrawn from the auction. The mansion and grounds only reached bids of £35,000 which was lower than the reserve.

One of the most notable purchases was Lot 47, entitled 'the manorial rights over Hindhead commons including the Devil's Punch Bowl, Gibbet Hill, etc. 750 acres of timber included'. Separate lots included the common land areas at Haslemere, Grayswood and Witley. There had been concerns in 1899 that the Hindhead common land was being despoiled by the apparent disregard for the area shown by Whitaker Wright as Lord of the Manor. There were reports that residents had seen gangs of workmen with an 'infernal' machine taking earth and plants for use in the landscaping of Lea Park. Whilst it was also understood that Whitaker Wright did not know what was happening, the work nevertheless stopped. But the local anxiety over the future of the land remained and there was a view that it should be protected. The moment to act came with the auction and the Haslemere Commons Preservation Society appealed for local funds chaired by Sir Robert Hunter who lived in Three Gates Lane, Hindhead. Its members started to gather names who would guarantee the purchase sum. £2,200 was raised by the due date. The auction was attended by Francis Muir and Mr. Miller for the committee and by Laurence Chubb who was Secretary of the Commons Preservation

Society. The bidding started at £2,000 and quickly went to £3,000. At the last minute, Mrs. Thackeray Turner pledged another £500 and the committee secured the plot for £3,625 which was in fact the reserve figure. The shortfall was made up with further local support. The land was transferred on 30th December 1905 and then further transferred to the National Trust on 22nd March 1906. Hindhead was the first Trust property to be managed by a local committee.

The family had watched these events from their residence at Lower House, knowing that the days of this home were finite. They would have to leave. Whitaker's Will had been proven by his widow on 11th July 1904 and the sum of £148,200 was available. After the auction, Anna Wright approached the estate agents and negotiated the purchase of the adjoining Winkford and Parsonage Farms. She then lived at Parsonage Farmhouse and on the farm with her two daughters and son. The young Whitaker Wright farmed the lands. It was an unexpected but welcome change to their situation. They could have some certainty and some life within the community that had taken them to their hearts. They continued to be regarded with warmth and affection. Anna could not recover from the events and her devotion to Whitaker.

She walked along the track and down the steep, narrow Church Lane with its tree-topped, high-sided backs of sandstone that rarely allowed any sunshine along its length. It was less than a mile from Parsonage Farmhouse to Witley Church. She entered the gate and passed the church carrying its 1,000 years of history with rustic solidity. She walked across to the grave and knelt at its side. Alone and in the afternoon sunshine, she reflected. She looked at the inscription on the side, bearing his name together with his date and place of birth and his date of death. Ironically and wrongly, Prestbury had been given as his birthplace. She did not know and it did not matter. She thought of the day when her own name would appear on the other side of the grave. The huge and ornate memorial she had erected at its head dominated the surrounding graves. She looked at the inscription. She had used the Song of Solomon: 'Until the day breaks and the shadows flee away.' The other inscription was, 'He loved the poor.' As always, she placed a few coins beneath to be taken eagerly by the local children as they later emerged from the nearby school. She gave solemn thanks and gently cried. Her head was full of gratitude and her heart full of peace. Her decision to stay in England where the children had grown up allowed her this regular devotion. She would never lose her belief in him, nor her love for him.

She looked up to see her son. He was a handsome image of his father. He had finished his farming duties for the day and had come to take her home. She remarked that it had been some journey from one tiny village in Cheshire to another tiny village in Surrey. They thought of the travels and turmoil, the trials and tribulation along the way. They recalled his stories and anecdotes. They wondered what had made the man. As always, they concluded that he had determined his own life. They stood together for a moment by the grave and then started the steep walk back home. The light faded and silence pervaded.

Printed in Great Britain
by Amazon